THE SATANIZING OF THE JEWS

Origin and Development of Mystical Anti-Semitism

By JOEL CARMICHAEL

FROMM

Fromm International Publishing Corporation
New York

First paperback edition, 1993

Printed in the United States of America

Library of Congress Cataloging-in-Publication Data
Carmichael, Joel.
    The Satanizing of the Jews : origin and development of mystical anti-Semitism / by Joel Carmichael.—1st U.S. ed.
        p.   cm.
    Includes bibliographical references.
    ISBN 0-88064-152-5 : $10.95
    1. Antisemitism—History.   2. Christianity and antisemitism—History.   3. Judaism (Christian theology)—History of doctrines.   4. Christianity and other religions—Judaism—History.   5. Judaism—Relations—Christianity—History.   I. Title.
DS145.C37   1992
305.892'4—dc20   91-46274
                                                       CIP

CONTENTS

FOREWORD

Hatred of outsiders is commonplace; anti-Semitism is unique.

Unique because of its source, its intensity, its duration—indeed, its very nature—it is a major component of European, as well as of Jewish, history over the past two thousand years, and in the twentieth century has had a decisive effect on the world. Its literature is vast, the details endless.

The word "anti-Semitism" itself, to be sure, contains elements similar to the countless varieties of animosity and prejudice that characterize vulgar xenophobia, but in the case of the Jews these elements are given special potency by a mystical dimension that identifies the Jews with a concept beyond themselves. It is this dimension—the root of what I shall call mystical anti-Semitism—that has lent a special tincture to the fate of the Jews.

Mystical anti-Semitism has nothing to do with the Jews. This outsize dimension, which is what makes anti-Semitism a definable subject, is to be found in Christian theology—though it was to be transferred, as we shall see, to the pseudo-scientific theories of "racism" that began to proliferate in the last third of the nineteenth century.

The disproportionate weight of the Jews in the world arises from their key role in the Christian drama. In the universe framed by Christian theology, the concepts of "Jews" and "Christians" have an undeniable balance that, while statistically absurd, reflects the fundamental theme of Christianity—the world of God and the world of the Devil. Since the Jews have not accepted the Christian God, they have ipso facto been arrayed alongside the Devil in Christendom.

Nor can the Jews be dislodged from this eminence through such flaccid ideas as tolerance. The rationale of Christianity requires the presence of the Jews not only because of their historic role in the genesis of Christianity, but also, and primarily, as the counterpoint needed to highlight the fundamental theme of the Christian Bible.

The chief difficulty in disentangling mystical anti-Semitism from the various kinds of xenophobia that often accompany it, as well as from expressions of hostility rooted in ordinary group conflicts, is that the word "anti-Semitism" itself is generally felt to be self-explanatory: it is simply another way of saying "dislike of Jews." Yet on reflection, it is instantly obvious that two entirely different ideas are involved, two distinct orders of magnitude.

One is the banal category of "ethnic" slurs applied to members of groups different from one's own; the other is different—its magnitude is cosmic. One is on the human plane: Jews may be called sly, deceitful, pushy, arrogant, sycophantic, stingy, ostentatious—indeed, anything disagreeable. And of course individual Jews may well be any of these things. The other category is unique: Jews have been called "Christ-killers," "enemies of God," "devils," "enemies of the human race." They have been considered utterly, eerily, and inhumanly Evil.

Astonishingly, perhaps, no surprise is felt at the fusion of such differences of scale. Jews themselves may accept these quite disproportionate ideas as arising from the same attitude—as being simply forms of "anti-Semitism."

Yet it is plain that mystical anti-Semitism is animated by a rationale that is quite different from the conventional disparagements, however exaggerated, of outsiders. At bottom, that rationale is the profound idea that Jews are both evil and mysteriously powerful.

It is surely this concept of essential Evil, plus occult power, that distinguishes anti-Semitism from all other group hatreds. And it is just this mystical hyperbole, this transformation of seemingly ordinary people into a mysterious "Power," that accounts for the radical Jewish inability to grasp its nature. The indifference of Jews to the fundamental ideas of Christianity has skewed their perceptions and led to an overconcentration on the banal theme of being "different."

The Jewish experience in Christendom will be seen to be different in kind from the animosity often encountered by Jews under Islam, especially during the past couple of generations of Muslim hostility to the State of Israel.

Beginning with the indigenous life of the Jews in their homeland, I shall survey the collision with Hellenism, the efflorescence of the idea of the Kingdom of God, the agitation against Rome and the great revolt of 66–70 A.D., the foundation of the Christian Church, and the evolution of Jewry in Christendom.

I hope to distinguish the infernal aspect of anti-Semitism, rooted originally in a theological structuring of the world, and trace its migration, through the secularization of modern Christendom, to Auschwitz.

THE JEWS AT HOME: The Kingdom of God and the Roman-Jewish War

The antiquity of the Jews has made it natural to trace anti-Semitism to the remote past. Historians, in discussing the phenomenon that has been familiar since long before the Middle Ages, have often made much of "classical anti-Semitism." I do not think that relevant; still, a very swift glance backward may be appropriate.

The ancient history of the Jews, as recorded in the Bible, can be summed up concisely: The wanderings of the Hebrew Patriarchs in the second millennium B.C., the descent into and the Exodus from Egypt; the formation, in the first millennium, of the Hebrew tribes into a people by the tradition of the Revelation at Mount Sinai; the Great Settlement in the Promised Land; and the emergence of the Hebrew monarchy that reached its apogee in the empire of King David and his son, Solomon.

After Solomon the realm was divided into two kingdoms, Israel and Judah; one was smashed by the Assyrians in the seventh century B.C., the other by the Babylonians in the fifth. After conquering Babylon later in the fifth century, the Persians then restored Jewish autonomy on a small strip of land around Jerusalem. Thus, by the time of Alexander the Great's conquests in the third century B.C., which reduced Persian power to Persia proper, the Jews were once again on their own land in Judea, Samaria, and Galilee. Here the biblical account comes to an end.

In addition to the resettlement in Judea, Samaria, and Galilee, the Jews were still scattered far and wide in communities established as a consequence of the Babylonian exile. After Alexander they were submerged in a tidal wave of Hellenism, spread over a vast area that brought together many peoples who were also steeped in Hellenism. During this Hellenistic expansion after Alexander, accordingly, the Jews were already a people renowned for its antiquity and its unique religion.

Jewish life developed extensively outside its political and religious center in Judea, Samaria, and Galilee. The opening up of the Middle East and its cultural homogenization by Alexander and his successors created new cities: as a result of the growing trade relations between Palestine and its neighbors, the deportations, the mercenary colonies, the slave trade, the emigrations, reinforced by the steady involvement of Rome from the second century B.C. on, the importance of the Diaspora (the Jewish communities living outside the center in Judea) steadily increased.

The Babylonian exile had reshaped the Jews in a new and decisive sense: unlike pagans exiled after defeat in war who mingled with local populations and disappeared—a common feature of countless deportations—the Jewish settlements outside Judea retained their identity while accepting the Jerusalem authorities as their religious and therefore, in a sense, their political leaders.

Alexander's conquests changed the nature of the Middle East fundamentally: the notion of a vast society clinging to universal ideals revolving around Greek language and culture replaced the earlier congeries of relatively sealed-off states and societies. Whereas absorption in Babylonian culture would have made one a Babylonian, absorption in Greek civilization made one not a Greek, but a citizen, more or less, of the world.

As traders and artisans, the Greeks had been an important factor in the life of the Middle East long before Alexander: educated Greeks were curious about the peoples whose lands they had been infiltrating, but generally only from the point of view of fitting them into various Greek speculations about the world. But comments about the Jews—initially innocuous, or at least not hostile—are skimpy, unfocused, and indifferent to their reality. After their first contacts with Jews, for instance, some Greeks described the Hebrews, thought to be ruled by priests, as having been descended from the Hindus, about whom equally little was known.

Before the spread of Hellenism the Jews had no difficulty in accommodating their relations with their neighbors. Their belief in the One God was not strange: all peoples had gods of their own. But the collision with the universal civilization of the Greeks created a problem: if the One God was in his nature universal, how could he after all be limited to one people?

The tension among the Jews between these two polar characteristics—the Creator of the Universe, who nevertheless had a special relationship to Mount Zion—had sustained the Jews for centuries, but now the universal factor in the equation was to collide with the universal claims of Hellenism. And it was this collision that was to generate the "classical anti-Semitism" made much of by some students: the hostility felt for Jews as a collective body after their absorption within the sphere of Hellenistic governments.

That hostility had nothing to do with economics: the Jews in the Diaspora were, if anything, generally despised as paupers, with rare exceptions; they were, in the main, farmers and artisans. It was their religion, in and of itself, that made for difficulties. It set them apart in a sense in which different pagan communities worshipping different gods were not set apart; though the mere fact of the Jews' One God was not strange in itself, the barrier created by the demands of ritual made social intercourse difficult. The Jewish cluster of beliefs and customs seemed a kind of bizarre arrogance, the bodiless God a form of atheism, the observance of the Sabbath, incomprehensible to the ancient world, a proof of morbid indolence.

The built-in tolerance of pagan religious feeling made it seem natural for all peoples to have their own gods, each valid for his own people, but Jewish laws and customs tended to separate Jews from their neighbors—the kosher laws, the for-

bidding of intermarriage, all the national religious command-
ments and prohibitions, including circumcision, the annual
contribution to the far-off Temple, and the celebration of
national-religious festivals. The mere fact that the groundwork
of Judaism was a universal proposition of human equality, that
all human beings were brothers by virtue of being children of
God the universal father, must have seemed to those pagans who
took it seriously an empty abstraction, as well as a form of
hypocrisy.

But all these social and communal frictions reflected, so to
speak, the world at large; they were an organic part of the normal
byplay between overlapping groups everywhere. In the case of
Jews under the Persian Empire, to be sure, there was an outsize
element in the irritation Jewish separateness seemingly caused
the Persian rulers, an irritation preserved in the Book of Esther:
"There is a certain people scattered abroad and dispersed in all
the provinces . . . their laws are different from those of all other
people . . . therefore the king should not spare them" (Esther
3:8).

But even this view of the Jews, which runs counter to the
cosmopolitan tolerance for which the Persian Empire was celebrated, is different in kind from the element of "mystical"
anti-Semitism I intend to distinguish: for the Persians, Jews on
Persian territory were an impediment to statecraft; they were
not different by nature.

Friction between the Jews and their neighbors did not acquire a cutting edge for generations after Alexander the Great's
conquests. The Jews, subject after the destruction of the Persian
state to regimes created by Alexander's successors—the Seleu-
cids in Syria and the Ptolemies in Egypt—were rapidly assimilated at least to the means by which international culture was
transmitted: the Greek language, which joined Aramaic as the
natural language of educated Jews everywhere; in Egypt and
Syria, Greek became another Jewish vernacular. The vast work
of translating into Greek the Hebrew Bible was undertaken in
Alexandria in the second century B.C., though practically speaking, to be sure, it was read only by Jews—part of the wholesale
Jewish accommodation to Greek culture, similar in a way to the

Jewish effort (epitomized by Philo of Alexandria) to synthesize the ancient Hebrew ideals with the allure of Greek cosmopolitanism and the adulation of rationality.

It was precisely the charm of Hellenistic culture, after most Jews had been steeped in Greek politics for a century, that created a violent backlash among pietists. The backlash took the form, essentially, of a civil war against those Jews whose seduction by Hellenism entailed the negation of Jewish separateness. A convergence between the Jewish aristocracy, which was longing to drop parochial Jewish beliefs and customs, and the statecraft of a Greek king (Antiochus IV Epiphanes) determined to homogenize his diverse subjects, provoked a violent reaction led by the Maccabees in 163 B.C.

The Maccabees regarded both Greek rulers and Jewish apostates alike as their enemies. They wrested Judea from the Greek dynasty and restored Jewish sovereignty in Judea; they founded the Hasmonean regime, which for almost a century endured as a more or less independent state, larger than Egypt, larger even than Solomon's empire. They had restored a Jewish national state, which became once again a factor in the Middle East.

From the time of the Maccabees actively malicious legends about the Jews—the substance of "classical anti-Semitism"—began to circulate. The Greek view of the Jews, indeed, acquired a sharp focus essentially through the political interest aroused by the Maccabee revolt.

A legend originating around half a century after Alexander —to the effect that the Jews, once rulers of Egypt, had been driven out by the Egyptians as lepers—had been put into a history written in Greek by Manetho, an Egyptian priest, and circulated as fact by Greco-Roman historians. This was no doubt a way of establishing plausibility: it was natural, in attacking contemporary Jews as corrupt and barbarous, to extend the concept back to their origins.

A fiction was circulated about Antiochus Epiphanes finding a golden donkey's head in the Temple sanctuary in 170 B.C.: the point of this story was that even though the Jews made much of their bodiless, invisible god, what they were really worshipping was simply a donkey. Antiochus was also supposed to have freed a Greek who was being fattened up by the Jews in order to be butchered afterward and devoured in accordance with their customs.

Many Greeks called Jews "atheists and misanthropes," as well as recklessly mad, and at the same time, cowards.* Among the Greeks and Romans, however, Jews were hardly ever referred to as "cunning" or the like, nor were they regarded as clever businessmen.

There was, of course, a reciprocal interaction between hostile reports inspired by enmity between the new state and its political rivals, and the intraethnic hostility in the Jewish Diaspora, in which the separateness of the Jews living among their pagan neighbors was exacerbated by their privileged position in the Roman Empire, owing to the Roman acceptance of the antiquity of their Scriptures. These Scriptures, though scarcely read by pagans, nevertheless warranted Judaism in the eyes of the Romans as a *religio licita*, an officially franchised religion. It was quite normal for the Jews, in the universalistic empire of Alexander's successors and in the Roman Empire that had absorbed them, to have all the rights of national-religious autonomy, like all peoples. Yet in the case of the Jews this included exemption from certain civic duties bound up with pagan religions. This type of exemption became a natural cause of friction.

In the great urban centers of the eastern Mediterranean, the status of the Jews came somewhere between the highest caste of the privileged Greeks and the underprivileged "natives," such as the Egyptians; the Jews made up a substantial part of the population in Egypt (in Alexandria they amounted to some 40 percent). In Palestine, curiously, though they comprised the basic population, they were, in the cities created there by the Greeks and later by the Romans, inferior: in such cities they were considered foreigners, just as they were in countries where they had been settled for generations, such as Egypt.

But the conflicts between the Hasmonean state founded by the Maccabees and its rivals began to be overshadowed by the rise of the Roman Empire. The whole of the eastern end of the

---

* Josephus, *Against Apion*, 2. 14, 148.

■ 6 ■

Mediterranean became a buffer zone between the expanding Roman Empire and the Parthian (Persian) state in the East; the Hasmonean state itself, which had managed to maintain its independence for about a century, slipped into the hands of the Romans in 63 B.C., when Pompey marched into Jerusalem and set his foot in the hitherto inviolate shrine of the Temple.

The Roman Empire had responded to Hellenistic universalism by itself swallowing all of Greek culture, thus becoming its chief channel, while supplying that culture with a military and administrative apparatus that from the first century B.C. was in full swing as a swallower-up of peoples. Judea, Galilee, and Samaria, all with dense Jewish populations, became part of the web of Roman protectorates, though for a generation an autonomous regime was headed by a Jewish king, Herod the Great.

Oddities and all, Judaism fascinated many pagans. From the time of the Jewish Diaspora—extending throughout the Roman Empire and far beyond to Mesopotamia, exceeding in importance and numbers the Jewry of Judea itself—there were countless converts to Judaism, either full converts or, more commonly, "God-fearers," pagans who worshipped the God of Israel but ignored various prescriptions of the Torah, notably circumcision and the kosher laws.

The Jews were in fact a substantial minority in the Roman Empire, perhaps as much as 10 to 12 percent of the population. Socially, they were not distinguished from their neighbors, except possibly by their poverty, at least outside Judea and Galilee. By trade they were generally farmers (no doubt the majority), or else craftsmen, traders, artisans, laborers, or soldiers. Hardly any were merchants. On the higher levels of society, they were imperial officials: knights, senators, legates, even praetors.

But they were not merely individuals or communities scattered through the Empire. They were felt to be a sort of state: their capital, in their own and hence in Roman eyes, remained Jerusalem. The Diaspora was understood as an appendage, spiritually speaking, of a genuine, ordinary capital: it was the Diaspora of a people that on its own terrain led a normal existence. Jerusalem was the center of all religious life. Every adult male Jew, regardless of where he lived, was supposed to pay an annual tax to the Temple; these voluntary taxes seem to have been paid more readily than the taxes of the various countries they lived in.

The Sanhedrin, the administrative-legislative body in Jerusalem, established all important dates: the beginning of the month and the year and all the festivals, especially Passover, the great festival celebrating the emancipation of the Jews and their formation as a people. Swarms of pilgrims went to Jerusalem every year, especially during Passover. There was an intimate interaction between all Diaspora colonies and Jerusalem.

The Hebrew Bible—the library of history books, prophecies, consolations, castigations, legislation, proverbs—had accumulated over the centuries following the Persian restoration of the upper-class Babylonian exiles: it had gradually become a canon, equally valid in the Diaspora and translated, accordingly, into the languages spoken by Jews (mainly Greek and Aramaic): this canon was "The Book"—or "Books" (Biblia)—for all Jews everywhere.

The general mood of hostility to the Jews, widespread in the population and especially among some of the more influential thinkers, was not reflected in law: despite the restiveness of the Jews in Judea, Galilee, and Samaria, which no doubt underlay occasional upheavals in various parts of Diaspora Jewry, the state itself did not single out the Jews for special legislation. Judaism remained a constitutionally acknowledged religion: in the first century the privileges and exemptions of Jewish communities in the Empire were not touched.

Yet the formation of a militant, intransigent resistance to the Roman state, which had begun before the death of Herod the Great in 4 B.C. and was to swell into a massive insurrection in 66–70 A.D., was to have consequences that far transcended Palestine, and Rome itself. The resistance, led by "Zealots"—zealous for the Hebrew Scriptures, especially the Torah—was to be the germ of a new religion.

This religio-political resistance had intensified under the reign of Herod's successor, Archelaus, whom the Romans dismissed a decade later: Judea was integrated directly into the Roman administration, and a succession of Procurators were sent out from Rome to govern the increasingly mutinous Jews. The rapacity of these Procurators, superimposed on the religious fervor of the Jews, created a constantly increasing turbulence, which lent a special edge to the hitherto somewhat fuzzy canards circulated about the Jews in the Hellenistic world. The rather abstract calumnies about Jews as "lepers," about human sacrifices in the Temple, and so on, were to be given a special charge by the constant agitation that culminated in the rebellion of 66–70.

The rebellion threatened the Romans for two reasons: on the practical plane, it endangered the road to Parthia (Persia), Rome's greatest enemy and never conquered. On the more complex social and intellectual plane, converts to Judaism were beginning to abound not only throughout the Empire, with its far-flung Jewish Diaspora, but on the highest levels of society and the state.

The armed resistance to Rome arose from the concept of the "Kingdom of God," to be heralded by a "Messiah." This notion had begun churning up the minds of many Jews in the aftermath of the collision with Greece some two centuries before, in the Maccabee rebellion; now, in the first century, this same concept focused the Jewish conflict with Rome.

The idea itself was very old: before the formation of the Hebrew monarchy, Jews in theory were meant to live directly under God. This idea was revived again after the collision with Hellenism, and with greater intensity after the subjugation by Rome.

Essentially, the Kingdom of God had a simple theme: The world was badly skewed. In particular, the fortunes of the Jews, the Chosen People, were at a low ebb; exiled by a pagan power from the Promised Land, later ruled and exploited by other pagan powers, their condition was manifestly intolerable.

To many pious Jews the imminent future seemed clear: the chastisement of the Jews—their "trial"—would eventually come to an end; God would reenter history once again, as he had with the Revelation on Sinai, the Great Exodus, and the Conquest of the Holy Land, and restore his direct reign in the world, incidentally restoring the fortunes of the Jews. The Kingdom of

God would be a total material transformation of the world, brought about by the will of God.

Initially, the Messiah had been thought of as a human being, but under the influence of the various calamities of Jewish history in the preceding centuries, many Jews also began to visualize the Messiah, while human, as decked out in various otherworldly accoutrements and performing a semidivine function. Thus the notion of a living Messiah meant that the revival of the Kingdom of God had an ideal and altogether current, active program, political as well as religious.

Some Jews were content merely to *believe* that the Kingdom of God was imminent, but others took it for granted that they could, so to speak, help it along by action—against the pagan powers and their accomplices among the Jews, that is, the aristocracy and the higher priesthood, who were either active allies of the Roman state or else "quietist," prepared to wait passively for God to accomplish his purpose. Thus the agitation for the Kingdom of God, which had begun during Herod the Great's reign, began swelling after the absorption of Judea into the Roman administration in 6 A.D. Lacking a client-king since the death of Herod the Great a decade before, the Jews confronted the Roman state face to face.

Perhaps the cardinal factor in the Kingdom of God movement of agitation, what made it a political crisis, was the conviction of its imminence. Had it been merely an ideal whose realization lay in the indefinite future, or one that, while imminent, did not depend on any action, it might have been accommodated by the Romans in their general indifference to the religion of their subjects. But the conviction of activist believers that something could, and *had*, to be done, there and then, was to lead to a major upheaval.

Jesus of Nazareth, too, heralded the imminent Kingdom of God: appearing about 30 A.D., during the reign of Tiberius, when Pontius Pilate was Procurator of Judea and the country was seething with messianist agitation, the person of Jesus gave rise to the new religion, which took shape through the Incarnation —an idea inspired by his death.

The origins of Christianity constitute a vast subject. I have written about it in several books from a purely secular point of view.* From the point of view of mystical anti-Semitism, however, two themes only are relevant: the interpretation of the Kingdom of God, and the Incarnation. I shall take the liberty of extracting from the vast literature on Jesus, St. Paul, and the formation of the early Church what I regard as the key factors in the origin of mystical anti-Semitism.

The actual account of Jesus' life—of Jesus the man, independent of his titles—is meager, in terms of both duration and incident; his career seems to have unfolded within the space of a few weeks. And the substance of his activities is summed up even more tersely: he came, as it seems, announcing the "Kingdom of God," fell out with the authorities (Roman and Jewish), and was crucified as "King of the Jews"—a rebel against Rome.

Since Jesus was executed by the Romans on a charge of sedition—recorded in all four Gospels, and stated by Tacitus as a plain fact—the authorities evidently considered him one of the activist believers in the imminent Kingdom of God, with its corollary, the extinction of the Roman power.

It is of some interest that two of Jesus' grandnephews were brought to Rome a couple of generations after his crucifixion on a warrant of arrest; they were given a hearing by Caesar Domitian, Vespasian's son, and released only after showing that they were politically innocuous.** Moreover, Paul refers to Jesus casually, in a context of no particular interest to himself, as a descendant of King David (Rom. 1:3), who was of vital importance to a pretender to power.

These two facts seem to heighten the likelihood that the movement of agitation led by Jesus was a major secular as well as religious event, which culminated in the war of 66–70. The movement associated with Jesus, accordingly, had a contemporary socio-political importance that was necessarily downplayed, as we shall see, by the tradition that was to spring up in his name.

The earliest Gospels, written long after Jesus' death, record

---

* *The Death of Jesus*, New York: Macmillan, London: Gollancz, 1983; *St. Paul's Timetable*, Munich: Bertelsmann (German), 1982; *The Birth of Christianity: Reality and Myth*, New York: Hippocrene Books, 1989.
** Eusebius, *History of the Church* 3. 18.4–20, 7, Baltimore: Penguin, 1965.

a series of postponements of the Kingdom, from the "at hand" of his debut, to the fortnight or so after his disciples would have returned from a tour of the land, to the statement that some of those hearing him speak would be alive when the Kingdom was installed.

What was to trigger the new faith was the belief in Jesus' resurrection, a belief that itself was quite simple: Shortly after the Crucifixion, a follower (Simon Peter, "The Rock") had a vision of Jesus not merely alive, but glorified at the right hand of God. This vision did not, that is, establish a mere resurrection of the physical body—such as the miracle ascribed to Jesus of, say, Lazarus's resurrection, which would end with Lazarus's normal death—but an actual affinity, as it were, to God. Initially, however, the Vision did not necessarily imply a *deification* of Jesus: it could also be interpreted as meaning merely that Jesus had been a human being who was elevated by God.

Before the formation of Christianity, in fact, two main interpretations took root:

One accepted the Vision as proof of Jesus having been the Herald of the Kingdom of God, the Messiah, which did not imply that Jesus in his lifetime had not been an ordinary human being. God, after all, had chosen other human beings to carry out his will—Abraham, Isaac, Jacob, Moses, Joshua, the Prophets.

This view could be accepted by devout Jews for at least a limited time. Believers in the Kingdom of God might well have thought God intended to choose Jesus as the Messiah as part of his plan to rectify the workaday world and restore the fortunes of the Jews. The Resurrection would then have been a way of reserving Jesus, so to speak, for a role in the future that would overcome what seemed to be the catastrophe of his execution.

This was the source of the notion that Jesus was coming back to earth once again, this time in Glory, as Herald of an enterprise that would consummate God's will. This was all the easier to accept since the concept of the Messiah had in any case come to absorb many otherworldly elements: it was possible to believe that an earthbound enterprise could function alongside cosmic celestial factors.

This notion of Jesus as the Jewish Messiah accounts for the tradition (crystallized in the Acts of the Apostles) that the immediate entourage of Jesus—his brother Upright Jacob, Simon the Rock, and others—hastened to Jerusalem after the vision and awaited Jesus' Return in Glory while praying "assiduously" in the Temple of Jerusalem. (Jerusalem was, of course, the supreme place for cosmic events to be reflected on earth.)

But this interpretation could not be maintained for very long; the second interpretation—the Incarnation, the actual deification of Jesus—soon prevailed. This fundamental idea became the foundation of the religion in which the Jews were to play a special role.

On the face of it, to be sure, the very notion of Glorification contained the potential of infinite expansion. And that expansion began on the very soil of Jerusalem, when some Jews from the Greek-speaking Diaspora deduced what seemed to them to be the ineluctable consequence of the Glorification of Jesus: If God had indeed intervened in human affairs by Glorifying a human being, that meant not only that Jesus had been confirmed as Messiah, but that he had also been made divine himself; moreover, the Torah, the bedrock of Judaism, was now obsolete. This notion may underlie the execution, a few years after Jesus' death, of Stephen, a Greek-speaking member of the messianist group clustered around the Temple.

Now, though the vision of Simon the Rock had launched the new faith, it was the conceptual expansion involved in the deification of Jesus, the Incarnation as worked out by Paul, that was to create a framework for it.

Though very nearly an exact contemporary of Jesus, Paul, also a Greek-speaking Jew, never encountered him, but had a vision of his own, as it seems, of Jesus speaking to him from Heaven. It was this vision that gave him a burning conviction of the imminence of the Kingdom of God, a conviction that remained with him, despite postponements of the immediacy, to the end of his life.

Paul's basic ideas—elaborated, apparently, from those of some unknown predecessors—were to provide the new faith with its theology. Though his main ideas, revolving around the worship of Lord Jesus Christ as the Incarnation of God and Lord of the Universe, and the parallel abrogation of the Torah, were to repel most Jews, Paul considered Israel nevertheless to be the premier people because of their covenant with God. Indeed, he considered himself a pious Jew who was responding, uniquely, to the exigencies of a new era in history—the imminent establishment of the Kingdom of God.

It was precisely in striving to articulate this idea of the new era in history, begun with the Resurrection and Glorification of Jesus, that Paul developed the ideas that were to underlie a new institution—the Universal Church, in which Jews were to be assigned a portentous role whose aftereffects are what I am discussing.

Paul was trying to resolve what was, for him, an historical puzzle: If Jesus had not only been singled out as the Messiah but was also the "Son of God," the human being in whom God had incarnated himself and allowed himself to be "sacrificed for many" through the Crucifixion, it must have meant the beginning of the new era imminently expected by the Kingdom of God activists. The titanic fact of the Incarnation meant that the Kingdom of God, or at least the "Messianic Kingdom" immediately preceding it, was, for Paul, already there.

The puzzle that perplexed Paul arose out of a simple dilemma: If the process leading to the Kingdom of God was in train, why had it not already been accomplished? Why were Paul and his generation not *already* in the Kingdom of God, consummating the World's End? How could such a cosmic process, set in motion by the Divine Will, begin without being immediately completed?

In coping with this conundrum, which for him was by no means theological but a problem of real-life, temporal history, Paul contrived an explanation that was to bring about, unforeseeably for him, the framework for the transformation of the Jews into an otherworldly entity.

Long after Paul's death, his grand ideas—the Incarnation, the Redemptive Crucifixion, the Sacraments, the Mystic Body of Christ, the Mystic Church itself—were to become the substance of Christian theology, but the preamble to their interaction—contention between superhuman forces—was dropped.

Or rather, one single element, accounting for the Jewish rejection of the Incarnation, was retained—with fateful consequences. Paul's explanation for the hiatus between the Resurrection of Jesus Christ and the advent of the Kingdom of God rested on the assumption of a real conflict between Devil forces and God forces: the Angels, who for Paul were maleficent, opposed the Kingdom of God, the God forces promoted it.

In this struggle Paul, who thought himself unique in understanding the true significance of the Crucifixion and Incarnation and their relationship to the Kingdom of God, regarded the Jews as "blinded"; the blindness of the Jews made up the "Mystery" of their rejection of the Incarnation. But the blindness of the Jews, who incomprehensibly failed to grasp what for him was obvious, would be brief. Ultimately their eyes *had* to be opened, since Israel was an essential part of God's plan. Paul's remarks about the Jews did not refer to what they were, but to their "mysterious" behavior at a given moment. "Israel has been blinded . . . until the fullness of the pagans have gone in, then will Israel all be saved" (Rom. 11:25, 26).

It is evident that this idea, in principle reassuring to the Jews, is predicated on the actual advent of the Kingdom, which was taken for granted by Paul and countless Jews of his generation.

During his lifetime Paul's activities seemed ineffectual, partly because of the unchallengeable supremacy of the Temple, both in Palestine and in the Diaspora, and partly because the turbulence in Judea under a succession of Roman Procurators kept rising to ever-higher pitches of intensity as the Kingdom of God activists, violently opposed to the commonsensical quietism of fellow Jews, made an increasingly determined effort to smash the imperial administration and revive Jewish sovereignty.

The countless Jewish communities scattered through the Empire, as well as the Jewry of Parthia, were all affected, in varying degrees, by the messianist fervor. In a society churned up by deportations, enslavements, upheavals, and calamities attendant on the constant wars following the breakup of the Greek dynasties through the expansion of the Roman Empire, even pagans had been touched by the ideal of universal redemption through the advent of the Kingdom of God.

In this mood of expectancy, the news of the Vision on the Sea of Galilee seems to have spread like wildfire. It was carried by unknown pilgrims from Jerusalem to other Jewish centers in the Diaspora very soon after it occurred. It must be emphasized that Jesus' activities took place against a background of social turbulence: the Kingdom of God movement, simmering from around the time of his birth, encompassed major portions of the population.

Despite the tradition that sprang up much later—of the Kingdom of God as a purely spiritual idea—Jesus, as a Kingdom of God activist, was part of the movement of agitation that had begun to mount in violence toward the end of Herod the Great's life, a few years before Jesus' birth. For two generations the most energetic men in Palestine were Kingdom of God activists: they believed in taking action against the Roman Empire in order to compel God, as it were, to intervene in history once again and restore sovereignty to his people in a regenerated world.

It was the agitation for the Kingdom of God "at hand" that brought about the Roman-Jewish war of 66–70. Though the Kingdom of God activists differed in many respects (some were republican, some social levelers, some monarchists), all opposed Rome.

The occasion of the war was the application of the focal theme of the Kingdom of God activists, expressed in the fundamental credo of Judaism: "Hear, Oh Israel, the Lord is our God, the Lord is one." Understood dynamically, the practical implications of this credo were clear: the pagans had no right to rule over devout Jews, and in particular, had no right to tax them. This religio-political rallying cry of the Zealots, in their many varieties, had penetrated the Temple milieu; a priest's refusal to make sacrifices to the Roman Emperor was a declaration of war.

The very first engagement with Roman troops, outside Jerusalem, ended with the quite unexpected, inexplicable rout and total destruction of a Roman legion. The Zealots were encouraged: certain of God's intervention, they interpreted the slaughter of the Roman legion as a sign: with it, a four-year struggle began.

On the Jewish side, the insurrection against Rome was complicated by a civil war between the Jews themselves: the peace party, headed by King Agrippa II and his sister, Queen Berenike, largely supported by the aristocracy and the upper strata of the priesthood, opposed the war as a mad adventure, doomed by the might of Rome and by God's support for the Empire, for which the evidence was precisely its success.

The Jewish royal family had had great hopes of playing an important role as a client of Rome in the East. The death of Nero, after the insurrection had begun, had opened the way to a number of upstarts: Vespasian, the general who had conquered Britain, was financed by Agrippa II and his sister, who enabled him to pay the troops needed to crush the Jewish uprising. Vespasian, soon to become Caesar, left his older son Titus to conduct the campaign against the Zealots; a love affair between Titus, who was in his early twenties, and Queen Berenike, a celebrated beauty, much married and somewhat older, was to be consummated by marriage.

The Zealot forces in Palestine were split into three factions, yet their intractability created a serious crisis for the Romans who, after achieving control of the country as a whole, forced the Zealots to fall back on Jerusalem, where, after a siege of unmatched ferocity, the soldiers and population alike were ultimately worn down by starvation. Finally, despite a promise to Queen Berenike, Titus destroyed the Temple by fire. Huge numbers of Jews were enslaved and exiled.

The Jewish royal family came to Rome to witness a remarkably elaborate Triumph: the four-year-long struggle against the Zealots had been one of the hardest-fought battles in Roman history. The war made it impossible for Titus, now the heir apparent, to marry a Jewish princess, despite recognition of the royal family's loyalty to Rome. Berenike, dismissed, left for her estates in the East; Titus, a legendary hero owing to his prowess during the war, remained in Vespasian's shadow for ten years, to die of illness after only a short reign as Caesar.

It is conventional to stress the harshness of Roman rule as an explanation, though perhaps only a partial one, for the ferocity of the Jewish uprising in 66. Yet it is obvious that the fanaticism shown by the Zealots and like-minded activists had little to do with the Romans.

Before the war the Roman administration had been lenient toward the Jews: there was no interference with Judaism as such (in any case, the Romans had no interest in their subjects' religion); Jews were exempt from acknowledging the divinity of the Emperors (except for a brief crisis under Caligula), from serving in the armed forces and in civic offices where their religion might have hampered them. In Judea itself they were given substantial autonomy.

The Maccabee uprising two hundred years before had been, after all, essentially a civil war: its target had been the largely hellenized Jewish aristocracy. But the Kingdom of God activists who rose against the Romans in 66 had the support not only of the mass of the population but of large sections of the aristocracy and priesthood. Those quietist Jews who accepted Roman rule did not do so as part of an apostasy from Judaism: even though the Kingdom of God activists regarded all collaborators with Rome as enemies, apostasy was by no means a current threat, apart from some distinguished individuals (such as Tiberius Alexander, Titus's supreme general in charge of the Jerusalem siege).

The uprising of 66, accordingly, had a positive factor—an upsurge in religio-national militancy. The very fact of the Kingdom of God movement, the notion of reviving Jewish sovereignty after the absorption of the whole area by the Roman Empire, struck both Romans and others as so strange that the defeat of 70 seemed a judgment of the gods—atheistic impiety, arrogance, and insolence had been punished.

THE FORMATION
OF THE CHURCH

CHAPTER TWO

The importance of the Roman-Jewish War, not only for the Jews but also for the new sect of believers in Jesus, can hardly be overestimated. The war brought about a split between the Jewish messianists in Palestine and the followers of Jesus in the Diaspora. It became a matter of life and death for his followers to dissociate Jesus, a messianic leader crucified by the Romans only a generation before as a rebel, from the activists who were carrying on a ferocious war against the Romans *now*—that is, from those who were actually doing what Jesus and his fellow messianists had only tried to do.

Jesus, after all, had been executed as a Zealot, that is, as a Kingdom of God activist, and no doubt for having seized the Temple (if the Gospel fragments indicating an actual seizure are to be believed: driving out the money-changers, being armed, preaching in the Temple for three days, and so on). This dissociation was all the easier to accomplish because of the "transcendental" otherworldly, universalist speculation articulated by Paul soon after the vision itself. This current had evidently made some headway; it enabled members of the new sect all over the

Roman Empire, and especially in Rome, to claim with sincerity that for them Jesus had never been an activist at all: for them the Kingdom of God was a "Kingdom not of this world." The new sect could whitewash the Romans and explain the execution of Jesus as the result of a Jewish conspiracy.

This was what gave rise to Mark, the first Gospel, which underlies Matthew and Luke. In Mark the Kingdom of God is denatured, that is, emptied of its activist content and etherealized, while Jesus, despite his undeniable identity as a Jew born in Palestine, is set at odds with his immediate Jewish background—his family ("Who are my mother and my brothers?") and the Pharisee and Sadducee parties in Palestine—and turned into a transcendental Son of God for all mankind.

This notion is consummated in the Gospel of John, the fourth and latest of the Gospels, no doubt written at least 150 years after Jesus, in which the transcendentalizing of the Christ is carried out still more extravagantly. For John, the Jews—"children of the Devil" (8:44)—represent an eternal principle of Evil: they are simply the Damned. As for Jesus, he is not a Jew at all. Indeed, he is scarcely human; he is an impenetrable, cosmic mystery. Prince of the True Light, he contends with the forces of Darkness, epitomized by the Jews.

Thus the Gospels, for all their deceptively bucolic atmosphere, in reality carry out in practical terms the intent of Paul himself—Jesus is magnified beyond the confines of Judaism and Palestine, beyond the parochial interests of the Kingdom of God activists, elevated beyond vulgar combat, and identified with the transcendental principles elaborated by Paul. It was the Gospels, supplemented by the letters of Paul, which survived by selection the oblivion that befell most of the letters he must have written, that formed the backbone of the New Testament a couple of centuries later.

Paul's lack of influence during his lifetime is evident from the very condition of his letters (much hotchpotch, very few letters extant, one entirely trivial letter, and so on). While the Temple stood, his ideas could make no headway. Even before the Temple was destroyed, there had been a proliferation of opinions about the meaning of the Resurrection: from Paul's letters we know of different "parties." With the Temple gone, they could compete with each other in what had become, so to speak, an open market. Thus it was the elimination of the Temple that enabled Paul's ideas, passionately formulated, to attract some groups of believers in Jesus, and eventually to dominate their farflung, still amorphous milieu.

This was possible, however, only through a singular quirk: a radical, quite unconscious reinterpretation of Paul's main idea, a reinterpretation imposed by what may be called a negative event: *the world did not end.* And because the world failed to end, nascent Christianity was to incorporate the Jews into a new world theory, which no longer derived its rationale from worldly conditions, but from the realm of ideas.

For the pagan world, the defeat and humiliation of the Jews, while not unwelcome, had no particular significance; it was on an entirely mundane level. The defeated Jews by definition had no power, nor did their God. But a new world theory, Christianity, was to restore power to the Jews—a dark and sinister power. It gave a *meaning* to the Jews that was to become the mainspring of mystical anti-Semitism, the singular idea I am discussing. And in the course of a few generations, this theory was to encompass the changing status of the Jews.

The extinction of Jewry as a territorially anchored nation proved to be a watershed in world history; for the world at large the effect of the destruction of the Temple in Jerusalem, a catastrophe for the Jews, was to clear the way for Christianity. Had the Temple survived, its unchallengeable authority would have constituted an impassable barrier during the initial stages of what was to become a new faith.

From a purely material point of view, to be sure, the importance of the Roman-Jewish War and the destruction of the Temple might seem exaggerated; after all, the Jewish state in Judea had been subjugated by the Romans for some time. Hasmonean independence had ceased generations before, from the time Palestine had been enveloped by the Romans in 63 B.C., with an interval of independence, restored for a mere three years (under Agrippa I in 41–45).

Still, even though Vespasian and Titus wiped out all vestiges of independence for good, the Jews were not disturbed in their religion, nor was their legal situation infringed on either in Judea or in the Diaspora. For that matter, the Romans, during the very siege of Jerusalem, had allowed the Jews to build another center in Judea (Jabneh), with a hereditary patriarchate, which in some spiritual sense could be thought of as replacing Jerusalem. For some time this center in Jabneh, under the descendants of the celebrated Hillel, supposedly of the royal house of David, exerted an almost monopolistic authority over Jews everywhere.

Nor was the elan of sovereignty entirely extinguished; in 115–17, only a generation and a half after the debacle of 70, Jewish communities in the Roman Diaspora, strengthened by the immigration of refugees and Jews ransomed from slavery, had become so powerful that they took advantage of Trajan's campaign against the Parthians to foment bloody riots in Libya, Egypt, and Cyprus.

For that matter, in Judea itself, despite all the massacres, devastations, and expropriations, the Jews recovered so quickly that only fifteen years after these riots another rebellion was launched under Bar Kochba, against whom Emperor Hadrian had to send his best general. The Bar Kochba revolt, summed up by Theodor Mommsen, "had not its match for intensity and duration" in the history of the Roman Empire.*

After the Bar Kochba fiasco Jews were forbidden access to Jerusalem altogether. The new city, crowned by the sanctuary of the supreme god of the Romans, "Jupiter Capitolinus," and by a monumental statue of Hadrian as warrior, was named Aelia Capitolina in his honor (his middle name was Aelius) and in that of the Capitoline Triad, Jupiter, Juno, and Minerva. Circumcision was made a capital crime for Jews, though not for Gentiles, including converts (this was rescinded by Hadrian's successor).

Jerusalem, the "Holy City," was now closed to Jews. "Judea" vanished: the Romans renamed the country after some ancient inhabitants, the Philistines, so that it came to be called, for a

---

* Theodor Mommsen, *The Provinces of the Roman Empire*, transl. W. Dickson, vol. 2, chap. 11, London: Macmillan & Co. Ltd., 1909, p. 224.

time, "Syria of the Philistines," then "Syria-Palestine," later abbreviated to "Palestine." This last name was revived by the British Mandate of 1919 and used to extend over both sides of the Jordan River (a geographical notion based a little vaguely on the Bible).

Hadrian's harshness toward the Jews has been taken by many as a reflection of Tacitus's views, though there is no real reason to seek an explanation beyond the natural exasperation of the Roman administration.

The debacle of 70 transformed the status of the Jews. As a people they were entirely humiliated in the eyes of the pagans generally, especially, in fact, the non-Romans: the vast sacrifices of blood and property in Judea, the burning of the Jewish capital and the celebrated Temple, the eradication of the High Priest-hood and the Sanhedrin, the bulk sale of cheap Jewish slaves in every city in the Roman Empire, all had a stunning effect.

Moreover, the victor of the war, Vespasian, the first of a new dynasty, transformed the annual voluntary Temple tax into a legal head tax for all Jews in the Diaspora as well as in Judea: the tax was allocated to the building and maintenance of the temple in Rome—a temple to Jupiter, to boot. (This *fiscus judaicus* was for some time collected by force.)

Thus, on top of the general catastrophe of the war, the Jews were singled out among all the inhabitants of the Empire by a unique obligation, that is, by a special status vis-à-vis the state. This created a precedent that was to remain effective for centuries and was constantly referred to by the heirs of the Empire. In the Middle Ages, for instance, any special legislation could find its validation in this special Jewish head tax: it was not merely the symbol but the actual legal basis of their subordination.

Practically all world histories regard the fall of Jerusalem, and the destruction of the Temple in 70, as the end of the Jews as a national entity, even though it was not until 637 that the Muslim-Arab conquests, which led to the gradual settlement of Arabs from the second third of the century on, wholly dejudaized Judea and Galilee.

Jews too have traditionally regarded the debacle of 70 as the beginning of the *real* Diaspora—that is, a Diaspora without a center. It is the strange fact of this existence of a Diaspora without a center that was to provide the historical background, so to speak, for what was to evolve into the "Jewish Question" in the nineteenth century. In the consciousness of Christians, the homelessness of the Jews after 70 A.D. was something uncanny.

On the basis of all previous experience, it would have seemed evident, and was taken to be so, that with time the Jews must vanish. A people scattered over a huge area that had previously been linked to a solid center of authority, as to the hub of an enormous wheel, was now expected to disappear through the normal processes of attrition, assimilation, and absorption in the culture of the host countries. Indeed, without a center, spiritual and physical, as Jerusalem and the Temple had been earlier, how could mere scattered individuals and small communities withstand the pressure of a dense cultural environment?

Yet strangely, the Jews did not disappear, even after the debacle of the Bar Kochba revolt in 135. They never merged with surrounding populations, nor did they accept in their hearts the seemingly mandatory verdict of the military outcome of ethnic conflict: rather, they clung to their religion, their customs, their separateness.

From a religious point of view there was deep satisfaction among the pagans at the Jewish debacle in 70. The Creator of the Universe, who had singled out the Jews among all other peoples for his special concern, had been shown up, it seemed, as a mere superstition. What was the value of such a god if he could save neither his own people nor his Temple, celebrated throughout the world for its splendor and beauty?

The destruction of the Temple had plainly been a major Roman objective. Though the Romans had for decades been unusually fair-minded to the Jews in the Diaspora and in Palestine—despite the corruption and depredations of most Judean procurators—once the activists had launched an actual revolt, it was obviously prudent to destroy their resistance utterly. The fate of the Temple, as the symbol of the spiritual arrogance of the Chosen People, summed up, in the Roman view and indeed in the view of all ordinary pagans, the total degradation of the Jews.

The arch (still in Rome today) erected to Titus, the conqueror of Jerusalem, by his brother, after Titus's early death, acclaimed Titus as "the first to destroy a city that before him all marshals, kings, and peoples had either besieged in vain or had not attacked at all." The triumphal coins featured on one side Titus's father Vespasian, the general who had passed on to Titus the task of reducing Jerusalem, and on the other Judea, as a woman, crushed in mourning under a palm tree, cowering in front of an arrogantly victorious Roman soldier. The Arch of Titus also shows the Menorah, the gold tabernacle, and the silver trumpets, all carried by Roman warriors wearing laurels. It is an impressive depiction of how the Jews in defeat appeared to the Romans—smashed in their devastated land, their god defeated, shattered, dethroned, and driven out of a Temple burned to cinders.

The pagans in the Diaspora, who had been attracted by the idea of the Kingdom of God, with the implications of universal redemption taken out of its specific national-religious context, now turned against the Jews in their midst. Jewish colonies in Alexandria, Antioch, and Cyrene, for instance, were called "enemies of God" who had been punished by the Zealot debacle.

The Roman-Jewish War of 66–70 refocused the hostility to the Jews in practical terms. In the minds of many leading Romans, it established them as congenital firebrands, troublemakers, and rebels.

Tacitus, for instance, denounces the Jews as the source of "subversion of the three main pillars of Rome—religion, country, and family." He seems to be referring both to the war in Palestine and to the attraction of Judaism for many upper-class women, still legally under their husbands' thumbs, for whom Judaism held out a vista of freedom.

Tacitus's entire account of the Jews before the war was based, curiously enough, on literally nothing but the disparaging legends that, as history, were worthless even at the time, all the more so since the Greek translation of the Bible had been in existence for centuries. Even though Tacitus grew up after the Roman-Jewish war, his would-be historic-ethnographic study was primarily intended to be a work of propaganda. He was determined to demonstrate that the Jews were mere rabble, odious to gods and men alike, capable of finding recruits only in a Rome that had become a seedbed for everything vile and abhorrent* (very similar to the portrait of the Jews in the writings of Cicero, Horace, Seneca, and Juvenal).

The importance of Tacitus's hostility to the Jews can scarcely be exaggerated: not only was he an authority in antiquity and the Middle Ages, with the Renaissance and the rediscovery of antiquity his influence was renewed—to endure, strangely enough, down to the present.

Palestine, and many centers of the Jewish Diaspora, lay athwart the main roads to Parthia, the only serious—and never conquered—enemy of the Empire. The Roman legions, who had to use the great highways from Egypt to Syria and Mesopotamia to be able to confront the Parthians, were constantly at risk: they were under permanent threat from Jewish insurrectionists en route. For both the Romans and all those pagans who had made their peace with Rome, the Jews seemed congenitally headstrong—opposing to the blessings of peace and prosperity an invisible God who had unaccountably chosen as his own this people of superstitious xenophobes.

Yet even after the debacle of 70, Judaism as a religion retained its influence in the Roman upper classes: for that very reason, many Romans, while smarting under the despotism of their own emperors, from Nero before 70 and Domitian afterward, resented the Jews as subversive of Roman moral standards in general. After the defeat of 70 many Roman intellectuals regarded Judaism, now infiltrating even the lower and middle classes with new ideas, as inherently dangerous.

Still, the military-political animus against Jews, considered as organized rebels, did not, perhaps surprisingly, bring about any changes in the Roman legal code. Even though Tacitus's venomous attitude toward the Jews, rooted in the conditions of his own day, was to play a role much later, as we shall see, it did not affect Roman policy toward the Jews as such at the time. It was the germination of Christianity that was to have the most enduring consequences for the Jews.

In the aftermath of the Roman-Jewish War, the idea of the

---

* *Annales*, 15, 44, in Salo W. Baron, *A Social and Religious History of the Jews*, vol. 1, New York: Columbia University Press, 1960, p. 191.

Kingdom of God began to fade as an immediate prospect, and above all as a source of emotional energy. Among Jews it was well-nigh extinct by the time of the Bar Kochba debacle of 135. Postponed to a remote future, it could no longer provoke action. Among the recruits to the new faith, too, it was fossilized a generation or two after Paul.

While the Kingdom of God idea had been alive, the differences among the various interpretations of the Resurrection of Christ had been harmonized by the high expectations of those who believed in the imminence of the Kingdom; had it come about, of course, all divergences would have been nullified. The Jewish believers in Jesus' special role as the Son of Man—a synonym for Messiah—simply expected Jesus to return in Glory as part of the installation of the Messianic Kingdom leading to the Kingdom of God. The Son of Man, the Messiah, had a meaning only in the cosmic drama.

Though Paul's view of the Kingdom of God was more visionary—there was to be no sexual life in the Kingdom of God, nor any divisions between mankind—the Incarnation, for him, was an historical event. God was of course eternal, but his Incarnation in a human being was temporary; it was meant to bring about another state of the universe that would, in turn, be eternal—the Kingdom of God. Once that was accomplished, God could, so to speak, withdraw his Incarnation.

For Paul, the man Jesus, while in some abstract way embodying the essence of God, had the appearance and personal circumstances of an ordinary human being. For that matter, the actual details about Jesus in the first three Gospels do not reflect the belief in the Incarnation: Jesus seems quite human.

Had Paul's theory of the hiatus between the Resurrection of Jesus and the Kingdom of God been correct, all his ideas would have been realized by the installation of the Kingdom, and thus nullified—by their success. As it was, the Son of Man–Messiah idea simply withered: those who had believed in this modified, nontranscendental notion either drifted back into Judaism, or joined the coteries gripped by Paul's transcendental ideas. And for the semipagan and pagan coteries converted to the belief in the "Lord Christ Jesus," the World's End no longer meant anything; hence there was no role for the Lord to play in it. For these coteries the concept of "The Lord" created mystical exaltation at the very moment of worship, there and then. It became, so to speak, a current condition of nature, a stasis of reality: the "real presence" of the Lord Christ Jesus during the very act of communion of his worshippers.

The transformation of the Mystic Body of Christ from an ad hoc mechanism in Paul's scheme into a condition of the universe meant that the Sacraments too, which for Paul were merely quasi-magical, since their purpose would be obviated once the Kingdom of God replaced the Natural World, became totally magical. In and for themselves they could change the substance of reality. In this way the Mystic Church as a whole became a magical instrument for the attainment of salvation.

The basic structure of Christianity—a Divine Being condescending to incarnate himself in a human being, who is then sacrificed for the salvation of others in the struggle against evil—is on the face of it a cosmic myth. But while myths dealing with the activities of pagan gods were restricted in scope by the general limitation on all pagan gods—none of them supreme, all subject to a primordial world order, all subject to Fate—when the pagan gods were replaced by Yahweh, Creator of the Universe, the myth embodying this, that is, the Incarnation, became infinite in its turn.

And the vast drama of the cosmos, which for Paul revolved around the collision between the forces representing God and the angel forces representing Satan, lost its dramatic power— the tension between opposing forces. In Paul's mind, while God had not yet conquered, he soon would. But with the elimination of an actual space of time at the end of which there would be a change, and the establishment of the Church as a permanent element in the universe, the Church itself became a condition of nature: salvation, accordingly, could come only through the Church.

Fundamentally, Paul's views arose out of his passionate conviction that the natural world was about to be transformed, the Kingdom of God installed. Paul's basic ideas—the Being-in-Christ, the Mystic Body of Christ, the Sacraments of Baptism and the Eucharist—were merely the antechamber to the Kingdom of God at the World's End. They had been elaborated only in order to bridge the hiatus between the Resurrection and the inexplicably postponed Kingdom of God.

A couple of generations later, when the hope of the World's End had faded, Paul's ideas were unconsciously dislocated from the concept that had given them their rationale. What finally made Paul's ideas appealing was not the theory he had worked out logically from the premise of the imminence of the World's End, but the intellectual vehicle created for the emotions by his powerful prose, which found a natural audience in a vast cosmopolitan society rent by upheavals of various kinds and no longer to be solicited by the purely Jewish World's End theories.

Paul's projection of hope for a future that was felt to be implemented, emotionally and conceptually, in the here and now, proved potent enough to serve as the basis of a theology he himself had never dreamed of. Since his general view, despite its Jewish matrix, could be addressed to mankind at large, the target of Christian propaganda generations after Paul, his writings could become the groundwork of a new canon at the very moment that their intellectual framework—actually their point —was dropped.

Paul's idea of the Incarnation, its function as a manifestation indissolubly linked to, and made meaningful only through, the World's End, was now integrated with nature. It successfully accomplished the work of reintroducing into the normal workaday world the sacrality that had been eliminated by the Jews a millennium before.

Thus Paul's history-bound, physical view of the World's End simply withered and fell away, to be replaced by the Church Fathers' theory of the timeless magic inherent in the notion that the fusion of the Spirit and the Flesh, mediated by the Church, had merely been exemplified for the first time in the case of Jesus. Salvation through identification not with the Body of Jesus, but with the Flesh, was a continuing miracle—a process embedded in nature and realized through the Sacraments of the Church.

But if the Church had become a condition of nature, an integral element of the world-stuff, the same effect was achieved on behalf of the Devil. In Judaism there is no autonomous Devil: the Devil, like everything else, is entirely subordinate to God.

Occasionally, for purposes of his own, God allows Satan to try something on his own, generally as a "test," but Satan cannot conceivably resist God: the very concept is absurd.

Hence, with the elimination of the contest between God forces and Devil forces underlying Paul's ideas, and with the establishment of the Church as a permanent condition of the world, Satan becomes autonomous—that is, the world is governed by both God and the Devil—the Church is the only way out.

But when the Church itself remained forever the very foundation stone of a universe in which God had *already* come, and was permanently, visibly, and tangibly present, interwoven with the fabric of the workaday world in the shape of the Church looming above all things, with the figure of God's only Son, conceived of as God himself, also present, the grandiose conception of the Incarnation became the most fundamental fact not merely of religious doctrine but of all life.

When Paul's concept of the Incarnation ceased to be a mere adjunct of the World's End, when it became part of everyday life in a Church intended to mediate salvation through the magical Sacraments, the result, for the Jews, was to expand, boundlessly, their role in the cosmic economy. Their role was magnified precisely by the unwitting magnification of the scope of the Incarnation by Paul's instinctive acceptance, as it were, of the all-powerful Jewish God, Creator of the Universe. Thus, if the Jews were to be the symbolical crystallization of the forces of evil on a scale commensurate with the infinite power of Yahweh, they naturally became the equivalent—in reverse.

Hence the "conversion" of the Jews, which for Paul was an indispensable element of the World's End drama, was shifted to the indefinite future, as the immediate World's End itself was forgotten. In the doctrine to be elaborated by the Church Fathers from their misperception of Paul's timetable, the Jews were not to be exterminated, to be sure, but they could not be redeemed either. They were held hostage, so to speak, and obliged to survive in misery and degradation as Witnesses to the Triumph of Christianity and as an emblem of the opposition that the Church Triumphant alone stood out against.

Hence, with the collision between God and the Devil no

longer Paul's historical, contingent idea, but instead a state of nature, the Jews were left with no role to play but that of being on the side of Satan—his ally, agent, and kin: they now represented, quite simply, the very principle of Evil.

And what was to lend this profoundly simple idea a most peculiar, indeed unique, potency was a concomitant of the Jews' identification with the Devil—they were *powerful*. That is, they shared in the power of Satan, who, though of course incapable of conquering God, could not, on the other hand, be vanquished—at least not while the Church existed.

Because the Jews had been embedded in Christian Scripture in its earliest stages, their refusal to acknowledge the Incarnation was not remotely comparable to the failure of other non-Christians, in the future, to become converts. Muslims, Hindus, Buddhists, Confucians, and so on were not to be considered demonic for clinging to their beliefs in the teeth of missionary zeal: they were merely crippled by ordinary human fallibility.

If Paul's absorption in the imminent World's End had been understood by the second generation after the destruction of the Temple, he would have been no more than an historical curiosity. But a century after his death his writings were solidly established; they required only a new interpretation. While Paul's place in the canon was unshakable, some of his ideas were forgotten, others reinterpreted.

The Church Fathers (Origen, Tertullian, Chrysostom), having abandoned the expectation of the Kingdom of God, welded Paul's ideas together and interpreted them as part of a *new* philosophy, in which the Church, eternal and universal, the reflection of God on earth, was confronted by the enemies of God, the children of Satan, the Jews, whose paramount function was to epitomize the struggle of the Devil forces against God. Thus the Jews, in Paul's mind a temporary ally of the Devil forces, had become the Counter-Incarnation on earth all by themselves. What had been, for Paul, their error became, for the Church Fathers, their nature.

The foundation of this view was eventually laid down in the Christian Scriptures, long after Paul, to be organized as the New

Testament. In the Scriptures themselves, to be sure, the consequences were not yet drawn: Paul's comments, in their own context, are ambiguous. But the Scriptures were also the foundation, properly interpreted, of the Church Fathers' doctrines generations later. And the interpretation was naturally based on the overwhelming fact that meanwhile Paul's great idea—the imminence of the Kingdom of God—had simply been forgotten. Thus the Jews, in fact powerless since their defeat and dispersion, were to embody a strange, eerie power, despite all appearances, through their being integrated with a new world view that assigned them their peculiar status—enemies of Jesus Christ, and hence of God, through their rejection of the Incarnation.

It is obvious that this concept—timeless, mythical—marks the first, and indeed the fundamental, formulation of what must now be called mystical anti-Semitism, in sharp contradistinction to the sporadic hostility to the Jews that had existed before. This new cosmic theory shifts us to a different terrain; it is a terrain that has survived down to our own day. In the twentieth century, indeed, this view of the Jews has, as we shall see, received a stunning exemplification.

All previous attitudes to the Jews, no matter how virulent, envenomed, hate-filled, were nevertheless no more than exaggerations of a real human situation—group frictions, political rivalries, social irritations, and so on. Greeks and Romans had regarded the Jews as xenophobic, intolerant, arrogant, atheistic. But all these traits, even if expressed with hyperbole, were common expressions of animosity or political outrage. Under the Roman Empire, when the Jews were considered intractable, Roman irritation was a response to a simple fact—they *were* intractable. The never-ending outbursts of rebelliousness—on behalf, moreover, of incomprehensible ideals—justified their reputation as troublemakers, a reputation that after the debacle of 70 was compounded, very satisfactorily for their enemies, by the stigma of political and military defeat.

All such attitudes, common for generations because of the situation of the Jews, and rooted to some extent in classical literature—known, to be sure, only to a small elite—were now encompassed, absorbed, and transformed to create an image that was entirely new—a demonic vision rooted in a new ideology.

The Jews had become demonstrations of a concept escalated, as it were, to another, cosmic plane: no longer mere people— irritating, maddening—but entities with a *meaning*, rejected, and above all *damned*, by God (the original meaning of "Damned Jew"). The corollary of this was, of course, that all those who saw this in the Jews, and were implementing what they saw, were doing no more than carrying out on earth what God had ordained in Heaven.

This original theory—perhaps unique in history in bestowing cosmic meaningfulness on ordinary people—was elaborated by the Church Fathers during the end of the first and the beginning of the second century. It was an essential part of the general process, not of rejecting Judaism—this was ruled out by the accepted accounts of Jesus, the Apostles, and Paul—but of absorbing Judaism, and indeed all Jewish history, into the Church.

The Hebrew Scriptures were taken into the Christian canon *in toto*: they were thought to show the road to Jesus Christ, who thus became the consummation of more than a millennium of Jewish tradition. They were all adopted en bloc so as to make them conform with the paramount assertion of the new faith, that all major claims of Christianity, being in their nature divine, had naturally been predicted in bygone ages. In this way all the spiritual leaders of past Jewry were taken to have been preexistent Christians, while all living Jews were denounced as worthless. This claim was itself founded as it were organically on the ancient writings in which the Hebrew Prophets had systematically castigated the Jews as having failed to live up to the demands of their own religion.

All messianic prophecies—that is, since the Babylonian Exile, and even from before, since Messianism, after all, was deeply rooted—were wrenched out of their down-to-earth historic context and applied to Jesus and to Christianity. The Jews were deprived of the right even to hope for a better future, while all the prophetic denunciations of actual Jews in the past were extended, congealed, and hypostatized as applying to the *essence* of Jews eternally. In this way the Curse of Cain could be considered to apply to the Jews, killers of the Deity, until the end of time. In the words of Irenaeus, Bishop of Lyons in the second century: "If the Prophets had only realized what an abuse was to be made of their exhortations, so that eventually they held a blessing for all people *except* the Jews, who were to get nothing but curses, they would, no doubt, have burned them."[*]

Thus, whatever was taken by the Jews to be positive in Judaism was turned by the early Church Fathers into something negative. The image of the Messiah was split into two: the positive element was taken to have been consummated in the figure and the concept of Jesus Christ, while the Messiah as believed in by Jews appeared to Christian thinkers as an arch-enemy— as anti-Christ, an emanation of Satan. The Jews themselves, accordingly, were understood to be no longer children of God —as in their own estimation they had been, regardless of individual derelictions of behavior—but the sons of the Devil.

The Church Fathers, writing in the first three centuries after the germination of Christianity, constructed a typology of Jewry that was entirely new in history—the Evil Jew, accursed, so to speak, in his nature, who chooses the Golden Calf over God, who even rejects his own salvation in favor of an immediate earthly advantage. In this devastating Christian conception, Judas, who in this view betrayed Jesus, his God and Savior, for thirty pieces of silver, was taken to be the archetype of all Jews—that is, a satanic character, pure evil, who does evil for its own sake. For how, after all, could a mere thirty pieces of silver outweigh salvation? This potent symbol of Evil was to be embedded in the new myth of the Jews as arch-exponents of Evil in the universe.

The key element in all this was the stupendous fact that Judas, symbol of the Jews, and the Jews as the collective symbol of Evil, were evil precisely because *they knew what they were doing*. They were in no sense pagans, outside the Light through mere ignorance. The Jews, knowing the truth of Christianity, nevertheless rejected it. It was this Evil through knowledge that was a paramount element of the alliance of the Jews with the Devil—was, indeed, the source of their kinship with him.

---

[*] Cited in Alex Bein, *The Jewish Question*, Teaneck, N.J.: Fairleigh Dickinson University Press, 1990, p. 68.

There was now in the world, accordingly, a community of human beings, bound together by blood as well as by beliefs, who despite all appearances could be thought of as evil by nature—and on a scale, moreover, that made them the counterpart and enemy of God. It is obvious that the eeriness of this conception of the Jews lies in just this contradiction between their apparent helplessness and their hidden power.

During the era in which Christian doctrine concerning the Jews was formulated by the Church Fathers, the Jews stood out as having been dramatically undone, over a long period of time, by the Roman Empire. Their most obvious characteristic, in the countries in which they were now sojourners, was their uprootedness, their dispersion as wanderers in a hostile universe, their inability to control their own destinies. It was precisely this condition, indeed, that was thought to be their punishment for having remained Jews.

As individuals, too, they were generally engaged in pursuits that seldom rose above the ordinary. Even those Jews who acquired riches and influence could not raise the level of Jews collectively, but were considered merely ordinary individuals who had been successful in specific situations.

To the extent that pagans were aware of them at all, the Jews were mere pariahs. And for the masses being christianized, they were the very symbol of defeat, a punishment for rejecting God. How, then, could the notion of Jewish power be sustained? How could it be made convincing?

It would seem necessary to suppose that the split in the notion of the Jews, as being simultaneously powerful and helpless, was made possible by a split in the mind: on the upper levels of perception, the Jews could be seen clearly as being what in fact they were; on the lower, symbolizing levels of the imagination, they could stand for the awesome, eerily invisible power of endless Evil. Double vision may be an inborn feature of the human imagination: a specific phenomenon contemplated through the prism of a general conception is not only understood but perceived in a special way.

In real life this could be manifested by a failure to notice the contradiction between the eerie power of the Jews and the obvious fact that they could be harassed, savaged, and destroyed at will. Thus people were not baffled by the failure of the Jews to use their demonic powers to save themselves from mistreatment that sometimes went as far as large-scale massacres; their evident inability to defend themselves did not, somehow, invalidate the notion that they were all-powerful *secretly*.

Double vision is necessary to explain the persuasiveness to so many people of this radical misconception of ordinary reality. As the diametrical opposite of the true Jewish condition, it is the most striking element in this inflamed cosmic fantasy of Jewish power. For pragmatically, the obvious fact of Jewish helplessness leaps to the eye: all authorities, both ecclesiastical and secular, could and in fact did handle Jews with complete arbitrariness, and with immunity, for many centuries, down to the modern era.

It was this conception of the Jewish role in the universe that was to constitute the "problem" of the Jews for Christian thinkers. For if the Jews, guilty of crucifying the Lord Christ Jesus and rejecting God, had been damned for centuries, why had they survived at all?

The classic answer to this conundrum was given in the fifth century by St. Augustine, refocusing theologically Paul's straightforward, simple historical view. Paul, as we have seen, thought the Jews God's people despite everything; when the Kingdom of God was finally installed, a few decades or so after the Resurrection, all would be set right. For Augustine too, the Jews remained God's people, but since the Kingdom of God had now been postponed to the remote future, the current status of the Jews was, for all practical purposes, permanent: having entirely invalidated their "chosenness," they were now accursed, scattered over the face of the earth, homeless, enslaved by princes and peoples, and forced to worship Christianity, the true heir to that "chosenness." *That* was why they had survived—to be eternal witnesses precisely to their own guilt, as well as to the truth of the prophecies embedded in their own Scriptures, now properly understood only by the Church, and to be witnesses too to the very Triumph of that Church.

Augustine's view became the official view of the Church: it guaranteed the Jews a place in the world view of Christianity— though it was, to be sure, a negative place, just as it had been for Paul—but now, with the time element forgotten, expanded and eternalized.

Perhaps a crowning irony was that the evolution of Christian doctrine, which was to prove such a burden for the Jews, also created a counter-balancing factor, an integral part of its very structure, that acted as a brake on the very oppression of the Jews that it simultaneously explained and justified. That brake, as we shall see, was to preserve the Jews as a people.

The Jews themselves naturally played no role in the formation of the theology that cast them in such a sinister role. Once the history-bound ideas of Paul were recast as theology, and the Jews transformed into the exemplification of a concept, the phenomenon of mystical anti-Semitism soared far beyond their comprehension. It would be no exaggeration to say that for Jews as a collectivity it was to remain a peculiarly irrational form of hatred.

It took several generations for Jewish national consciousness to change. Jews had to transform their view of themselves as a people that, even though widely scattered, had a territorial center, to a people with no land of their own and hence with no reason not to migrate from place to place.

With the debacle of 70 and the various mutinies and insurrections that followed around the Mediterranean, until it seemed that the will to sovereignty was extinguished after the abortive Bar Kochba revolt in 135, the need for resignation was finally internalized. Successive military defeats had given rise to a feeling that steadily grew and spread throughout the Diaspora—armed struggle was hopeless. God had handed down his verdict: for the foreseeable future it was to be the destiny of the Jews to have no center on earth, or rather, to have as their true center a spiritual one—what many centuries later was to be called (by Heinrich Heine) a portable fatherland: the Hebrew Scriptures.

For some Jews, by the end of the second or third generation, the "problem" of Jewish existence under a pagan power and outside a center no longer meant anything: they accepted the Roman Empire, not only externally but in their hearts. Others, who inwardly rejected Rome and all it stood for, also rejected Judaism: the dismay over the fall of Jerusalem in 70, and especially the destruction of the Temple—thought by pious Jews to be literally impregnable—seems to have accelerated the abandonment of Judaism by many Jews, veering away from the Pharisees, who were to live on in the rabbis of succeeding ages down to our own day, and joining various groups of the new Jesus cult, which before the triumph of Paul's Christology included many ordinary Jews.

For a time it was possible to be both a Christian and a Jew. Before the evolution of Christian theology—when the belief in the Messianic status of Jesus involved no principle, but could be thought a personal or political idiosyncrasy—and before the definitive extinction of statehood with the Bar Kochba debacle in 135, Christians were in fact regarded by the Romans as a species of Jew, partly because of the involvement of Jesus and his partisans in the messianist agitation against Rome, and partly because the new theology had not yet coagulated.

Because of this, even though it had been essential during the war of 66–70 for the believers in Jesus to dissociate themselves from the Zealots in Jerusalem, the slowly growing Christian community nevertheless benefited for a long time from the legal status of Judaism. But when that became impossible, because of the evolution of theology in the Christian community, on the one hand, and the gradual intensifying of self-defense among the Jews, on the other, the communities were permanently split. By 135 it was no longer possible to be both.

Still, the bulk of the Jews in the Diaspora both of Rome and of Parthia, as well as the Jewish communities scattered around the Mediterranean and Arabia, clung to their religion and customs. Their very existence demonstrated the feeling that must have animated them—that the Roman victory meant nothing to them, either collectively or as individuals.

From the religious point of view, after all, there had been no distinction of principle between the activists and the quietists in the insurrections against the Romans: for the Zealots the help of God had been indispensable both theoretically and, as they rightly thought, practically. For both quietists and activists the struggle against Rome had been, at bottom, a struggle for the same Kingdom of God on earth.

Thus pious Jews even after the defeat did not interpret the defeat as the defeat of God—an incomprehensible idea. It was simply that God had not approved of that kind of struggle—that the concept, crystallized in the phrase "Forcing the End" (of History) or "Forcing the Kingdom of God," had not found favor with God, who had other plans. Thus pious Jews in the Diaspora felt it natural to cling still more ardently to their God.

It was just this reaction on the part of the Jews that struck the antique world as bizarre, uncanny: why did the Jews not draw what was obviously, in terms of common sense, the true conclusion—that their God himself had been shown up by his opponents, that he had lacked the power to defend either his Temple or his people, in short, himself, against his opponents? How was it that even after the fall of the Temple and the national humiliation, people *still* considered God the only God and looked down on the gods of the pagans with scorn, called them frauds, nonexistent? That even after the titanic defeat of 70 they went on insouciantly propagating their belief? How could such arrogance be explained?

The crowning oddity was that the propagation of Judaism after the defeat of 70 was eminently successful: there was a steady influx of pagans who seemed to accept the Jewish version of the debacle—indeed, were impressed by the authoritative assurance of the Jews even after the debacle, and themselves became Jews. Thus, from the general pagan point of view, the Jews, in the teeth of the evidence, even in the countries to which they had gone after being driven out of their own country, still clung to a defeated and humiliated god.

The belief in God's uniqueness and benevolence on behalf of his Chosen People led to a further internalization of the objective situation: the verdict of history was also the verdict of God, was in fact the same thing. This was, of course, the fundamental theory of Judaism. And after the consolidation of the Diaspora, that is, the digestion of a new fact of life—the vanishing of the national center in Judea—the Jews who remained Jews accepted that too as the expression of God's will. This acceptance was facilitated by the gradual shift in the locus of religious practice from the centralized services in the Temple of Jerusalem to the synagogues that at first, after the Return from Babylon, had paralleled the services in the Temple and then, with the disappearance of the Temple, replaced the very concept of centralization by the independence of small communities that freely accepted the Scriptures as their basis.

In this way the knowledge of the Scriptures was democratized: without a priesthood, every Jew could read, understand, and grapple with the Scriptures on his own. Just as the notion of a Divine Plan had been the unique fruit of Judaism from its inception, so the knowledge of the Torah was part of the patrimony of each and every individual Jew—a notion that was also unique in history.

Thus the Dispersion too could be seen as part of the Divine Plan: the messianic ideal of a restoration to Zion in a regenerated world could be regarded as a method of bringing the Light unto the Nations.

To be sure, the efficacy of this general theory could cut both ways: the Divine Plan was also taken over by Christianity, with a contrary twist: the blindness of the Jews was also part of that Plan, together with the notion that the conversion of the Jews had to be accomplished before the general regeneration of the world took place in the far-off future. Thus, on the level of argument, any solution was precluded by the contrary parallelism of the claims.

A root of Jewish optimism—the élan to survive, in the teeth of general hostility—could be found in the concept of the "Birth pangs of the Messiah," the notion that the Kingdom of God was to be heralded by dislocations, upheavals, slaughters, massacres, suffering in general. Thus the travail undergone by Jewry in Christendom could be interpreted by the pious as precisely a reason for hope: the greater the suffering, the better!

But perhaps the chief source of hope was the mystical belief in the Messiah.

Originally thought of as a flesh-and-blood human being carrying out God's will in the manner of the Prophets who preached God's word, the Messiah, after the successive disappointments of the actual upheavals fueled by the Messianic hope in the first century and afterward, became a misty, indefinite figure of the remote future. While pious Jews were meant to believe in the Messiah as though "he might come today," in practice the hope was held out only for the End of Time. This might have implanted a grain of optimism in the Jewish masses, giving them a sort of elasticity that helped them survive the burdens of their environment. Since the masses were wholly integrated with their Scriptures, with no priesthood or other authority intervening, the fusion of the theory and the hope it underlay might have given the Jews both a sort of psychic independence and an intellectual and emotional prop for sustaining it.

On the institutional level, the vast work of the Talmud created a framework for the life of Jewry in exile. Practically speaking, it secured Jewish communal existence administratively and legally. The Talmud was supreme in all aspects of Jewish communal life except insofar as one of its own precepts—that the Law of the Land is the Law—constituted a basic, common-sense concession to reality: in practical affairs Jews were governed by the authorities of whatever country they were in.

The Talmud was compiled, gradually, as a surrogate for the World's End, which, evidently postponed, made it imperative for the ideas, beliefs, and behavior of Diaspora Jewry to be organized. It was the workaday underpinning for the mystical belief in the Messiah: while the Messiah was "tarrying," the Talmud established order in the exiled communities for life to be carried on in accordance with God's will.

The Pharisees had been distinguished by their emphasis on the "Oral Law," a method of interpreting Scriptural prescriptions and prohibitions so as to adapt them to changing circumstances. This Oral Law was now organized, around 200, into the Mishnah (Instruction), supplemented over the centuries by the Gemarah (Completion), a record of the discussions in the academies in Palestine and in Babylon and the decisions based on debates, recorded observations of notables, anecdotes, and pious expositions. This was finally set down in writing in a definitive form in 500, then closed. Thus the Talmud (work of instruction), consisting of Mishnah and Gemarah, became the fully authoritative exponent of the Halakha, or proper way of life, for some sixty generations of Jews down to the modern era.

In countless details the Talmud, a comprehensive commentary on the Hebrew Bible, summed up commands, prescriptions, prohibitions, and customs that, taken together, "hedged off" the life of the believing Jew from the life of everyone else: not only the succession of festivals and working days, leading to the New Year's annual atonement, Yom Kippur, but every moment of the day was accounted for, from the cradle to the grave. It was a living realization of a famous passage in the Pentateuch (Balaam's curse-blessing in Numbers 23:9): "A people that lives alone and mingles not with others."

Thus what had seemed to the peoples of antiquity as the self-isolation of the Jews was reinforced in a variety of ways. To the Christians of Europe, who knew even less about the various "hedges" around Jewish life in the Talmud than had been known in antiquity about the Hebrew Scriptures themselves, this accomplishment of a people that no longer even lived in its own land made the Jews seem more uncanny than ever.

The "hedging" did not mean, to be sure, that Jews were cut off from society: on the contrary, there was an organic interaction between Jews and their neighbors with respect to language, clothing, housing, organization, way of life, and culture in general. But this could scarcely have an effect on intimate life: as before, Jews could not dine out with their neighbors; intermarriage was out of the question; nor could Jews in Christendom participate in the life of the state, for a long time intertwined with the Church.

This situation was consolidated after the Muslim conquests of the seventh century put a stop to the isolated revolts that had been common in the eastern Mediterranean, in which Jews in Palestine had taken part in armed conflicts between Byzantium and Persia. With the Muslim conquests the rise of Islam, which for the time being took Palestine too out of the sphere of Jewish hopes, the verdict of God and history was finally accepted: "the Jews left the ranks of warring nations and put their fate altogether in the hands of God."* This lasted until the Zionist move-

---

* Y. F. Baer, *Galut*, transl. Robert Warshow, New York: Schocken Books, 1947, p. 19.

ment of the late nineteenth century, whose goal was the restoration of a Jewish state.

Until the present day, however, the uniqueness of Jewish existence in Christendom has not merely been epitomized by the oddities of Jewish life and customs; it has been illuminated, as we shall see, by the macabre refulgence shed on Jewry by its satanic role in the universe.

THE FOCUS
OF THEOLOGY

CHAPTER   THREE

Though a theory to encompass the strangeness of Jewry was perfected during the first few generations after the formation of the new religion, its impact was not felt among the populations of Europe for a long time. The christianization of Europe took centuries.

In the second and third centuries, converts to Judaism were a significant phenomenon. This was natural: after all, the Jews were the people of the Old Testament, adopted en bloc by the earliest Christian orthodoxy; simple-minded Christians tended to consider rabbis the ablest interpreters of the most ancient texts, venerated by the Church itself. For instance, the author of the Latin Vulgate, St. Jerome, inevitably turned to Jewish consultants for basic instruction. The Jewish calendar itself, at a time when calendars were superstitiously venerated, was followed by Christians for more than two centuries.

It took a long time for the Church to congeal into a hierarchical structure: no effective control could be exercised over the interpretation of the sacred texts by the Christian communities that were gradually spreading throughout Europe and the Middle East. Sects and schisms proliferated; many of them over-emphasized, from the point of view of the later Church, the "Jewish" view of things, which might well be difficult to "refute," since it was embedded in texts necessarily revered by the Christian authorities. Nor were the Jews so far wrenched out of normal society that they could be held to exemplify the wretched condition in which they were supposed to be frozen. For many centuries, in short, the status of the Jews was relatively untouched by the stringencies of doctrine.

During the first few centuries the denunciations of Jews scarcely ever utilized the real elements—social frictions and irritations—in the coexistence of Jews and Christians. It was not the social reality in the era of the Church Fathers that kindled hatred of the Jews—a nineteenth- and twentieth-century cliché of dogmatic social theory—but the obsession of the elite with a metaphysical theory.

Though hatred and ostracism of the Jews were a theological mandate, in ordinary life Jews were not touched by it until much later. In everyday life real Jews were largely exempt from the theological logic of the "Damned Jew," the surrogate for Satan on earth. The "Damned Jew," castigated, vilified, denounced in the anti-Semitic tracts of the Church Fathers, did not engage as yet the emotions of ordinary Christians. Thus the "Damned Jew" existed as it were outside real life, perhaps in a realm of abstract ideas that does not impinge on it. The sweep of metaphysics soared far beyond real-life Jews.

For many years Judaism, even after the debacle of 70, retained great magnetic appeal because of its antiquity, its simplicity, and its undeniability as the background of the Savior and thus, in Church theory, as the source of Christianity itself. In the earliest period of Christian proselytizing of pagans, there was indeed a natural tendency to regard the Jews as the "people of God," if only because of their descent from the Biblical Patriarchs as well as their identity as founders of Christianity.

This is obvious in the very attacks by the Church Fathers on the Jews, in denunciations of a bizarre violence that at the same time indicate normal relations between Jews and their neighbors.

John Chrysostom (344–407), for instance, was infuriated by

the respect, goodwill, and friendship enjoyed by the Jews among their pagan and Christian neighbors; his fury was inflamed by the failure of the pagans and Christians to grasp the metaphysical horror of the Jews. Chrysostom was not only a fiery orator, but very learned; no doubt he represented the consummation of the mystical revulsion against the Jews collectively: he created a mold for the image of Jewry that became the exemplar for the mystical conception of the Evil Jew. His diatribes were remarkable:

> Brothel and theater, the synagogue is also a cave of pirates and the lair of wild beasts . . . Living for their belly, mouth forever gaping, the Jews behave no better than hogs and goats in their lewd grossness and the excesses of their gluttony. They can do one thing only: gorge themselves with food and drink . . .

For Chrysostom, the source of the stunning iniquities of the Jews was their "odious murder of Christ." For this there could of course be "no expiation possible, no indulgence, no pardon." The Dispersion of the Jews was brought about not by mortal men, but by God himself; by "the wrath of God and his absolute abandon" of the Jews. "God hates the Jews forever."*

Chrysostom was not of course alone in his castigation: here is another instance of the peculiar infusion of a theological idea with passion:

> Slayers of the Lord, murderers of the Prophets, enemies of God, haters of God, adversaries of grace, enemies of their fathers' faith, advocates of the Devil, brood of vipers, slanderers, scoffers, men of darkened minds . . . congregations of demons, sinners, wicked men, stoners and haters of goodness. (Gregory of Nyssa)**

This view of the Jews, restricted for a few centuries to a small elite, gradually began to spread, along with the spread of Christianity.

The expansion of Christianity, in tandem with the slowly

---

* Chrysostom, *Homilies*, 6:4, 6:2, 1:7; delivered in Antioch, cited in Edward H. Flannery, *The Anguish of the Jews*, New York: Mahwah, 1985, pp. 47, 48.
** Ibid.

growing power of different states, was itself rather slow, but from the early part of the fourth century on, the Church began to extend its influence over society at large, in particular from the time the state itself, under Constantine (313), officially sponsored Christianity.

Constantine had initially decreed a form of tolerance toward non-Christians, based on the prohibition of idol worship as well as of emperor worship. By eliminating the barrier between pagans and nonpagans, this might have been thought to ensure further tolerance with respect to the Jews, but when Theodosius I made Christianity the actual state religion (392), tolerance came to an end. Fanaticism, embodied in a state institution, was now directed with special force against the Jews. The metaphysics of the Church was soon solidified. What had been mere views beforehand were, from the early part of the fourth century on, rammed home systematically and energetically, through two channels, the legislation of the Church itself and that of the state.

From the fourth century on, religious festivals, which had been substantially the same for Jews and Christians, were deliberately differentiated: the circumcision of Christians, even of Christian slaves, was now forbidden to Jews; this was swiftly followed by prohibiting the conversion to Judaism of all non-Jews, while Jews were forbidden to prosecute Jewish converts to Christianity. The social transformation effected during the first few centuries after the consolidation of Christianity was thus profound.

Before, the Jews had been the same, socially and professionally, as the peoples they lived among: they were, like everyone else, farmers, artisans, and, in the upper strata, merchants. But very soon they were placed in a category of their own. Most important, they were forced off the land, indeed, forbidden even to own land.

In Palestine the interdiction on the ownership of land resulted from a policy under the Byzantine Empire and the Church, which was sustained later on by the Muslims after their conquests in the seventh century. Elsewhere it was enforced by legislation. Jews were also excluded from the army, the civil services, and the respectable professions. Also, in accordance with the principle that Jews were ipso facto forbidden to rule over Christians, they came to be forbidden the possession of Christian slaves. If a pagan slave became a Christian his Jewish owner was obliged to free him out of hand (the only problem was that of compensation, whether with or without).

Forced into the cities, Jews naturally turned to commerce, though here too, during these first centuries, not disproportionately. Substantial numbers remained artisans, especially in the East, and in the higher strata, physicians.

The legislation after Constantine directly affected Palestine: Jerusalem became a purely Christian capital—studded with magnificent buildings, the visible symbol of the Triumph of the Church and conversely of the Divine Curse. The throngs of pilgrims who journeyed to see the places where the Savior had lived and suffered became torrential. Christianity was now the total and exclusive heir of all Jewish claims. Jews were squeezed out of the country, very nearly altogether: the Patriarchate of Jerusalem was abolished (425).

The dispersion was now well-nigh total, but the immigration of Jews into other countries did not proceed in an organized manner: they did not arrive as either conquerors or colonizers, but simply in order to survive as best they could wherever they settled. For many centuries, no doubt, individuals and small groups felt a lively identification with Palestine. This sentimental survival made it natural for them to regard their new dwelling places as not permanent, that is, as not a true substitute for Palestine.

On the other hand, however they thought of their ancient homeland, it remained in the realm of ideas. It did not help them materially, nor did it sustain them in any way. Individuals and small groups naturally tended to live in one place with their own people. In the case of the Jews, this was all the more important, since it was also a requirement of their religion: a "good Jew" cannot live alone. It was only in compact groups that children could be given religious instruction and the prescriptions of the Scriptures carried out.

All this was, of course, limited to the Jews themselves: there was no question of proselytizing among the peoples in whose midst the Jews were now settling. The colonies founded by Jews in this unorganized, haphazard manner were merely extensions of other, equally shapeless colonies of immigrants clinging together: no doubt the prelude to the compulsory ghettoization of the Jews later on.

The very style of colonization was another demonstration that from the very beginning Jews were settling down in different countries as foreigners: the question of how long they would stay was always open. Thus, whether or not they were regarded as foreigners in the legal sense—this varied through the ages— they were always regarded as aliens vis-à-vis the natives. There were three basic categories, accordingly, in which the Jews appeared expressly alien: in religion, as foreigners, and in terms of the law of the land they were settling in.

Especially where the Bible was authoritative—that is, in all countries where Christianity became dominant—it was natural for ordinary people to regard the Jews as coming from the Holy Land, that is, as foreigners by definition, driven out of their own country—for accepted theological reasons—and now living as aliens elsewhere.

The theological explanation given of this apparently simple situation—that the Jews had been driven out of their homeland in punishment for murdering the Savior, as taught by the Church—merely lent an uncanny element to the whole situation. This widespread and rather natural view made it easy to accept the basic idea that the Jews were accomplices of the enemies of Christendom—first of all, of course, since the seventh century, of the Muslims; for centuries large numbers of Jews had been drifting from their territory into Europe, and had been engaged in trade with them ever since.

This general attitude—minus, to be sure, the theological explanation—was of course shared by the Jews. No matter how long they stayed in any country, for centuries they felt no inner bond to that country, even though they quickly adopted its language and customs.

Thus, regardless of economic prosperity, and despite their increase in numbers and their lucrative livelihoods, houses of worship, and so on, Jews did not feel themselves to be on their own land, even though they might have acquired it as real estate. Anchored in their religion, they felt themselves to be "abroad," at least until the coming of the Messiah, who would arrive in due course, gather them all together from the ends of the earth, and lead them to their own country.

Meanwhile, Jews had been moving around Europe for centuries. Until the eighth century most had lived in Asia, North Africa, essentially in the Byzantine Empire, and in the countries conquered by Islam in the seventh and eighth centuries. But from the eighth to the twelfth century, the movement of population was reversed: the bulk of the Jews shifted from Asia to Europe, and from the twelfth to the late fourteenth century on, down to this century, most of Jewry has been contained within Christendom.

From remote antiquity Jews had been in Greece, around the Aegean, Italy, Spain, southern France, and in the Roman colonial towns on the Rhine. But after the folk migrations of the first centuries A.D., after conversion had given the newly christianized pagans a special zeal—as in Spain, under the West Goths, as well as in France, northern Italy, and so on—all these ancient settlements were nearly wiped out, to be succeeded, from the tenth century on, by the immigration of Jewish newcomers from far away, from Catholic Spain and the Byzantine areas. They came, above all, from territories that had fallen to Islam, a world regarded by the Christendom of the early Middle Ages as inherently strange, uncanny, and hostile.

If we take a bird's-eye view of the tensions surrounding the Jews in Europe, just before the outbreak of the long-drawn-out crisis initiated by the First Crusade in 1096, we shall see an apparent relaxation. In Germany, for instance, special privileges were given the Jews in 1084 and 1090 (in Speyer) to facilitate their settlement; the privileges included special rights for a merchant guild. The bishop, turning his episcopal seat into a city, made a point of boasting of having gone out of his way to attract the Jews in order to "augment the honor of our region." He had made them settle outside the residential districts of the other citizens and placed a wall around their own, so that "they would not be bothered by the mischief of the rabble."*

They received the right to exchange gold and silver freely throughout the city and to buy and sell whatever they liked; to govern themselves and employ Christian servants and keep Christian slaves. These rights of 1084 were confirmed and expanded by Holy Roman Emperor Henry IV: in a further Privilege (of 1090) it was explicitly forbidden to seize any Jewish property of any kind whatever; Jews received "the full right to trade their possessions honestly with any person and to move about freely and peacefully in our territory, to engage in commerce and business, to buy and sell."** Compulsory baptism and torture for the purpose of extorting confessions were forbidden; injuring or murdering a Jew was liable to severe punishment.

These privileges reflected their status as a special sort of outsider, rather like the status of a colony designed to attract foreign merchants.

All this was, of course, on the level of daily civic life. At the same time, as the dispersion of the Jews was gradually consolidated, what had previously been a mere socio-political fact was given by Christian theology a special symbolical, metaphysical *meaning*. Just as the collective Jewish rejection of the Savior had a special meaning in the cosmology of the nascent faith, so the Diaspora itself—though already in existence for five centuries —was now taken as a divine punishment for the murder of God. By the end of the eleventh century—the beginning of the First Crusade—the complex of concepts and attitudes worked out by the Church Fathers and summed up by the phrase "Damned Jew" was to encompass all Christendom.

The growth of Church power was naturally accompanied, as Christianity seeped throughout Europe, by a comprehensive effort to inculcate its dogmas. These dogmas, meant to interpret and illuminate all aspects of life, equally naturally included the basic theory of Good and Evil, whose cornerstone consisted of precisely the historical element of Christianity as interpreted by

---

* Cited in Bein, *The Jewish Question*, op. cit., p.147.
** Ibid.

the Church—the role played by the people among whom Jesus had appeared and by whom he was betrayed, now augmented by the dimension of an invisible but eerily looming power derived from their kinship with Satan.

This primordial mystery—with its bewitchingly sinister conflict between God and the Devil, its mobilization of horror at the blood-curdling cosmic drama, the conquest of the still-unconquered and always-to-be-opposed villain, the Damned Jew—was the centerpiece of the theology transmitted to the masses. Though the intellectual element in this mystery, the theology proper, might not have been taken so seriously as the Church would have wished, the role of "The Jew" sank deep into the symbolizing recesses of the mind.

While the Church sustained its dialectical view of "The Jew," simultaneously damned and—as Witness to the Truth—sacred, what uneducated Christians saw about them was not an idea but living people. Though the authority of the Church could force living people into the embrace of a theological abstraction, the result was not to intellectualize the public perception of living Jews, but to emotionalize, so to speak, the abstraction.

In its way the abstraction was, after all, subtle, rather cerebral: perhaps only educated people could grasp its force. What ordinary people perceived was only the most conspicuous element of the Church theory—Jews were certainly powerful, certainly damned, and certainly *there*. The universal human tendency to lump groups of people together under some generalization was thus given a horrifying twist: these people, damned by God, limbs of Satan, and enemies of mankind, were, despite their apparent humanity, not really human at all.

The "sparing" of the Jews merely illustrated a profound consequence of the Incarnation. What would otherwise have been mere exoticism, a cluster of normal dissimilarities between different groups, was escalated by the Jewish role as a Counter-Incarnation to a level of lofty horror that, in the very process of "sparing" the Jews, heightened their demonically powerful character.

This theory, linked to persistent Jewish stubbornness in refusing to mingle with the population—despite many individual cases of intermarriage, in which Christian spouses would generally become Jews—in clinging to their odd customs, in their peculiar eating habits, must have heightened their demonic quality and made them all the more uncanny.

The ideology, so to speak, of sponsorship through dogma underlay various decrees, both Papal and ecclesiastical, that protected the Jews as residents of Christendom and shielded them against maltreatment (massacre and plundering) in general as well as against forced conversion and the like. This view was also, of course, in force at the inception of the Church Fathers' extension of Paul's groundwork, and was later more fully worked out (by Thomas Aquinas, Bernard de Clairvaux, and so on).

In any case, even if the harmonious, subtle Augustinian theory of the need for Jewish survival could have had any effect at all, it could only have been during periods of tranquility: in times of distress and upheaval the common down-to-earth horror at the mere fact of the existence of Jews would prevail—to become, as we shall see, a source of countless atrocities.

It was during the era launched by the First Crusade that the "double vision" referred to above achieved its characteristic balance—between the intensity of a sophisticated idea, suffused with emotion, and a down-to-earth reality that enabled ordinary people to torture and kill their victims without becoming aware of invalidating the very idea by that fact alone. The mobs that fell upon Jewish communities could actually believe Jews to be embodiments of satanic power at the very moment of witnessing their total helplessness. One must assume that these mobs were incited simultaneously by horror of their satanic enemy and by glee at the ease with which they could undo him.

Thus the efforts of the Church to impress on the masses its demonic theory of the Jews created a strange counterpoint: the propaganda of the Church was emotionally so potent, from its natural links with the numerous demons already infesting the human psyche, that mass outbreaks against Jews achieved a ferocity from which the authorities themselves were bound to recoil. In social life as a whole, what for the Church was the conceptual puzzle of Jewish survival was subordinated to more down-to-earth passions. If some of the subtlety of the sophisticated explanation of Jewish survival, based on Augustine, filtered down to ordinary Christians, its only effect on them was to reinforce just this uncanny element in the bizarre metaphysical image of "The Jew," damned, a limb of Satan, yet preserved—by God himself.

When mass emotion overflowed, when the masses drew, so to speak, in ordinary life the natural conclusions of Church logic, they saw no reason why "Damned Jews" should not be treated as the awesome enemies of Christendom and of mankind that the Church itself had declared them to be. The second half of what for the Church was a syllogism—that just for that reason the Jews must be preserved—was emotionally sterile. The very concept of "sparing" the Jews because of their sacrosanct role in the Divine Plan put them still further beyond the human pale: it was like sparing Cain the Murderer because of metaphysics.

For centuries the doctrine about the Jews elaborated in the second and third centuries by the Church Fathers was confined to the small, relatively sophisticated milieu of the clergy and its educated intimates: for a long time there were no outbreaks of violence. There was no systematic persecution of Jews in Europe (except in the seventh century in Spain, under the West Goths); attacks on Jews had been sporadic (on individuals or specific communities). And while a certain background of violence is implied by occasional reactions—for example, a decree of the Mayence Town Council, at the beginning of the ninth century, to the effect that the killing of a Jew was not a misdemeanor but a real murder—such incidents were rare.

By the end of the eleventh century, however, with the preparations for the First Crusade, the general situation of Jewry in Europe began to deteriorate. The Crusades, with a renewal of fervor for the Kingdom of God, were no doubt the watershed between the theoretical underpinnings, so to speak, of mystical anti-Semitism and its expression in daily life.

It would seem that Christendom was permeated by theological concepts whose symbolization had struck root in mass emotions. Christian awareness of Jews as an uncanny, powerful entity had been integrated with society as a permanent condition. From the end of the eleventh century on, Jews were there to be rejected and hated, and in addition plundered and murdered.

During the eleventh century the Church leaders, reacting against centuries of laxness, corruption, administrative indolence, and dependence on the kings and nobles who controlled Church appointments, undertook the reform of the Church, restoring its autonomy and, concomitantly, their own prestige as the spiritual elite. The purchase of ecclesiastical offices (simony) was reduced, clerical celibacy was insisted on. The laity were occasionally drawn into propaganda against recalcitrant clerics; the Church itself would denounce some of its refractory personnel as servants of Satan.

But toward the end of the century the religious energies unleashed by the Church initiative for reform overflowed into the population at large, itself now inflamed by intense plebeian fervor, a hysteria generated by the conviction of the imminent advent of the Millennium, a contemporary version of the Kingdom of God agitation of the first century that now attacked the established Church.

The fundamental Church claim, for instance, that ordination as such established the potency of the priesthood came to be overridden by ardent plebeians insisting that the function of a priest had to be complemented by personal merit, by an "apostolic" way of life (grounded in the Church's perception of Jesus' followers), of which amateur exemplars, lay "apostles" roving about Europe, had long been common.

The concept of the Millennium goes back to the Revelation of John (Chapter 20); it is the thousand-year reign of Christ and his "priests"; Satan is cooped up in the "abyss" until the cosmic battle takes place, at the end of which he is "flung into the lake of fire and sulphur . . . there to be tormented day and night."

This revival, or echo, of the imminent Kingdom of God was to enthrall plebeian millenarians for centuries. Beginning at the end of the eleventh century, they began agitating for the total reconstruction of society as indispensable for the World's End. The clergy came under systematic attack as "corrupt," the upper classes as oppressors.

Though some millenarians were peaceable ascetics, expecting the Millennium to be a distillation of spiritual values, the most fanatical, the most ruthless, the most extreme millenarian sects were those that focused the commonplace resentment of socio-economic distress into an intense, all-embracing revulsion against the world. For such fanatics, who for centuries were to teem throughout Western Europe, the fantasies of World's-End redemption projected a regenerated world in which blissful innocence would be achieved through an apocalyptic massacre. The people who necessarily had to be exterminated were on hand: the "rich," the clergy—and the Jews. It was only after such a cosmic slaughter that the Kingdom of the Saints—the holy executioners—could be established.

Thus, in evaluating mystical anti-Semitism as a phenomenon, the end of the eleventh century, with the First Crusade and the flood tide of plebeian Kingdom of God insurrectionaries, can be taken as the foundation of mystical anti-Semitism in its modern form. It was then that the work accomplished in the second and third centuries by the Church Fathers to establish the image of the Damned Jew began bearing fruit on a massive scale.

The tidal wave of millennial agitation showed that despite appearances and all rational perceptions, the World's End idea, which had seemed by the second century to be fossilized, retained enough latent energy to galvanize masses of people once again and generate explosive upheavals. Large parts of Western Europe were steeped in a torrent of revolutionary millenarianism.

The mass agitation was aimed at the pillars of the social order—the Church, the aristocracy, the emerging bourgeoisie. Though sometimes intertwined with Papal activity, it was essentially, in all its activist variations, hostile to the Church hierarchy as inherently corrupt, a manifestation, precisely, of the corruption of the world, and hence necessarily a target of the Kingdom of God fever aiming at a new world.

The First Crusade, for instance, launched by the Papacy in 1095 as part of a broad strategy to restore Christian unity under the aegis of Rome (by providing Byzantium with enough manpower to repel the Seljuk Turks), was transformed by hordes of fanatical plebeians into a turbulent movement of social agitation. For them, the notion of capturing Jerusalem as a way of obstructing and damaging Islam was too cold-blooded and objective. They transformed into the most acutely personal religious fervor.

And even though these new seekers of the Kingdom of God

were intensely hostile to the Church, and were in fact burned at the stake in large numbers by the Church authorities, their most intense passion was directed at the Jews, who for them remained the personification of the very principle of Evil built into the current world. Their hostility to the established Church enabled them to disregard its doctrinal restraints on the murder of Jews.

If the expressed aim of the Crusades was taken at face value—wresting the Church of the Holy Sepulcher in Jerusalem from the Muslim infidels—Jews living in the small towns and villages of Europe would seem quite irrelevant. But that was not the reality perceived by the mobs inflamed by the Crusades: not merely had the Jews occupied a focal position for centuries in the world view of Christendom, they were also visible everywhere—as merchants, property holders, and money lenders. The convergence of these two factors, the ubiquitous activity of Jews interpreted by the overpowering concept of the Jews as sons of the Devil, was from then on to place them at the flash point of any social upheaval. A wide variety of political and social movements, countless currents in the endless flux of life, could find a convenient target in the Jews.

From the very outset of the First Crusade, the ardor stoked up to fuel it was fateful for the Jews. The intensification of religious fervor heightened to fever pitch the preaching for the Crusade itself; it was normal for Crusaders and the mobs accompanying them to celebrate the beginning of the arduous journey to the east by massacring small communities of Jews in France, the Netherlands, and Germany. It was evident to them that the Jews, notorious enemies of God and agents of Satan, were just as much or even more the enemies of the ardent Christians on their way to the Holy Land to free it from the infidel, indeed, were exactly the same enemy closer to home. And it was equally natural, to be sure, for the massacre of the Jews to yield material benefits by way of plunder and pillage.

It was during the Crusade of 1096 that the first great massacre of European Jews took place. It was independent of the armies of the nobility; the inflamed plebeians alone carried out the same slaughter among the Jews in Europe that they were to carry out a little later, in an even more concentrated butchery, in Palestine among the Muslims, especially in Jerusalem. The same theme was to be repeated during the Second Crusade a half century later (1146), when, for instance, masses of ordinary Jews were massacred in Normandy and Picardy.

For these plebeians the massacres of Jews in Europe and Muslims in Palestine were only the first act of a World's End enterprise on the very verge of consummation: the destruction of Satan. The plebeian hordes busily engaged in bloodshed felt themselves spurred on by the looming horror of the Anti-Christ.

The hatred of these millenarians for corrupt clerics and rapacious nobles, selected as it were functionally from the general population, was evidently different in kind from the loathing of Jews. The massacre of Jews had nothing to do with the specific activities of individual Jews, even though one real-life category, usurers, could be said to illustrate the mystical theme of "The Jew" as limb of Satan. The very existence of the entire people was taken to be a satanic activity. These plebeian massacres were of course opposed by the aristocracy and the Church summits, both in Europe and Palestine. The aristocrats leading the Crusaders generally made energetic efforts to deflect the blood lust of the mobs, and indeed saved many Jews.

It was their combination of visionary extremism and ruthless violence that distinguished these medieval Kingdom of God activists from other plebeian revolts, strictly circumscribed by low-key local aims, that also proliferated throughout the Middle Ages.

Such plebeian rebels, generally led by "messiahs," living "saints," and the like, who sounded like heirs of the Kingdom of God fever that had enthralled Jesus and Paul, and that had been expressed most bizarrely in the Revelation of John, were to ravage Western Europe from the end of the eleventh down to the mid-sixteenth century. The effects of the various heresies revolving around this focal idea were not evenly distributed, to be sure: the Rhine valley was a continuing theater of operations; Belgium and northern France subsided by the mid-fourteenth century; in south and central Germany, slipping into the mainstream a little late, the agitation continued until Luther's Reformation.*

Thus, for centuries Central and Western Europe was churned up by this ancient idea, by the conviction that the Kingdom of God was at hand. Fantasies ran rife throughout the people concerning a new paradise on earth, the elimination of suffering, the conquest of sin—a regenerated world, with the corrupt clergy and the rapacious nobility replaced by a kingdom of saints. These fantasies were validated by the authority of Scripture—properly understood, of course, by them alone. Spontaneously arising sects succeeded and complemented each other. For all of them The Jew remained the primary target.

Perhaps most significant, as a general tendency, was the magnification of the malefic element in this revival of the old Kingdom of God idea. The medieval fantasts had distorted the ancient concept of a Messiah of the World's End, "The Christ," and created an equally pregnant opponent, the anti-Christ of the World's End, the exact opposite of the Christ in all respects. This high degree of polarization produced the emotionally charged symmetry of Good and Evil: millenarians represented the Christ; the Jews, the Anti-Christ.

It was no doubt the plebeian character of the turbulence unleashed by the First Crusade of 1096, itself the outcome of the ripening aversion to the Jews, that in and of itself for many centuries reinforced that aversion and consolidated it as an integral part of Christendom. From the end of the eleventh century on, the situation of Jews, not only in Germany and France, but all over Europe, steadily worsened. When ghettoes were established at the beginning of the sixteenth century, the alienation of the Jews was given institutional expression.

At the outset, the Jews themselves, as at practically every other outbreak of heightened persecution, had no inkling of trouble. Even after the First Crusade had actually started, in France, and French Jewish communities were being slaughtered, German Jews, appealed to for help, gave it without, ap-

---

* Norman Cohn, *The Pursuit of the Millennium*, London and New York: Oxford University Press, 1972, p. 53.

parently, considering themselves in danger. The first massacre of Jews in Germany (Mayence, 1096) found them wholly unprepared.

This was indeed to be a theme of countless disasters in Jewish history, most recently with the mass murder of European Jews in the twentieth century. It would seem to indicate the great difficulty Jews have had in grasping the nature of mystical anti-Semitism. The advent of violence was invariably a surprise; Jewish communities found it inconceivable that neighbors would turn on them: reports from outside, credible, perhaps, only as abstractions, were discounted as of no immediate personal concern.

The massacres of the summer of 1096 and their aftermath gave rise to a custom that was peculiar to the Jews: the so-called "Sanctification of the Name"—collective suicide to avoid forcible conversion. In view of the categorical Jewish prohibition of suicide, the very notion of mass suicide for such a reason may well be a reflection, ironically, of Christian martyrology.

The primary consequence of the Crusades for the Jews was the destruction of their economic base in the Diaspora; Jewish livelihoods were simply wiped out. In addition, the notion of Palestine as a real place, as their actual former homeland, was extinguished for centuries.

Christendom became more and more pervasively conscious of the Jews. The ancient theme of Jews as murderers of God was rammed home with exceptional force during the Crusades and their preparation for the very reason that it was no longer an abstraction, but an adjunct of a practical activity: the Jews could now be felt to be something real and actual—a real enemy of real people, Crusaders who were determined to risk their lives living up to a high ideal.

The gradual permeation of the European masses by a theology filtering down from the hierarchy of the Church through the local priesthood was accompanied by the evolution of certain nuances in the theology itself.

In the twelfth and thirteenth centuries the theory of transubstantiation was developed, the dogma that the flesh and blood of Jesus were literally present in the consecrated Host and wine; this reinforced the cult of the Eucharist, a fundamental sacra-

ment of the Church, and consequently gave a conceptual basis
to the spread of miraculous tales about the Host. Indeed, the
profound contrast between the Host as a wafer and the Host,
properly understood, as constituting the actual flesh and blood
of the Savior, in itself reinforced the other-worldly mysticism
inherent in the very concept.

This gave another twist to the definition of the Jew as a
maleficent pariah and enemy of God: the charge of the desecration of the Host, made palpable by the novel doctrine of
transubstantiation. The doctrine contributed, moreover, to the
development of a further theory that Jews were engaged in fabricating a conspiracy against the Savior and against Christians
at large. This became part and parcel of another charge, which
had been maturing from the middle of the twelfth century on
—that the Jews required Christian blood for ritual purposes.
These two charges no doubt reflected the central conviction of
mystical anti-Semites: that the Jews were not ignorant, but
knowingly evil.

Rationally, of course, these notions were inherently non-
sensical: if pious Jews were forbidden even animal blood by the
Bible, how could they require Christian blood for their ritual?
Similarly, if by definition the Host, symbolizing a rejected Savior,
was nonsense to them, how could its desecration have any meaning? Nevertheless, the "blood-murder," though energetically denied by Pope after Pope, remained a rooted belief among masses
of people. There was a profound feeling among ordinary Christians that there was, indeed, something wholly inhuman, uncanny, and monstrous about the Jews: the eeriness inherent in
the concept of the Incarnation kept bursting through its theological subtleties.

Ordinary people found it difficult, perhaps, to identify fully
with the concept of the Savior as God-man: the guilt arising out
of this perception of one's own unworthiness could naturally be
projected on to the "witness people," the Jews, once the people
of God but now flung outside the universal communion of Christendom, there to play out their satanic role.

The obsession with the notions of ritual murder and the
desecration of the Host paralleled a third obsession: the development and consolidation of the image of the Jew as money-

lender. This exemplifies what was to become a standard phenomenon: the mingling of two types of hatred—the commonplace resentment of an aspect of social need, and its eerie, other-worldly illumination by the glare of metaphysics.

Usury was banned by the Church for centuries. Even in the modern world, in which credit and its modalities occupy a central place, people living by their own labor commonly feel there is something loathsome in making money by lending it. In the Middle Ages this feeling was all the more intense and widespread because credit had not yet been integrated with the economic system, and had no legal place at all: in theory the economy, broadly speaking, was based on a natural law revolving around the notion of a "fair price," while needy people would be given alms, whose reward could only be prosperity in this world or the next, but could not have a material form. Thus interest in any form was prohibited.

The Church's interdiction of interest was based on the Bible and of course on Aristotle.* According to the verses in the Bible (Deuteronomy), only foreigners could charge interest; the converse was applied to Jews, considered foreigners, who were thus allowed to charge interest.

Because of this simple accommodation with the expanding European economy, for which credit was indispensable despite all legal and ethical opposition, the Jews were allowed to perform the role of moneylender, which interacted as it were organically with the heightening of the opprobrium attached to them in any case. Themselves accursed, they were performing a function that was also accursed by God as well as by the Church. Accordingly, the general ban on interest of all kinds—common to Judaism and Islam as well as Christianity—left the Jews in Christendom playing a role, of great value to princes and governments as well as to private individuals, that was both essential and at the same time repellent, and in particular often aroused the hatred of their clients.

Thus it was natural for the Jews, regarded collectively as

---

* Luke 6:35, Exod. 22:2, Lev. 25:35–37, Deut. 20–21; Aristotle, *Politics*, 1.10 (quoted from Bein, *The Jewish Question*, op. cit., pp. 99 f.).

eerily powerful, camouflaged demons and murderers of God, to find themselves summed up by a supernatural image superimposed on a down-to-earth social activity: usury came to be thought of as another manifestation of Satan. Hence, even when the usefulness of the economic functions permitted to them was accepted, however grudgingly, there could be no carry-over into a feeling of "tolerance"; the very usefulness itself contained an element of vexation. This supernatural notion of the Jew as moneylender, anchored in the Middle Ages, has survived to this day: it is a cliché in all European literature, even in countries, such as Russia and Poland, in which Jews were almost never usurers at all.

By the time of the Crusades, the dogmas of the Church with regard to the Jews were well established; the Crusades added nothing new, conceptually, to the theory of the powerful Damned Jew. Practically speaking, however, the Crusades, accompanied by the growth of Papal power, gradually centralized the social position of Jews in Western Christendom. The growth of the Papacy unified Christendom as it were bureaucratically, while at the same time the Crusades heightened enormously the intensity of mystical anti-Semitism. The obsessive element inherent in mystical anti-Semitism was now a fixed element in a pattern that was to endure to our own day, with different forms of expression and no doubt, as we shall see, with different emotional emphases, but nevertheless anchored in a socio-psychological superstructure.

The gradual spread of Christianity, ironing out on the religious plane the ancient fragmentation of peoples, languages, and ethnic identities in Europe, followed by bureaucratic centralization after the Papal successes, left the Jews less and less leeway for social maneuvering. This made it easier and easier for the Church Triumphant to implement its legislation concerning the Jews. It also entailed the old concept of "sparing" them as witnesses to the Truth of Christianity. In the decrees of the Fourth Lateran Council (1215), the zenith of anti-Jewish Church legislation, the Preamble laid it down that Jews were to be protected not as human beings enjoying the benefits of the civil order but because of their special role in the Divine Plan.

According to this Council, applying Augustine's theory, Jews could not be forcibly converted to Christianity, their cemeteries were not to be desecrated, nor were Jewish corpses to be exhumed and defiled. Further, no Christian had a right to kill or rob Jews as such. This last prohibition, to be sure, had to be formally renewed ten times from the beginning of the twelfth to the thirteenth century: for nontheologians, the sublety of the reasoning was elusive.

The Jews were not, of course, the main concern of the Council of 1215; on the contrary, of the seventy resolutions contained in its report, only the last four dealt with the Jews. The Church, only just emerging from the Albigensian conflict in southern France, was still coping with a cluster of perennial problems— splits, heresies, internal reforms. Nevertheless, these last four resolutions had a tremendous effect in systematically disadvantaging the Jews wherever the Church reigned, which by now was practically everywhere in Europe. The Jews were struck most by Resolution 68, which without specifying details ordered a special garb for all Jews—the "Yellow Badge," which established a portentous and enduring principle: Jews were to be distinguished outwardly too from Christians.

All such restrictions on Jews—indeed, any form of visible stigmatization—naturally had the effect of reinforcing the feeling that brought about the stigmatization in the first place. The sight of anyone being punished arouses in most people a feeling that there must be some good reason for it: people are punished because they ought to be. The imposition of the Yellow Badge was thus an element in the beginning of the Inquisition and the comprehensive campaign against heresy that preoccupied Christendom for centuries.

Jews were particularly endangered by the numerous campaigns undertaken against heretics of all kinds before and during the Middle Ages. A common charge directed at any heresy was that of "judaizing": it was considered a quality inherent in any form of belief or organization that rejected the dominion of the Church. During the Hussite wars (1419–36), for instance, countless Jews were savagely persecuted after attacks from the pulpits throughout Central Europe stigmatized them as abettors of the militant heretics inspired by Jan Hus.

The Church authorities were in a logical bind: they had a perfectly good reason, after all, to regard Jews as heretics through the very fact of their clinging, knowingly, to Judaism, since according to doctrine Christianity was the true heir of what had formerly been Judaism. Hence it would have been understandable, in a sense, indeed entirely cogent, for Jews to be considered heretics of the first water. From the fourth century on, in fact, many Churchmen wrote in favor of the identification of Judaism as a Christian heresy.

On the other hand, it was unreasonable to call them heretics, since they had never been Christians to begin with. This line of argument prevailed: no official statement condemning Jews as heretics was ever formulated. The obstacle of the counter-argument—that Jews must survive as a Witness to the Truth—could not be overcome. At the same time the folk feeling, understandably, was that Jews really *were* heretics, and in fact the worst of all. So, even though the Church did not make the decisive leap into a decree of heresy, and its propaganda restricted itself to the use of the theologically innocuous, though of course damaging, epithet "perfidious," the general feeling prevailed that Jews were "natural" heretics as well as natural sorcerers, devils, and so on.

In the eleventh and twelfth centuries, the totalitarian church felt itself to be harassed by a rash of heresies—Catharists, Albigensians, Luciferans, Neo-Manicheans, Waldensians, Passagii. The tension over heresy was palpable and dangerous: when the Inquisition was established in the thirteenth century to deal with it, the conviction of the Jews as heretics per se would have been enough to wipe all of them out, either physically or, as happened to many Jewish converts to Catholicism (Marranos), religiously. Thus the logic of the Church prevailed against the intolerance general in Christendom, and restrained the Church's own extremist tendencies. The Jews were saved, once again, by the same logic that confined them to semi-enserfment.

In the case of the Inquisition, of course, there was a natural inspiration in the distrust of forced conversions, often thought to be in all probability fraudulent. Since the Inquisition was charged to investigate all conversions, Jewish converts automatically fell under its authority. Aside from instances of Jews being forced to accept baptism and then immediately afterward charged with heresy, there were obviously many fraudulent conversions among Iberian Jewry. With time, of course, and the succession of generations the new faith was accepted, so that today in many parts of Spain whole communities can recall without any particular emotion their remote Jewish forebears.

It was natural in any case for the Church to intervene at will in Jewish affairs: in the early thirteenth century the Jews themselves precipitated a crisis when Maimonides, the celebrated Jewish philosopher and rationalist, was attacked by Orthodox Jews in Montpellier; they asked the Dominicans, codirectors with the Franciscans of the Inquisition, to treat Jewish "heretics" as they would Christians. At the end of 1233, in consequence, all the Maimonist books were seized and the first Hebrew books were ceremonially burned. This was to be repeated by the Inquisition in many places with many books, including the Talmud, the violent campaign against which has had repercussions down to our own day. The denunciation of the Talmud, and the attributing to it of a broad range of depravity, has served to focus a vast amount of hatred.

It is this quality of hatred that surely stands out above all others in the propaganda against the Jews from the inception of Christianity to our own day. This hatred on the part of Christians is naturally projected onto the Jews: it is they who are accused of being full of hate—cursing Jesus and Christians daily in their routine prayers, conspiring to bring about the physical destruction of Christians, and so on.

This feature of mystical anti-Semitism meshed very well with large-scale political situations, such as the tug of war with the Moors, in the eighth and ninth centuries, and with the Turks, from the end of the fifteenth century. Jews were very naturally associated with the Muslim (Moorish and Turkish) enemies of Christendom, just as they were with countless Christian heresies.

The association of Jews with various heresies had its comic side: at the very moment when Luther was pointing out that baptism meant the "return of the Jews to their ancestral religion," he and his partisans were being denounced by the Church in Rome as "heretics and Jews"; for his part, Luther responded by accusing, as enemies of Christ, heretics, Jews, Turks and—

papists. During the sectarian disputes of the sixteenth century the word "Jew," used as an epithet, was hurled back and forth with abandon.

Heresy was of course intimately linked to sorcery and to the Devil himself. It must be emphasized that in the medieval imagination the Devil was a genuine living being: he could be thought of as the source of homely pranks, practical jokes, and mild persecutions of neighbors, as well as of titanic catastrophes. From the thirteenth century on there was a real Devil cult, formally sponsored by the Church, disbelief in which was not only unorthodox but actionable. The linkage between heresy and sorcery established a belief in sorcery as something profoundly significant; it became a fixed element, as it seems, of mass psychology.

The connection was evident: since heresy was obviously the Devil's work—the only possible explanation for the otherwise incomprehensible deviation from orthodox faith—it was natural for heretics to be castigated as agents of the Devil. This was facilitated by the evident fact that before the Church became totalitarian, it regarded with horror early heresies, such as Gnosticism, partly because of their attraction for so many. It was natural to equate sorcery and heresy, since the Devil was, of course, the king of sorcerers.

When, at the end of the thirteenth and the beginning of the fourteenth century, sorcery was finally placed under the formal control of the Inquisition, it was not conceived of as merely illicit, forbidden acts, but as a form of heterodox belief. Sorcerers and heretics were lumped together: all heretics were called sorcerers, all sorcerers heretics.

Poisoning, too, was ascribed to heretics and sorcerers alike: this was so common, in fact, that a charge of poisoning was very likely in and of itself to lead to a further charge of sorcery. And a papal bull of the early thirteenth century (Gregory X) routinely equated heresy of all kinds with a variety of loathsome practices, such as sexual intercourse with toads, orgies conducted by black tomcats, and so on. This had the natural effect of stressing the satanic element in the conception of Jews, felt to be arch-heretics even though the Church was restrained by its own logic from officially stigmatizing them as such.

The desecration of the Host—emphasized by the Fourth Lateran Council's acceptance of the doctrine of transubstantiation —thus routinely became a natural charge to lay against the Jews, by the end of the thirteenth century; magicians were notorious for using sacred objects, such as consecrated oil and water, crucifixes, biblical texts, and so on. This in itself reflects a naive belief, of course, in the magical qualities of the properties inherent in these objects.

Nor was this belief restricted to the uneducated laity; it was part of the belief of the Church summits as well. The clergy openly believed in the efficacy of all forms of sorcery; some Church dignitaries were even themselves well-known magicians, who used their special skills to detect heretics. When sorcery finally came under the Inquisition, astrology, a favorite of all levels of the clergy, was excluded from the category.

Thus the Church carried over the magical core of Christianity—the sacred role of the Church itself, as well as the efficacy of the Sacraments—into the domain of ordinary belief: quite simply, everyone believed in magic. The Church, after all, approved of magic—"sacred" magic, to be sure, such as consecrated water, relics, holy fire, selected miracles, and so on.

The Fourth Lateran Council was accompanied by a torrent of fables whose function was to make palpable the innermost conception of the Jews within the framework of Christian theology—that the Jews were really children of the Devil.

Against this background the Yellow Badge decreed at the Fourth Lateran Council filled the gap, as it were, between the normal-seeming appearance of Jews and their function in the theological sphere. It was around this time that people began to listen, with bated breath, to stories of how the Jews really had a tail and horns like the Devil, and even a distinctive smell, conceived of, evidently, as the opposite of the "odor of sanctity": theirs was the stench of moral corruption.

The Church authorities naturally took pains to protect the Jews against this form of popular demonology: that was required by the logic of theology. At the same time, the subtle, sophisticated, conceptual demonology of the Church and the gross, palpable, sensual demonology of the masses were indissolubly intertwined: the satanization of the Jews as part of the Divine

Scheme, according to the Church's view of salvation, brought about in the minds of nontheological ordinary people a concrete satanization on the plane of the senses: if Jews played a satanic role, it was because they *were* Satan, and, as Satan, were surely entitled to horns, tails, and a special stench.

All this affected, perhaps bizarrely, the status of medicine, one of the most ancient pursuits of Jews: at all times, in the Diaspora, Jewish doctors were well known, often preeminent. But during the Middle Ages Jewish physicians too fell under the suspicion of sorcery and witchcraft. This was of course quite natural: there has always been something inherently awe-inspiring in the role of a physician. Hence, since a physician has always been felt to be some sort of magician, the only question was whether his powers came from God or the Devil (one of the themes, of course, in the Gospels, when the "signs" of Jesus' power were ascribed by detractors not to God but to Beelzebub).

For a couple of centuries, from the thirteenth century on, Jewish physicians were considered to be working on behalf of the Devil; Christians were formally forbidden to have recourse to them. At the same time, Jewish physicians continued to be popular with princes; if this was a weakness, it was one permitted only to the rulers of society. According to a decree of the kings of Castile in the fifteenth century, there were "to be no physicians among the Jews except for the physician to the king." Thus the decrees directed at Jewish doctors were in effect only for ordinary people, since the bourgeoisie followed royalty in clinging to their own Jewish doctors.

In this way Jews were turned into the real-life centerpiece of a trio consisting of Devil, Jew, and witch: Jews participated in the mystic essence of potent evil emanating from this whole triangulated concept, in which the Devil uses real-life Jews and allegedly real-life witches to do his bidding.

For many generations the Devil, though a bulwark of Christian doctrine, was thought not to be visible on earth. Actual sightings of devils were generally regarded as pagan superstitions, in sharp contradistinction to magicians, who abounded and whose incantations were universally accepted as effective—provided, of course, that the magician was genuine.

But with the scholastics at the end of the thirteenth and

fourteenth centuries the Devil quickly found a place on earth—visible, palpable, and aromatic. Aquinas devoted his powers of ratiocination to demonstrating that even though devils could not actually digest food or make love, they could in fact have a visible physical shape, and by assuming the form of a female figure (succubus) and then, instantaneously, that of a male (incubus), were able to act as carriers of male sperm from a man to a woman. The children brought into the world in this way were not, to be sure, the Devil's own seed, but human, since the Devil had been no more than a mere carrier. (Aquinas also took it for granted that the Huns had been spawned by demons.)

During the following century these simple ideas were greatly expanded: from around 1320, within a couple of generations (50 years), a campaign was launched against the Cathars, who believed that it was not the God of mercy who governed the world, but Satan; hence the monitors of the orthodox faith (chiefly Dominicans) had to expose any traffic with the Devil, a paramount sin because of Catharism.

Thus there came about a fusion of two notions: on the one hand the attitude implicit in Catharism—hope resting on the Devil—became attractive to many Catholics, including, no doubt, countless psychopaths, and on the other, as a way of combating this major heresy, the Church itself sponsored the validity of the very notions whose reality had previously been poohpoohed. The demonology of the time was thus officially recognized: a bull of Pope John XXII—himself, it seems, a high paranoiac—denounced false Christians who "sacrifice to demons and worship them" and do countless shameful things to secure their aid in the most wicked schemes.

For a couple of centuries after the first witch burning (Toulouse, 1335) there was a flood of accusations, tortures to force confessions, and trials, all galvanized by what was felt to be the need to pin down the Devil's auxiliaries on earth. This confirmed not only the real existence of the Devil, but the details of everything anyone could hope to know about him: how he looked, behaved, and so on.

The interrogations, lasting for months, would inevitably produce the confessions required by ecclesiastical law. The interrogators themselves seem to have believed wholeheartedly in what they were doing: the portrait of the Devil they arrived at was evidently assembled from notions they had had about the Devil to begin with. The confessions, regarded as sincere, confirmed and reconfirmed all the Devil's attributes. Conversely, the victories of the Devil detectives confirmed the procedures that had produced the proofs: in 1404 the Inquisition reported with pride that 30,000 witches had been burned; if they had not been exposed, the world would surely have been destroyed.

The Devil was, of course, black: he had horns, talons, a tail, a goatee, and an insidious stench: all this was taken to symbolize both virility and lecherousness. The portrait emerges from the replies given under torture by the women accused of witchcraft ("wizards" were burned only exceptionally). Women, themselves the symbol of impurity and temptation, were naturally pliant tools of the virile Devil. This view of women no doubt complemented the official worship of the Virgin and its obsession with chastity.

The Devil, the personification of a cosmic principle, comprehensively opposed God in all respects; he could even nullify baptism, designed in Church doctrine to expunge Original Sin. Thus, the Devil descended from theology into the world, becoming a true personality, an actual being with agents, allies, and kinfolk, and entirely at home on earth, which he could claim as his own.

The monsterization of the Jews via caricature appeared in Germany during the second half of the fifteenth century. Their physical coalescence with the Devil was established by a series of symbolical and caricatural approximations, beginning with the horns and proceeding through tails and an insidious stench.

The horns seem to have been based on a mistranslation in the Bible: in painting and sculpture Moses always had horns (apparently through a misunderstanding of a word that meant "beams" or "rays"), but until the thirteenth century no other Biblical figure had them, not even the villains of the Gospels, the High Priests Hananiah and Caiaphas. This was merged with the pointed Jewish hat (the pileum cornatum), which from the end of the thirteenth century was a part of Jewish garb. From then on, Jews were constantly depicted with horns.

Around the same time a "Jewish nose" also began to be

made much of. Though rather few Jews actually had such a nose, and it was also fairly common in many peoples around the Mediterranean, to say nothing of the English aristocracy, the combination of a long, hooked nose and a misshapen figure was to become a staple of caricature down to our own day.

The physical projection of the Devil coincided with the crystallization of the maleficent, and infinitely powerful, Jews, whom experts, and even ordinary people, could learn to detect beneath the apparently ordinary garb of individual Jews, most of whom in Christian eyes were quite impoverished—again, of course, only apparently. All the notions about the Devil were absorbed into the legends about the Jews (tails, horns and stench).

The accusation of smelliness has, of course, been made by many peoples against their neighbors, but the special status of the Jew gave this curious fusion of qualities a unique theological significance. In the popular imagination the virility ascribed to the Devil turned the Jews, his counterparts on earth, into sexual athletes as well as redoubtable magicians, who were nevertheless—through the combination of contrasts associated with dynamic pathologies—also feeble and sickly.

By the erudite, the congenital sicknesses ascribed to the Jews were assigned to different tribes (extinct among Jews for millennia): thus Simon's descendants were supposed to bleed four days a year, the mouths of Benjamin's to contain worms, and so on. It may be significant that this notion goes back to a pamphlet (1630) by a Jewish convert, Franco da Piacenza: Jewish converts, indeed, were the source of many of the most grotesque legends about the Jews.

The net effect of all this—the amalgamation of satanism and the sorcery ascribed to the Jews—was to place them once and for all outside humanity, an aspect of the eerie occult. When not portrayed as devils themselves, Jews were shown as the Devil's intimates: engravings and paintings depicting Jews generally have devils located somewhere in the background; Jews are the mediators between Satan and those trying to sell him their souls.

The Church condemned marriage with a Jew as meriting both excommunication and death, since such a marriage was at best regarded as adultery. A Christian who married a Jew, or even lived with one, was liable to a charge of bestiality. A Frenchman living with a Jewess who had borne him several children, for instance, was convicted of sodomy and burned together with her: it was laid down that "coitus with a Jewess was exactly the same as though a man were to copulate with a dog."* Thus the Jews—whose Torah had no doubt originated the formal, legal opposition to sexual intercourse with beasts—found themselves the target of their own law.

For many centuries these obsessions were so widespread— they have indeed endured into the modern age—that it may be presumptuous to call them pathological: collective social behavior normalizes a great deal. In a world in which the terrors of the unconscious could be externalized in monsters of the most diverse kinds, notions about the Devil were really only further instances of the uncontrollable elements of the psyche. The difference was that, like the Incarnation, they were organized into an intellectual and above all a moral system: dislikes and fears could take on flesh, in the shape of living people who could be subsumed under some lofty idea and thus hated *legitimately*.

The tensions of the epoch naturally reinforced, or even generated, the obsessions about devils, witches, Jews, and so on. Much psychological stress was no doubt due to the social upheaval of the last centuries of the Middle Ages, the gradual but painful crumbling of the feudal order, the shakeup in social relations, and the agonizing passage of society through the rudimentary but dynamically evolving conditions of mercantilism, the predecessor of the early free-enterprise system. In this transition the Jews played an increasingly conspicuous role.

The anxieties naturally engendered by these processes made the presence of all "alien" elements particularly inflammatory: witches and Jews, converted or not, were paramount figures of popular fantasy. The emotional basis of the horror felt for Jews and witches alike was no doubt the same, but the relationship between the two phenomena had a curious seesaw quality: some-

---

* Joshua Trachtenberg, *The Devil and the Jews*, New Haven: Yale University Press, 1943, p. 187.

times Jews came before witches, sometimes vice versa. What remained permanent was the conviction of some profound organic relationship between them.

When the Black Death struck Western Europe in 1348, for instance, Jews became the universal scapegoat, partly because, thanks to their religiously grounded hygiene, they were less affected by the disease. There was a general conclusion that "some class of 'people' " must have poisoned the water supply with a poison made of spiders, frogs, and lizards—all obviously symbols of maleficent filth and of the Devil—or possibly, of basilisk flesh. Bewildered masses of people would blame successively the "lepers, the poor, the rich, the clergy," then, finally, the Jews, "who thereupon were almost exterminated."*

Later on, during the long-drawn-out wars of religion, it was the witches who replaced the Jews as the major scapegoat.

There was, to be sure, no conceptual problem in hating both "categories" simultaneously. In medieval Hungary, in an instance of the interchangeability of the two ideas, witches, upon a first charge being laid against them, would be pilloried in a public square, wearing a Jewish hat. And of course Jews were constantly being accused of witchcraft: in reports on the success of various campaigns against witches, Jews are generally mentioned, with the stress laid on one group or the other.

Another Church doctrine that came to affect Jews adversely was from Thomas Aquinas. Though he did no more than build on the foundations laid by Augustine, he extended Church doctrine to the civil order with respect to the Jews: in civil law, Jews were to be considered eternally the chattel property of princes, who were entitled, accordingly, to seize all Jewish property at will, the only proviso being that the Jews were to be allowed a minimum to live on.

Since the Church was on a constant alert for heretics, schismatics, and minorities of all kinds, massacres and burnings to death were commonplace. Christianity, to be sure, with its complex intellectual substance, was inherently subject to variations in interpretation in detail, but the Jews as a whole constituted

---

* Cohn, *The Pursuit of the Millennium*, op. cit., p. 87.

a special, uncanny kind of minority. Christians could, after all, move about and change their status while remaining members of society, but Jews could change only through conversion. As long as they did not convert, they remained different in *kind*.

The simple theme of mystical anti-Semitism that I am tracing through these complicated centuries naturally interacted with social developments. In the thirteenth century the economic situation of the Jews began a steep decline: the Jews, who had willy-nilly played an economic role that enabled them to survive, despite their status as pariahs, were gradually restricted in all aspects of life: their economic function was taken over by the rise of a middle class as well as by the development of banking in Florence and Siena during the thirteenth century, and by the rise of the Lombards in France. This parvenu middle class became the implacable enemy of the Jews: a fusion was brought about between socio-economic rivalry and the looming vision of The Jew as a limb of Satan, that is, as a cosmological phenomenon focused on earth in the activities of apparent human beings. This curious fusion was fortified and circulated by the deliberate propaganda of the great Franciscan and Dominican orders of the Church.

The Jews, sponsored earlier as economically useful, perhaps precisely because of their abject status, could now be dispensed with altogether. Thus for two centuries, from the end of the thirteenth to the end of the fifteenth century, they were massively persecuted; settlements of Jews in western and central Europe were sapped or wholly eliminated; Jews were largely wiped out. Their entire legal and social situation deteriorated radically.

It is enough to list the various expulsions: In 1290 Jews were expelled from England; this was followed by their expulsion from nearly everywhere in France under Philip Le Bel in 1306 (concluded in 1394), the mass murder and the destruction of about 300 communities in Germany; and the expulsion of survivors during the grotesque horrors of the Black Death (1348–49). At the end of the fourteenth century a Holy War was launched against the Spanish Jews (1391), ending a century later with the expulsion or forced conversion of all Jews in Spain (1492) and four years later in Portugal. This was supplemented by the expulsion of Jews from Prague (1400), Vienna (1421), Cologne

(1424), Mayence (1438), Augsburg (1440), the Tyrol (1493), Nuremberg (1499), Provence (1498–1506), and finally from the ancient Jewish settlement of Regensburg (1519). These formal expulsions were accompanied by countless persecutions in individual communities and districts, massacres, returns, and reexpulsions.

A massive segment of Jewry was simply wiped out during this period, partly by the Black Death, like so many others, and partly by the spasmodic convulsions referred to earlier. Jews vanished from places they had lived in for centuries, sometimes even longer than the "natives." England and France were to have no large Jewish settlements for centuries; Spain was closed to Jews until recently.

Streams of Jews fled in every direction: Iberian Jews reinforced the ancient communities in northern Italy and laid the foundations for a new Jewry in Holland, as well as in the Ottoman Empire, which welcomed them at once, thus giving them access again to Palestine.

Vast numbers of Jews found refuge in Poland, where for centuries they were to prosper, increasing in numbers until the Second World War: Polish Jewry, indeed, was to become the "crown" of world Jewry, and in the modern era to constitute the bulk of the Jewish communities in America, England, Germany, and Israel.

Russia proper was barred to Jews because of the so-called "judaizing heresy" that at the end of the fourteenth century was felt to be menacing Greek Orthodoxy in Russia. This heresy was in many respects similar to the Reformation in Western Europe: calling for a "return to the sources" of the Old Testament, the heresy was thought especially pernicious just because it kindled some interest in the Moscow Court. It was soon suppressed (although religious "dissenters" were to remain a common, if minor, phenomenon in Tsarist Russia for many years) and had the effect of barring Jews from Russia until the nineteenth century.

It was in the Middle Ages that masses of people became susceptible to mystical anti-Semitism: in all languages the very word "Jew" became an epithet. Religious instruction via the catechism—for centuries practically the only form of popular education—inculcated in even the youngest children the basic concept of deicide. At the beginning of the sixteenth century Erasmus summed it up: "If it is incumbent on a good Christian to detest the Jews, then we are all good Christians."

By the end of the Middle Ages, in short, the Jews were thought of in Europe as a sort of poison: segregated, defamed, loathed, hated. The figure of "The Jew" was well established: the purely theoretical concepts of the Christology worked out by the Church with such zeal during the first few centuries had finally been integrated with the perception of real-life Jews. Despite their visible presence, despite their human appearance, despite the communities of living Jews scattered about, the accumulated weight of cultural representation made it possible to view the Jews as inherently, eerily different—and powerful.

Ordinary people brought up on the liturgy of the Church, on sermons, learning the Gospels through Church interpretations, surrounded by sculpture and painting, hearing countless songs and ditties that all told the same story, found it natural to view the Jews not as human beings at all, but as incarnations of the Devil.

In the minds of Christians in the Middle Ages there was a flickering image, so to speak, of a real-life Jew: on the one hand, a person dressed oddly but looking, after all, human, speaking one's own language, dealing with one in all everyday concerns and activities, buying, selling, building, treating patients, and behaving humanly in the very act of practicing curious customs. On the other hand, this same person could embody an *idea*— the idea of being, in reality, not a human being at all but somehow occultly powerful, an emanation of the Devil, murderer of God, Christ killer, and so on.

Thus "The Jew" was not, after all, quite human: in the realm of the spirit he could play a weird role; the imagination of ordinary people, including the more or less educated summits, was full of spirits, demons, occult forces, witches, magicians, conjurors, soothsayers (not so different, to be sure, from the world of today). Hence it was, as it seems, child's play to see an actual Jew engaged in an ordinary human activity and to think of him or her, at the same time, as carrying out secret, eerily camouflaged activities of an entirely different, maleficent, and powerful nature. Double vision ruled with ease.

It was easy for people to see a Jewish doctor, for instance, as a manipulator of secret, evil spells, unknown poisons, strange enchantments that would spoil crops; or poisoning wells, desecrating the sacred Host, conspiring night and day to undo mankind on behalf of his master Satan, secret ally and consort. By the end of the Middle Ages "The Jew" was not only a concept in the minds of theologians, but a living entity in the minds of ordinary people.

We shall see in a moment the deep roots of this strange transfiguration of human beings. Even after the world of theology had been, as it might have seemed, shattered, and religious faith had been virtually lost, the secular imagination of many Christians could still regard the Jews as weird, alien, and horrifying.

THE AGE
OF THE PROTESTANT
REFORMATION

CHAPTER FOUR

At the end of the fifteenth and the beginning of the sixteenth
century a change loomed in Europe: the Renaissance, which
began in Italy and swiftly passed to northern Europe, brought
about a revival of interest in the heritage of antiquity. The ideals
of Greece and Rome, on the spiritual plane, were adopted with
a new zeal; the arts and sciences were cast in a new mold. A
new interest in the individual germinated. The unity of the
Church was ruptured: Protestantism, in various forms, made
deep inroads into the Papal monopoly; every form of Protestantism, after all, claimed the same heritage of antiquity.

The Bible as a whole, as well as the Gospels, now came under
independent scrutiny. Greek and Hebrew were studied by non-
professionals; increasingly the Bible was read by scholars in the
original Hebrew and Greek. In addition, the translation of the
Scriptures into vernacular languages overcame the exclusive
claim of St. Jerome's Latin Vulgate.

Thus the breakup of a centuries-old monopoly, whose main
target had been the strange existence of this nation of exiled
pariahs, might have been expected to ease things for the Jews.

And it is true that the growth of interest in the Bible as a living work, instead of as a repository of ecclesiastical authority, and even the stirring of interest, on the part of Christian scholastics, humanists, and religious reformers, in the Jewish mysticism of the Kabbala, had a direct influence on Christian faith.

Nevertheless, the status of the Jews did not fundamentally change. Indeed, in a sense Jews were even more alienated, if possible, from their environment precisely by the development of the humanist interest in history. At that time history was bound to remain essentially what it had always been: within the framework of the New Testament and of Church tradition, it was equated with the Church's version of the history of Christian Europe and its origins.

In this way the disintegration of rigid medieval society, for so long a straitjacket for the Jews, proved an even greater affliction. Moreover, as we shall see, the very breakup of long-established institutions was to exacerbate the spiritual climate of the elite, filter through to the masses, and, in the manner of all breakups, heighten social tension. Thus it was precisely in the period of transition that the rigidity and cruelty of the treatment of Jews intensified: the resolutions of the Fourth Lateran Council, for instance, were applied with particular harshness precisely during, and no doubt because of, the general change.

The emergence of Martin Luther as a schismatic within the Catholic Church might also have seemed to hold out some hope for the Jews: his initial approach to them (1517) was remarkably friendly; they were naturally hopeful. Yet their congenital optimism soon proved absurdly mistaken.

Luther's infringement on the Catholic monopoly—at first practical, tentative, without a principle, then a sustained, violent, and altogether extravagant revulsion (like everything else in his behavior)—did not entail an abandonment of Christian doctrine concerning the Jews, which was rooted, after all, in the earliest documents of Christianity: Paul's assignment of the Jews to a (temporary) satanic role and the Gospels' polemical dissociation of Jesus from them. The concept of the Jews as pariahs was as valid for Luther as for his opponents.

Luther in fact never challenged traditional doctrine concerning the Jews; on the contrary, his freeing of doctrine from the bureaucracy of the Roman Church merely presaged still greater hatred for them, a hatred that in the Church itself had been segregated, so to speak, as an element of theology, enabling the Church to act sincerely as defenders of the Jews even while its legislation made life difficult for them.

Thus a sober assessment of Luther's motivation for initially proposing that the Jews be dealt with more compassionately would have indicated how foolish this idea was. From the outset, after all, it was obvious that he was a fanatic, and that his reasons for indulging the Jews were grounded in a mere misunderstanding of their attitude toward their Scriptures.

Since Luther thought that the Scriptures, as the word of God, required no mediation on the part of the Church, that is, that ordinary people could grasp God's word without difficulty, he took it for granted that the Jews, who themselves took this view, would naturally agree with him, and at once become pious Christians of his own kind. His proposed "kindness" to the Jews, accordingly, was no more than a missionary tactic. When they failed to transform themselves, he naturally reversed his position. The abhorrence pious Jews felt for the doctrine of the Incarnation seems to have made little impression on him.

It was obvious, for that matter, that from its very inception his defense of the Jewish position on the Scriptures was no more than a side effect of his own defense against the charge of heresy launched against *him* (by the brother of Emperor Karl V, the Archduke Ferdinand). Luther had pointed out that Jesus was the son of Abraham, which was regarded as tantamount to denying the Immaculate Conception, and so on. This charge of a christological heresy seemed to Luther ludicrous, and while defending himself he merely thought of saying something that was both true and also attractive to Jews, presumably on the theory that they would be moved by Jesus' descent from Abraham.

After Luther's diplomacy missed its mark, he turned more and more violently against the Jews. He took up and stressed with characteristic tempestuousness the celebrated Church theme of Jewish blameworthiness; i.e., their full knowledge of their own wickedness. "They know perfectly well, these desperate rascals, that the New Testament is the book of our Lord Jesus Christ the son of God, and pretend they don't want to

know what it is."* Thus he merely expressed with greater violence the old theory that all Jewish denial of The Truth is mere
ill-will and satanic demonism.

By 1543 Luther's stream of anti-Jewish venom had culminated in two writings dealing expressly with the Jews,** both of
them outbursts of a primordial type of mystical phobia buttressed
by a sort of biblical erudition, by political ideas, and by the
religious ferment of the day, worded with intemperate force.

Twenty years before, during his "judeophile," missionary
phase, Luther had routinely scoffed at the old wives' tales of
Jewish well-poisoning, ritual murder, and sorcery; now he presented all these morbid fantasies as quite believable, and while
not, perhaps, factually accurate, as nevertheless an accurate
expression of the soul of The Jew. Luther had by now long since
given up the notion of converting Jews—"just as possible as
converting the Devil": he now wanted to expose them and their
lies for what they were, "so that we Germans can . . . know what
a Jew *is*, and defend our Christianity against the Devil himself."
This comparison with the Devil was a staple of Luther's rhetoric.

Luther was consumed by hatred for the God of the Torah,
that is, the Jewish God Yahweh; he thought the Torah had created an unbridgeable chasm between the Jews and Christianity,
and was itself the demonstration of their satanic nature. He
assumed, indeed, that he was doing no more than carrying on
St. Paul's struggle of fifteen hundred years before, which was
possible, of course, only if he disregarded Paul's view that the
"blindness" of the Jews was merely temporary.

Thus Luther's loathing of the Jews and his struggle against
them were in his mind an externalization of his inner struggle
against the Jewish God, Yahweh, now himself converted into a
sort of Devil, like his people the Jews, and hence a menace to

---

* Martin Luther, *On the Jews and Their Lies*, 1543, transl. Martin H. Bertram,
in *Luther's Works*, general editor Jaroslav Pelikan, vol. 47, Philadelphia: For-
tress Press, 1971, pp. 268–74.
** Ibid. and Martin Luther, *Vom Schem Hamphoras und vom Geschlecht
Christi*, Matth. 1, 1543, *Sämtliche Werke*, Polemische deutsche Schriften, Er-
langen: Carl Hayder, 1842, pp. 275–358.

God's true people, the Christians, the present heirs of the chosenness of the Jews and of their mission.

In this we see again one of the conclusions endlessly to be drawn from the Incarnation: obviously there could be no place for compassion in such a struggle against the Devil: it was a struggle—as it had been since the very genesis of theology—between truth and lies, that is, between God and the Devil. Thus the cardinal motivation of Luther, as of all for whom theology could encapsulate and express pathological phobias and hatreds, was bound to exclude, more or less by definition, all "humane" factors on principle: the Jews, as the very embodiment of Evil, were inevitably counterposed to the Incarnation of God in Jesus as the quintessence of the Good. In this way Luther was merely repeating, with his characteristically ferocious boundlessness, the focal theme of Christian theology.

If Nietzsche was right in saying that Luther was a medieval phenomenon merely protesting against the Renaissance and the blossoming of the sciences, then he can be considered a typical expression of a social malaise, crystallized with special potency in an extravagant psyche.

Luther's actual views were by no means original, nor was his hatred of the Jews. His attitude merely focused a general tendency. The breakup of the Catholic monopoly, despite its apparent change in premises, was no more beneficial to the Jews, by and large, than the previous era had been. Even friends of the Jews could defend them only by refuting certain specific misstatements, falsehoods, and so on, such as, for instance, in the question of burning or conserving the Hebrew Scriptures—friends of the Jews would want the Scriptures conserved for, say, scholarly reasons—or in assessing the value of some technical Jewish view with respect to some particular area of interest to theologians. It was vital for defenders of the Jews to avoid at all costs the slightest suspicion of heresy, a matter of life and death both then and for centuries to come.

Thus Luther's view of the Jews was no different, for instance, from that of Erasmus or Johannes Reuchlin (the celebrated Hebraist of the preceding generation): for Luther, too, the dispersion of the Jews was just one more proof of their damnation,

their fifteen-hundred-year exclusion from their own country—
a stunning demonstration of God's verdict.

Luther's denial of protection for the Jews, which had always
been incumbent on the Church, made things worse for them in
many respects, since his execration of them, retained from the
medieval Church, no longer had any theological mitigation.
Thus his addiction to violently abusive language—his habitual
references to Jews as "venomous and virulent," "thieves and
brigands," "disgusting vermin"—coupled with his growing and
soon enormous influence, was fatal to them.

To be sure, Luther turned the same explosive violence on all
his adversaries—especially, of course, the Pope—but the position of the Jews was obviously different in kind from that of those
who were more or less immune to his assaults. His lush rhetoric,
rooted in a fantasy in which erotic and scatological images ran
riot, made it natural for him to make much of, for instance, a
preposterous sculpture of a sow suckling a Jew, a typical form
of pornographic satire that was common, especially in Germany,
from the thirteenth century on. He also proposed practical measures, from outright expulsion to forced labor, the burning of
synagogues and houses, and so on.

Luther's fury against the Jews, after his disappointment at
their reception of his ideas, was characteristically violent: "What
then do we Germans want to do with this rejected, damned
people of the Jews?"

Advising "sharp mercy," he recommended the following:

> First, to set fire to their synagogues or schools and to bury and cover with
> dirt whatever will not burn, so that no man will ever again see a stone or
> cinder of them. This is to be done in honor of our Lord and of Christendom,
> so that God might see that we are Christians, and do not condone or
> knowingly tolerate [such] public lying, cursing, blaspheming of his Son
> and of his Christians . . .
>
> Second, I advise that their houses be razed and destroyed. For they
> pursue in them the same aims as in their synagogues. Instead they might
> be lodged under a roof or in a barn like the gypsies . . .
>
> Third, I advise that all their prayer-books and Talmudic writings, in
> which [such] idolatry, lies, cursing and blasphemy are taught, be taken
> from them.
>
> Fourth, I advise that their rabbis be forbidden to teach henceforth on
> pain of loss of life and limb . . .

Fifth, I advise that safe-conduct on the highways be abolished completely for the Jews.

Sixth, I advise that usury be prohibited to them, and that all cash and treasure of silver and gold be taken from them . . .

Seventh, I recommend putting a flail, an ax, a hoe, a spade, a distaff, or a spindle into the hands of young, strong Jews and Jewesses and letting them earn their bread in the sweat of their brow, as was imposed on the children of Adam (Gen 3) . . .

In brief, dear princes and lords, those of you who have Jews under your rule—if my counsel does not please you, find better advice, so that you and we all can be rid of the unbearable, devilish burden of the Jews.*

(At the Nuremberg Trials of the Nazi leaders after the Second World War, Julius Streicher was to point out that the one to be sitting in the dock was really Martin Luther, since the Nazis, after all, had merely "drawn the conclusions," so to speak, from everything he had said and written about the Jews.)

The most immediate consequence of the Reformation was the aggravation of the Jewish situation in countries still Catholic. It was around this time that ghettoes, first heard of in Venice in 1516 (a year before Luther's first public appearance) and mentioned in 1562, in a Papal bull, as a term for the Jewish quarter set up in Rome in 1556 on the left bank of the Tiber, made their appearance. Ghettoes were enclosed in Italy from the sixteenth century on; from the beginning of the seventeenth they gradually appeared in other countries (Germany and England); the word was absorbed into all languages.

The ghettoes expressed in tangible form the whole centuries-old process of stigmatizing the Jews, publicly and ostentatiously, as an alien community. It rounded off in the most strikingly visible way the implications of the Yellow Badge, the Jews' Hat, and the mandatory different attire in general. A compulsory streamlining of the normal colonization of immigrants, it made as evident as possible the alienation of the Jews in their actual habitations, in which, when the ghettoes were enclosed, they were confined as though in prison. The ghetto was, accordingly, utterly demeaning.

It must be understood, however, as a commentary on the

---

* *On the Jews and Their Lies*, op. cit.

anxieties generated by social change. Ghettoes became compulsory, with full rigidity and thoroughness, precisely in the first two centuries of the "modern era." Just as the old order began crumbling, spasmodically and unevenly, people no doubt felt a longing for their vanishing stability, and found it natural to give a physical embodiment to a hitherto spiritual complex.

But if the Reformation did not benefit the Jews, the Counter-Reformation launched by the Catholic Church was even worse. The rigidity brought about by the Counter-Reformation led to an intensified and literal application of the views of Augustine and Aquinas.

Jews were assigned quite naturally a major responsibility for the Reformation itself. It was obvious to Rome that the principal outrage of the heretics was their disdain for Church tradition, their astigmatic, ill-willed determination to "go back" to the sources by rejecting the Catholic contention that the sources could be understood only with the help of the Church tradition, which was, after all, itself as old as the sources (that is, Paul's Letters together with the earliest Church traditions). And in returning to the source of the Hebrew Scriptures, it had been natural for the heretics to receive instruction from Jewish scholars, if only in the Hebrew language. The very fact of discarding the Latin Vulgate meant that the Scriptures could be translated at will into any vernacular at all, with unforeseeably revolutionary consequences.

One of the chief factors in Luther's celebrity was, of course, his translation of the Bible into vernacular German, which had a tremendous influence thanks to his literary talent, even though he knew little Hebrew and less Greek. A result of Luther's primary innovation, that the word of God required no institutional mediation, this translation triggered a movement of vernacular translation throughout Europe in the wake of the Protestant Reformation: the impact of Luther's German Bible equaled that of the King James English version.

Protestantism was to split at once into many sects, each of them clinging to its own "orthodox" version of the texts. Nevertheless, as we shall see, the exposure to the public of the fundamental tendencies of the Old Testament—elementary democracy and the notion of a millennium based on justice—

was to bear fruit for many centuries, indeed, down to our own day.

There were substantial differences between the various streams of Protestantism. Lutheranism accepted Luther's ferocity against the Jews, based as it was on theology that was manifestly sound and consistent with traditional doctrine, but until the twentieth century Calvinism was to be far less hostile. Calvinism, with its belief in social values, energetic moral action, and the acceptance of individual responsibility, could accept the Jewish presence, while Lutheranism, founded on justification by faith, entailed the renunciation to some extent of civic obligations and hostility to faith as shown by "good works" (called by Luther a "Jewish belief"). Also, the Calvinists were more influenced by the Old Testament, which made them friendlier to contemporary Jews. French Calvinists, for that matter, were even rather pro-Jewish: to some extent they identified themselves with Jews because of their own oppression at the hands of the Church. In the Netherlands too, the situation of the Jews was relatively lightened, as also in Great Britain, after Cromwell, and in North America.

The malaise inherent in the erosion of the social order in the fifteenth and sixteenth centuries reinforced the phobias of the preceding centuries: there was an epidemic of witch hunts and devil mania, both of which intensified the persecution of the Jews, by now thoroughly established in the popular imagination as agents of the Devil. This identification, going back to the very beginning of the Church, was further deepened by a bona fide fear of devils, sorcerers, witches, and the like that enthralled the popular imagination. Everything that could be thought of as seductive, tempting, exotic, exciting—sexuality, sensuality, money, usury, the Jews themselves—was satanized. Everything seen as disturbing—that is, *all* change—was seen as Satan's work, ascribed to the Jews directly as his agents, whose sinister power, naturally, stemmed from their master.

Caricatures of Jews increased in violence: the invention of printing in the second half of the fifteenth century enormously accelerated the circulation of anti-Jewish lampoons. Hatred of Jews, firmly rooted in ideas and institutions, could now permeate the popular imagination through the growing variety of media:

flyers, pamphlets, woodcuts, and copperplates brought to life, through art, the ancient ideas concerning this eerie people of pariahs who at the same time had great though of course hidden power.

The notion inherent in the satanization of the Jews naturally created a popular image: Jews were thought to be plotting night and day in a vast conspiracy against Christendom. The image of the usurer making everyone else toil on his behalf, and of the Wandering Jew, which came into existence around this time, became popular, both in the mystical symbolic figure wandering eternally over continents and through epochs, desecrating the Host in various bestial caricatures and in the specific form of a pathetic peddler bearing his little bundle of tawdry goods while wielding diabolical power.

The Wandering Jew emerged in Germany in 1602: eight versions of a small tract came out the same year, to be followed by various European translations. By the end of the seventeenth century (1694) the figure of the Wandering Jew, also called the Eternal Jew, was well established in Germany. By 1714 it was established everywhere as a symbol of Jewry. Since the end of the eighteenth and the beginning of the nineteenth century, this symbol has become more diffuse, ramified, and widespread in all Occidental languages: beginning as a mere synonym for the fate of the Jews—the dispersion and wandering—it has since been charged with countless varieties of mysticism and the occult.

A well-known fact must be recalled: until well into the modern era, practically everyone in Christendom and Islam was illiterate (like most of mankind, to be sure). In Christendom, accordingly, the only view generally held was that of the Church. The Gospels and the Bible as a whole were read aloud in translation and interpreted by the lower clergy. Insofar as the text was learned at all, it was understood in that interpretation. When the Jews were mentioned, as they were bound to be during the major holiday, Easter, they were necessarily the subject of such interpretation; that was, indeed, the point of their being mentioned.

Thus "The Jew," as developed in the Christian interpretation of the Bible as a whole and in particular of the Gospel passages concerning the Crucifixion, became the primordial type of sinner, whose depravity was hammered home by endless repetition, the basic concept being ramified and embellished with constantly renewed overtones. The theme was central both in the catechism taught to children and in the sermons preached to adult audiences in church.

The net result of the Church teachings, which for centuries dominated every aspect of education, and which for hundreds of millions of people are dominant to this day, was the implanting of fixed symbols of an all-encompassing world view in the minds of people in their formative years. There seems to be a critical period in a child's life when heavily stressed concepts, and the symbols that point them up, can be so firmly implanted in his mind that they affect his behavior throughout life. And if repressed, during maturation, they can lead to extravagantly explosive conduct.

Moreover, the same theme of "The Jew" was enhanced and reinforced in all aspects of painting: every sculpture, every painting of the Crucifixion of the Savior, the martyrs, and the saints, was designed to drive home the central message. Songs, fairy tales, and the lives of the saints drove the same thought and image deep into the consciousness and of course the unconscious of many generations.

The reflection in cultural life was massive: the spate of literary production focused on the Jews inflamed multitudes. Passion Plays were put on annually, performed in the vernacular; they lasted several days, creating a mood of tension, awe, and feverishness. Their effect was heightened by the very technique of the casting: the "historical" element was disregarded entirely; the evil, scheming Jews in the Passion Plays were cast to remind the audience of local Jews, whose caricature was merely retrojected into a bogus historical background.

The purpose of the Passion Plays was, of course, to dramatize the events as seen by the Church, but the view of the Church was itself wholly demonological, and since the Jews were regarded as a permanent historical entity, it was perfectly plausible to take Jewish "types" from everyday life and project them into the demonological roles assigned them by Church tradition. The cruelty, perfidy, and malevolence of the Jews plotting against the Savior that was dramatized in the Passion Plays produced the most profound impression on audiences already exposed to lifelong conditioning that led them to hear and see the Jews in just such a role.

The basic theme of these Passion Plays is, of course, the traditional one, presented with dramatic highlights: The Jews have deserted God, since the Christians were now God's people. Jews are presented as having been stricken with blindness since the Crucifixion, following Paul's thesis that blindness had come upon Israel after the Resurrection, which should have opened their eyes. The Devil often appears in person, egging the Jews on against Jesus.

In the French drama *Le Mystère de la Passion*, the devils are at first in the forefront; then the plotting against Jesus is taken up by the Jews, the true malefactors, while the devils, now in the background, maintain a guiding hand. The conspiracy between Jews and devils is the key theme of the play: in the climactic scene they collaborate in spurring Judas on to his betrayal, howling with delight at their success. Jews, scoffing and crowing, twirling about the Cross on which Jesus is hanging in torment: this scene, theatrically most effective, is the culmination of the Crucifixion in many mystery plays in England, France, and Germany.

The myth was so pervasive that it did not require flesh-and-blood Jews to sustain it: "The Jew" had become such a structural necessity, so to speak, that his actual presence was not required—it was enough for him merely to be referred to. Even in countries with no Jews at all, such as the Netherlands after the Black Death, or after the expulsion of 1290 in England, where there had been no Jews whatever for centuries, the Jews could be harped on in literature in the knowledge that the concept of "The Jew" was still meaningful. Chaucer, for instance, treats it with relish in "The Prioress's Tale" (ca. 1386).

The notion of Shylock appeared in world literature for the first time in the fifteenth and sixteenth centuries. Shakespeare used it with characteristic modifications: his original version in 1595, followed in two editions by 1600, had been preceded by Marlowe's *Jew of Malta*, in which the Jewish protagonist, Barabbas, was a usurer, poisoner, hater of Christians, killer, hypocrite, and traitor—as well as morbidly ambitious. His only positive qualities were his love for his daughter—which may perhaps be taken as a softening of the portrait in the direction of humanizing it, as in Shakespeare's Shylock, whose fidelity to Judaism, of course, was interpreted nevertheless as typical arrogance and stubbornness.

These two plays interacted curiously with an historical incident: the personal physician of Elizabeth I was Rodrigo Lopez, a Marrano, who was also a diplomatic agent at the court as well as an interpreter. He was accused of high treason and of an attempt to poison the Queen: under torture, he confessed to everything and was condemned to death (February 1594). Lopez was called "that vile Jew . . . a perjured and murdering villain and a Jewish doctor worse than Judas"; while the mob, during his torture before being executed, yelled out, "A Jew! A Jew!"*

This event stimulated many current rumors about the Jews: the *Jew of Malta* was performed again, *The Merchant of Venice* was written: Shakespeare thus seems to have combined the traditional hatred of Jews, with the traditional focus on usury, and the real history of Rodrigo Lopez, though as usual Shakespeare's craftsmanlike preoccupation with writing effective speeches results in a slightly contradictory attitude toward Shylock, conceived of by Shakespeare's idolaters as indicating the profound complexity of the character.

Shylock could be expected to entertain ordinary audiences even though they could scarcely have known any Jews: the Venetians in the play were ordinary foreigners, with nothing to distinguish them, say, from ordinary Englishmen (as is true of all Shakespeare's plays with foreign settings). The audience could be depended on to see in Shylock the living epitome of qualities notoriously associated with the Jews in legend, literature, and art.

Still, though Shylock was to some extent humanized, he has always been considered a caricature of a Jew; the name itself soon became the equivalent of "usurer," even in gangsters' parlance. It was striking that in England, where the caricature of

---

* Alex Bein, *The Jewish Question*, op. cit., p. 158.

the Jews that was rooted in theology was beginning to recede together with the theology itself, the old portrait of the Jew was not, in fact, discarded, but was simply further developed by the artist's resources, and thus made more vivid than the arid stereotype of tradition. Since the end of the sixteenth century, accordingly, a hybrid symbol of Shylock plus the Wandering Jew has been roving through the English and international theater and world literature; a fusion of traditional mythology plus an echo or two of a reality distorted by the prism of that same tradition.

The technique of Shakespeare's semihumanizing of Shylock was to be indefinitely expanded in during the evolution of modern literature. Jewish stereotypes were to be gradually replaced, first by well-meaning, idealistic refutations of the maleficent image, then by admixtures of would-be naturalism, and finally, today, by more or less authentic naturalism.

The very fact, to be sure, that the satanic portrait anchored in mystical anti-Semitism had to be counteracted by absurdly unrealistic counter-portraits—in nineteenth-century English literature, for instance (Anthony Trollope's *Melmotte*, George Eliot's *Daniel Deronda*, Sir Walter Scott's *Ivanhoe*, George Meredith's *Tragic Comedians*)—as though the satanic caricatures were merely "unfair," no doubt indicates the unconscious plausibility of the ancient image.

At first glance it might seem strange that Jews survived the Middle Ages at all. It is true that the logic of the Church made it obligatory to "spare" them, but even though many Churchmen and members of the elite were quite sincere about the theological rationale of Jewish survival, it was surely far too subtle to have had much effect on the happily sensual anti-Semites in the masses.

The fact is that while it is atrocities that tend to be stressed, very naturally, in history books, they were exceptional. Though the concept of The Jew held real-life Jews in a vise of alienation, actual violence against them erupted rarely. And if the canvas being examined is large enough, the countless communities that were, in fact, wiped out were made up for, statistically speaking, in other areas or at other times.

It was only in moments of tension, during crises of social anxiety, that the concept of The Jew merged with familiar real-life Jews. The double vision of Jews, accordingly, as partly real human beings and partly Devil Jews could encompass all relationships between Jews and Christians in ordinary social life, with the concept of The Damned Jew lying latent, to become inflamed and externalized in moments of extreme tension.

Even after the symbols had permeated the masses, centuries after the theology explaining and justifying such symbols had been developed, the human psyche was healthy and resilient enough to segregate them in some compartment that did not come in contact with reality. The symbols could activate the masses, but only spasmodically: massacres would be unusual.

That is why Jewry was not extinguished in Christendom, and was not, indeed, to be collectively and radically endangered until the twentieth century, when, as we shall see, religion in its formal sense seemed to be drying up.

SECULARIZATION

CHAPTER FIVE

With the crumbling of the feudal order, with the discovery of America and the Far East, with the Renaissance and the rise of natural sciences in the seventeenth century, with the growth of a contemplation of the past and the beginning of the Higher Criticism of the Bible at the end of the eighteenth century, theology's grip began to slacken.

Traditional religion, and in particular the Christian tradition, began to be scrutinized. Dogma was analyzed, criticized, contested, overthrown. By the last third of the eighteenth century, the "Age of Enlightenment," although an explicit attack on Christianity as such was still taboo, the dogmatic presuppositions of Catholic and Protestant Christendom were splintered. Enlightened thinkers in France, England, and Germany plucked apart all aspects of traditional religion, reshaping ideas to meet the criteria of rationalism.

At the same time, the life of Jews all over Europe was being transformed. Segregation yielded to the shifts in world trade, whose traditional institutions began to break up with the dissolution of the feudal order they themselves had helped to bring about. The conquest of Constantinople by the Ottoman Turks at the end of the fifteenth century and the discovery of America—a new way around Africa—had set in train vast upheavals. Jews from Iberia, both real Jews and Marranos, had been playing a seminal role in the newly arisen trade centers in the Netherlands as well as in the discovery and exploitation of America. Jews, in fact, had begun performing new economic functions all over Europe: as administrators for the nobility, they had been occupying an intermediate position between the summits of society, the rising middle class, and the peasantry and laborers.

Mercantilism—an expansion of the economic markets on a new basis—finally shattered the feudal system in Western Europe, and the breakup of feudalism ultimately transformed Jewish life as well as the world. The "laissez-faire" stance of mercantilism gave the Jews an increasingly productive role that dovetailed organically with the reshaping of society. But the transformation of institutions and ideas was spasmodic, the reshaping of society explosive.

The Jews were affected adversely by the opposition to mercantilism among the "physiocrats" of the mid-eighteenth century; the resistance to the laissez-faire at the core of mercantilism took the form of an all-out onslaught on both its theory and its practice. For the physiocrats, trade as such was pernicious, and the peasants, in fact, were the sole "productive" class: trade and industry were "sterile." Thus the Jews, who during the breakup of the feudal order had facilitated the emergence of a different socio-economic base, found themselves still pariahs.

This mystical summing up of whole classes of people as either "productive" or "sterile" was itself, no doubt, an expression of anxiety arising precisely from the changes. The theory that a basic economic function such as trade or industry could be inherently sterile seems to be a form of mystical nostalgia. Such categorization was to accompany the social upheavals that began in the eighteenth century.

The movement of ideas that was to bring about the emancipation of the Jews began with the erosion of traditional Christian theology, reducing it to a simple belief in God—Deism—untrammelled by specific dogmas or rituals, and with the Enlightenment of the eighteenth century. Deism made it possible, for the first time, to discuss the actual status of the Jews.

The Enlightenment, which led up to, transcended, and generalized the ideas underlying the French Revolution, may be considered the summation of aspirations going all the way back to the Middle Ages: humanism, religious reformation, the natural sciences, the formation of the urban bourgeoisie, the transformation of international commerce, the development of the universities, the foundation of scientific academies.

"Nationalism" and "tolerance" were key words: the leading thinkers, whom the religious wars of the seventeenth century, which were exacerbated by endless dynastic contests, persuaded of the inherent futility and perniciousness of conflict, strove for a society in which human intelligence would generate a new order.

The theological and institutional structures of the Church—and for that matter all aspects of organized religion as a whole—were gradually eroded, as it seemed, by rationalism: pious optimism expressed itself in a general hope that both economics and society would soon be freed from the prejudices and superstitions underlying all institutions by the human mind, which would eventually sap and overcome the inevitable resistance from the churches, the privileged classes, and the retrograde economic summits of society.

The Emancipation of the Jews proceeded staccato, like social processes in general. In England, for instance, though there had been only a handful of Jews, some 8,000, in the middle of the eighteenth century (they had begun returning in the mid-seventeenth century after their expulsion at the end of the thirteenth) their status became a burning issue. Until the middle of the eighteenth century Jews could neither hold public office, buy land, nor participate in the colonial trade through the ownership of English vessels.

In 1753 an attempt was made to change this by passing a Naturalization Bill that would allow Jews to become citizens.

There was violent opposition to the Naturalization Bill, which was, in fact, soon repealed: yet the opposition did not touch on the real condition of the Jews in England but revolved, instead, around age-old stereotypes: most opponents of the Bill did not mention the arguments made by Deists against the Jews, but merely repeated the classical theory of divinely ordained Jewish dispersion and degradation, and the consequent outrageousness of improving their condition under a Christian government.

On the other hand, the centuries-long absence of Jews from England may have shielded them against the proliferation of current stereotypes, and thus made it possible for the Old Testament directly to influence mores, attitudes, and so on. In England, accordingly, the Deist criticism of the Bible, which had naturally ricocheted against the Jews, was not translated into personal hostility. In France, where there had been Jews for some time, at least in the East and the South, the effects of the Enlightenment were both more massive and more personal.

In its mainstream, the French Enlightenment—except no doubt for Montesquieu—was priggish: people were meant to conform with principles of "reason." Considering the validity of their own ideas to be absolute, the *philosophes* were determined to remake all mankind in their own image.

One might well have thought, accordingly, that the *philosophes*, whose ideas of equality, fraternity, and the rights of man were to be crystallized in the French Revolution, would have been bound to include the Jews. And formally speaking, the Jews were indeed to be emancipated, through the general principles encapsulated in the French Revolution: they were included by the force, so to speak, of logic.

Since the rationalist approach was inherently universal, the Jews had to be included, not only for humanitarian reasons, a natural byproduct of this whole humanist view, but because of the general conviction that *all* problems of society would yield to the benign application of common sense based on knowledge. This would naturally and inevitably lead both to tolerance and ultimately to a legal order valid for one and all.

The "return to the sources," that is, to the Old Testament (the Hebrew Scriptures), which was part of the whole reassessment of the Church tradition and institutions, and the acceptance of the Mosaic code as a standard for modern constitutions, which characterized the English and North American Puritans as well as the Calvinists in Geneva and Holland, might reasonably have been expected to lead to a "pro-Jewish" attitude. This was, for instance, a strong motive behind the welcome given the Iberian Jews in Holland in the seventeenth century, and for the tacitly approved return to England of Jewish merchants under Cromwell.

One of the first consequences of Deism might well have been the automatic emancipation of the Jews from the libels, slanders, maltreatment, and persecutions that for so many centuries had resulted from their role as surrogates of Satan. European Jewry was now concentrated in Eastern Europe: most Jews were small merchants, craftsmen, tradesmen, and the like. In the West their numbers were few: often on the periphery of society, they could not be thought of as exerting any significant influence. The rare individuals who distinguished themselves did so in conventional pursuits in which their Jewishness played no discernible role.

One might have thought, in sum, that with the beginnings of secularization in Western Europe the end of anti-Semitism could be seen as imminent. It could be only a matter of time before an age-old, ossified, and at last obsolete category of thought would dissolve of itself.

Moreover, apart from large-scale socio-economic evolution, the fundamental change in the outlook of educated people entailed first the gradual, then the precipitous downgrading of theology. If the curious status of the Jews was, in fact, due to the interweaving of theological factors with the emotions of the masses, then the attrition of theology, one might think, could only have benefited the Jews.

Indeed, it would surely have seemed inevitable that so profound an obsession as the status of the Jews in Christian doctrine would have automatically become obsolete with the decline of theology. The preoccupation with the Jews, after all, would seem to have been rooted in a specific historical situation—the emergence of Jesus, the ideas of St. Paul, the formation of the Church—that when scrutinized critically might reasonably have been expected to yield to empirical analysis.

How indeed could a collectivity of ordinary people, subject like all mankind to the laws of biology and physiology, have been expected to represent a cosmic principle? And how could that cosmic principle, assuming it to have been exemplified two thousand years before by events in Judea, have gone on finding its embodiment in the genetic continuity of a people scattered throughout the world?

Just as during the Kingdom of God hysteria that punctuated several centuries after the First Crusade in 1096, adding a manic element to the turbulence of the Middle Ages as a whole, so now, with the withering of theology, the apparent source of mystical anti-Semitism and hence of the age-old opprobrium attached to the Jews, it might have been expected that they could become a "normal" people: odd, perhaps, and with a sort of unity despite their dispersion, with a curious ancient religion and strange customs, but in no way *important.*

As a numerically insignificant people, now no longer, at last, conceived of as a cosmic force—a concept justified only by their role in the Divine Plan—they would have warranted only a fraction of the attention expended on the study of exotic peoples made fashionable by the Renaissance and the Enlightenment.

Yet the residue unwittingly inherited by the *philosophes* from Christian theology and more generally, perhaps, from the world picture of Christendom, made it impossible for them to consider the Jews simply as people to be reshaped like other human beings—more specifically, other Europeans. For the *philosophes,* the Jews remained, somehow, an irremediably fossilized social entity, with ineradicable traits stemming from an inborn nature that could not be modified.

Thus the French Revolution contained a core of mysticism with respect to the Jews: the general outlook of the *philosophes* had a gap through which inherited preconceptions of, masquerading as familiarity with, the Jews could slip through, rendering them as a collectivity essentially indigestible. It was not merely this or that element of ritual in Judaism, nor was it even Judaism as a whole, that was rejected as part of the "superstition" the *philosophes* were combating: the very essence of the Jewish "spirit" was taken to be hostile to mankind. Hence the most ancient legends about the Jews, legends stemming from

the mundane conflicts of ancient Jewish rulers with their opponents long before the germination of Christianity, were given
a new embodiment. Indeed, the attention paid the Jews by countless thinkers since the Renaissance and the Enlightenment was,
by any ordinary standards, staggering.

It can be explained only by a deeply rooted feeling that in
spite of their apparent insignificance, the Jews were still, somehow, powerful. Even when this was not stated explicitly, the very
concentration on them could have an effect only because their
occult power made them plausible as a counterforce to Christendom. The lengthy, passionate diatribes against them could
be explained only by this underlying assumption. Unconsciously,
the occult power attributed to the Jews was simply taken for
granted.

Immanuel Kant, for instance, who wrote about the Jews often
and in different contexts, took pains to reject Judaism as a religion entirely, and to devote a long, ferocious diatribe against
Jews:

> The Palestinians living among us . . . have through their usurious
> spirit . . . received the not-unfounded reputation of deceivers. It seems
> strange to think of a nation of deceivers, but it is just as strange to think
> of a nation made up of nothing but merchants, which are united for the
> most part by an old superstition that is recognized by the government
> under which they live. They do not seek any civil honor, but rather wish
> to compensate their loss by profitably outwitting the very people among
> whom they find protection . . . It cannot be otherwise with a whole nation
> of merchants, who are non-productive members of society.*

Johann Herder, in the last half of the eighteenth century,
also made much of the uniqueness of the Jews; he, to be sure,
praised their "folk" quality: ". . . If a history of the Jews from
all the countries they are scattered in were to be written, it would
be a show-piece of mankind, most remarkable as both a natural
and a political phenomenon."**

---

* Immanuel Kant, *Anthropology from a Pragmatic Point of View*, 1798, transl.
Victor Lyle Dowdell, London and Amsterdam: Southern Illinois University
Press, 1978, p. 101.
** Johann Gottfried Herder, *Ideen*, 1785, in *Sämtliche Werke*, 1877–1913, vol.
17, Berlin: Bernhard Suphan, p. 285.

Herder regarded the "Hebrew people as having been looked on since its very origin as a *genetic individual*, as a people;"* yet for that very reason he thought of them as an "Asiatic people alien to our part of the world:" and "since Israel in it prayers considers itself a people of its own, distinguished from all peoples, how could it be considered otherwise by other nations?"

And for the actual, living Jews of his own time, Herder, a man of great compassion and sensitivity, without really the slightest *prejudice* against Jews, wrote (1787) that the Jews, "God's people, once given its fatherland by heaven itself, have now been for millennia, indeed, almost since its inception, a parasitic plant on the trunks of other nations."**

This broad and simple conception, echoing, evidently, the most ancient theme of Christian theology, was to underlie all future forms of anti-Semitism: the metaphor of a parasite in the body of its host was to sum up the feelings of mystical anti-Semites down to our own day, both among the masses of the people and for that matter in the thin layer of the elite.

It must be recalled that whatever the content of the Enlightenment, its penetration of the masses was only gradual: the belief in witches remained common for many generations. A denial of the existence of witches would have entailed a total rejection of an entire world of received ideas—first and foremost, the cult of saints, as well as the magical instrumentalities embedded in the Church itself (the Incarnation and the Sacraments). If the departed could help the living by becoming saints, why should miscreants not make mischief as devils?

Long before the French Revolution it was obvious that mere ideas had not changed the emotional attitude toward Jews: on the contrary, the general ideas that led up to and were furthered by the Revolution quickly found a natural focus in a renewed judeophobia, merely transferred from the theological to another sphere. The *philosophes*, for instance, in a way sympathized with the Jews as the oppressed people par excellence, the most

---

* Ibid., vol. 24, pp. 63, 64.
** Herder, *Ideen zur Philosophie der Geschichte der Menschheit*, book 16, chap. 12, cited in Leon Poliakov, *History of Anti-Semitism*, vol. 3, transl. Miriam Kochan, New York: Vanguard Press, translation copyright 1975, p. 162.

notorious victims of Christian intolerance: since the *philosophes* believed in justice, and had sworn to destroy intolerance of all kinds, it was natural for them to express sympathy with the Jews.

Indeed, protests against the persecution of the Jews became clichés of eighteenth-century rhetoric, especially from hatred of the Inquisition, the bête noire of the Enlightenment. It was routine for eighteenth-century thinkers (Montesquieu, Lessing, Rousseau) to insist on the common humanity and the natural rights shared by Christians and Jews alike. Even though few went so far as to foresee a true emancipation of the Jews, the idea itself was adumbrated as early as the beginning of the eighteenth century (in 1714, by John Toland, the English freethinker).

But this attack on the Church, which might have been thought to benefit the Jews, soon turned to their disadvantage: the focus of the Enlightenment was not the Jews for their own sake, but as show-pieces for the attack on official Christianity. Pro-Jewish rhetoric was merely a formula for undermining the Church. Lessing's celebrated *Nathan the Wise*, for instance, produced a version of Judaism in conformity with the views of the *philosophes*, as a way of pointing up the backwardness of official Christianity.

Thus the Jews were turned into an abstraction whose principal utility now was as witnesses to the error of Christianity, just as before, in their degradation, they had been, theologically, witnesses to the Truth.

Real-life Jews continued to be regarded with suspicious aversion. The integrity of Jewry as a symbol of a concept remained untouched. It was only the locus of its function that was shifted, from theology to ethnology, and later, as we shall see—in the racial theories of the nineteenth and twentieth centuries—to biology. Throughout these shifts, the mechanism remained the same: the Jews continued to be identified with a repugnant concept, playing the same role of a pernicious and essentially indigestible species—or subspecies—of humanity.

The extravagance of the judeophobic attacks cannot be understood as arising out of expediency, as a mere ploy in the campaign against Christianity. The venomous hostility to the Jews, communally and individually, demonstrated most characteristically, perhaps, by Diderot and Voltaire, went beyond all reason. The diatribes launched against the Jews by the chief thinkers of the Enlightenment can be understood only as the products of a hatred far beyond the reach of rationality. It may have been nourished, to be sure, by mundane factors: perhaps a dislike of Jewish particularism plus resentment grounded in envy (of prosperous individual Jews). The tone went far beyond actual complaints: its spitefulness evidently had deep roots. It was exceeded only by the most virulent movements of mystical anti-Semitism in the twentieth century.

The extravagance of the *philosophes'* emotions really had nothing to do with religion per se at all. Christianity as such, to be sure, was for a long time immune to attack; it was, accordingly, natural for Judaism to be attacked in its place, since the Bible, the dogmatic foundation of Christianity, was also the foundation of Judaism; hence it might serve as the camouflage needed for the fundamental onslaught—on Christianity.

Yet this was its most superficial aspect: the difference was that there were no consequences for individuals from an attack on Christianity. In the case of the Jews, however, a rigorous identity was established and never shaken off between Jews as believers in Judaism and Jews as individuals. They were treated as an entity, in which strictures on Judaism as a religion entailed strictures on Jews as people.

This was to be characteristic of a process that transferred identifying Jews with one principle—during the heyday of theology with the principle of The Devil—to identifying them with some other principle. The Jews were to be successively identified with some aspect of evil, whatever it might be, which they were said to exemplify, symbolize, or epitomize. When the Jews were being attacked for their religion, as they continued to be after the rationalist attack on all religion, they were held particularly culpable of "superstition," which, unlike individual Christians, they could not simply shake off. During the era of nationalism, they were outsiders: for Socialists they represented the principle of noxious finance.

Denis Diderot, for instance, could discuss Judaism as a religion urbanely, indeed benevolently—much like d'Holbach, Voltaire, and other *philosophes*—yet he took pains to sum up the Jews in a definition that in fact soared far beyond either religion or culture: he created a stigma that was in its nature permanent and absolute.

Diderot expressed a predilection for the Pharisees, during their influential period, before the Jewish debacle of 70, but in discussing subsequent Jewish history he abandoned his interest in the Pharisees, even though since there were latter-day Pharisees—i.e., contemporary rabbis—it might have been considered normal to discuss them too. Diderot not only avoided this religious question, but shunted his interest in the Jews into a purely anthropological topic: their *nature*. He conceded that they should "subsist, since they marry and have children," but since their "religion and that of the peoples they live among do not allow them to be absorbed by them, they should live apart."*

This view was evidently merely a reformulation of a tendency we shall see expressed uninterruptedly throughout the secularization stemming from the late seventeenth century, a reworking of the classic theological view of the Jews, an echo of the mystical framework of Christianity—for in what actual society of real life could such an absolute, quasi-racial stigma mean anything?

Diderot's intelligence makes his lack of awareness of the connection between his quasi-biological characterization of the Jews and his putative sociological analysis all the more disconcerting. It was just this lack of awareness, indeed, of the connection between absolute theology and the unconscious carryover of theology into other realms, such as culture and biology, that was to be the leitmotif of all secular attacks on Jews.

This theological view of the Jews was ultimately what determined Diderot's opinion of them as objects of the fundamental reforms being promoted by him and other *philosophes*.

---

* Denis Diderot, *Oeuvres Complètes*, vol. 2, from his "Réponse à l'examen du prosélyte" (1763), Paris: Garnier Frères, 1875, p. 97 (author's translation).

Though he respected "true" religion and opposed only superstition, the distinction he made between Christians and Jews made it inherently impossible to salvage the Jews.

For the *philosophes*, believing Christians merely bore a sort of veneer of superstition, consisting of the mixture of credulity, superstition, and fanaticism imposed on them by the Jewish creation of Christianity; but since their essential character was sound—that is, not "oriental"—they might be regenerated if only they could be emancipated from religion. Jews, on the other hand, were credulous, superstitious, and fanatical by *nature*: in *their* case, religion was dictated by inherent character.

Voltaire's influence on both contemporaries and posterity was incalculable; no doubt it was the link between the mystical anti-Semitism of medieval Christendom and the "secular," still mystical anti-Semitism of the nineteenth and twentieth centuries. His role is all the more instructive since in many ways he was, of course, the architect of the ostensibly rational, secular Enlightenment. Yet at the same time it is obvious that he shaped the mystical anti-Semitism that was from the very outset embedded in the Enlightenment itself. His theory of the Jews as inherently alien constituted a sort of revolving door that enabled the social thinkers heralding the modern age—Fourier, Proudhon, Marx—to compose an amalgam that integrated the Church's theological hostility to Judaism with two still more ancient notions, alienness and race—both irremediable.

The explicitly theological aversion and the apparently non-theological aversion could coalesce in a tacit agreement that Jews per se were incapable of being emancipated, and hence were a peril for European society. Though Voltaire and the other *philosophes* did not deny that Jews, if they *ceased* to be Jews, could be assimilated, and while they also repudiated specific libels such as that of ritual murder, they undoubtedly played a key role in the later evolution of mystical anti-Semitism. The focusing of their main attack on Jewish parochialism amounted to saying that Jews as such were enemies of the state—a secular version, of course, of one strand of medieval mystical anti-Semitism.

Yet how could Voltaire graft onto his secular formulations the mystical anti-Semitism of the very Christian tradition he

spent a large part of his life attacking? It may well be that for
Voltaire, as for countless others, the Jews played the role of a
lightning rod for some underlying hatred, some unavowed or
unavowable emotion camouflaged by the intellectual climate as
mere "views."

For decades before the French Revolution, Voltaire was universally seen as the enemy of contemporary Jewry as well as of
the Jewry of the remote past. This is all the more striking since
in his day most of the Jews in France, to say nothing of Europe
as a whole, were eking out a meager livelihood on the fringes
of society. Voltaire's writings provided rich material for all those
who wished to embellish their hatred of the Jews with fashionable ideas.

As with other *philosophes*, Voltaire's hatred of Judaism derived from his onslaught on Christianity itself, and for that matter, on dogmatic religion in general: it was taken for granted
that the dogmatism of organized religion was the principal bulwark of antirationalism and of pernicious social prejudices. Because of this he took pains, like Spinoza to some extent before
him, to undermine the value of the Bible as an historical doc-
ument as well as a form of revealed wisdom: thus he demonstrated that Christianity had never been foreseen or predicted
in the Old Testament—the Jews of course agreed with that—
and that the Jews were in no way "Chosen" or in any way special
at all. On the contrary, they had always been inferior to any of
the peoples surrounding them.

To highlight his rupture with the Christocentric view of history anchored in the Church, Voltaire took pleasure in showing
that the Jews were nothing but a vagabond horde of Arabs
"called Jews," merely one more barbarian people, and in demonstrating this with the help of the Bible itself. But he accompanied this debunking with fantastic attacks on contemporary
Jews: what he and other Enlightenment thinkers did, in by-
passing the traditions of the Church, was to transfer to the remote
past the usual run-of-the-mill disparagements of the Jews of
their own day. Hostility to the Jews could easily be documented
from classical antiquity as well as from disparagements of the
Jews in the secular literature of the past.

Voltaire went to extravagant lengths to run down the Jews,

finding every conceivable reason to do so: from their inception they had been mere thieves; their Bible and everything civilization had credited them for had been largely borrowed from others, just as they peddled old clothes that they had merely refurbished and passed off as new. And just as their Yiddish was a vulgar jargon compounded of German and other elements, so in the remote past their Hebrew had been a jargon of Phoenician and Arabic. In a similar debunking style, Voltaire explained the Jewish prescriptions of cleanliness as having been imposed on them simply because they were by nature filthy and noisome, indeed stinking.

The only virtues Voltaire granted the Jews was their fecundity and their thrift, both qualities, in the context, obviously pejorative.

In this way Voltaire the Freethinker adopted from hostile biblical criticism as well as from the libels of antiquity a critique of the Jews of the past that obviously derived from the disparaging views of his own day. Since contemporary Jews were vulnerable to charges of usury, so Voltaire transferred the concept of usury to the most remote past, as though Jews had in their essence always been usurers.

Voltaire dismissed the notion of the Chosen People as a piece of abominable arrogance that had awoken in them a striving for world rule; that was what underlay their hatred of foreigners, harped on by Voltaire like so many others since Tacitus. At bottom, Jews regarded the land of others as their own: similarly, their ethics were limited to their relations with each other; in dealing with outsiders, anything went.

Voltaire was exceptionally vindictive: for him the very concept of monotheism, the Bible, and biblical history taken together—that is, the contribution of the Jews—was a grotesque interruption of human progress, which without it would have been initiated by the marvels of antiquity alone: for him, the Golden Age was Greco-Roman civilization. Thus the Jews, who in any case had been rightly attacked by various critics and opponents in antiquity, represented in their nature a disturbance of classical progress, begun in the remote past, but aborted. For Voltaire the issue was, accordingly, between Western culture, now about to recover during the Enlightenment from the Christian-Jewish contamination, and European progress without the burden of Jewry.

As a journalist and, in a way, an ex-Christian busily attacking the Church, Voltaire could scarcely use an explicitly theological argument against the Jews, yet it is impossible to explain his animus except through the "essentializing" treatment of the Jews in Christian theology.

In his summation of Jewish character (1771, in one of his last serious writings) he loses all balance:

> They are the most insolent of all men, detested by all their neighbors and detesting them all, always either robbers or robbed, either bandits or slaves, either murderers or being murdered turn and turn about . . . All peoples have committed crimes; the Jews are the only ones to boast about them. They are all of them born with the fury of fanaticism in their hearts, just as Bretons and Teutons are born with blond hair. I should not be in the least surprised if these people one day became a calamity for the human race.*

Voltaire plainly needed no religious argument to express a metaphysical hatred of the Jews: if they were "fanatics" by nature, as others are blond, their situation was evidently hopeless.

A year later, after making a brief survey of various religions, he says, addressing Jews:

> You seem to me the maddest of the lot. The Kaffirs, Hottentots and the Negroes of Guinea are much more reasonable and honest people than your ancestors, the Jews. You have surpassed all nations in impertinent fables, in misconduct and in barbarism. You bear the punishment for all that, such is your destiny."**

By adopting arguments from the ancient opponents of the Jews when the Jews still lived on their own land, and investing them with the absolute quality of theology while at the same time transposing the odium from theology to biology, Voltaire succeeded in reinforcing the notion of a Jewish collectivity with

---

* Voltaire, *Oeuvres Complètes*, vol. 28, in *Lettres de Memmius à Ciceron*, praising Cicero for a violent diatribe against the Jews (in the latter's *Pro Flaco*), Paris: Garnier Frères, 1879, pp. 439 f. (author's translation).
** Ibid., in *Discours d'un théiste*, p. 549 (author's translation).

certain ineradicable qualities. All this evidently served as a secular version of the eternal damnation of the Jews.

In his famous polemic against a well-known Jewish adversary (Isaac de Pinto) he displayed a total hostility toward Jews. Instead of signing the polemic with his usual formula, "Ecrasez l'Infâme!" he signed himself "Voltaire, chrétien gentilhomme de la Chambre du Roi Très-Chrétien," no doubt with his usual irony.

A major portion of Voltaire's vast output was devoted to highly colored tales of Jewish credulity and fanaticism, interpreted as serious threats to the very existence of European culture. For him, Jews were ignorant not merely because of their environment, history, and so on, but again because of their very nature.

The irrational intensity of the *philosophes'* anti-Jewish feelings itself demonstrated that its roots were embedded in a deep stratum of the psyche. It can be understood only as arising out of a basic emotion retained through some process of rationalization.

Mystical anti-Semitism is generally presented, of course, as being rooted in real life and not as in any way fantastic. Accordingly, "rational" explanations are generally given even for the most extravagant charges: out of a concern for plausibility alone, those looking for explanations will inquire into the early lives of mystical anti-Semites, look for the influences of Jewish acquaintances, and so on.

It is in fact a scholarly cliché that Voltaire turned against the Jews because of some rascally Jewish lawyer, but apart from his having begun fulminating against the Jews well before he had any such experiences (there were, indeed, a few), the very assumption that anything relevant could be learned from this is a tacit admission of the presence of mystical anti-Semitism. Otherwise, how could it be taken for granted that resentment of an injustice suffered at the hands of an individual can "naturally" be vented on a community?

It seems evident that the feeling of its being natural to generalize hatred from individual Jews to Jews as a group derives its persuasiveness from an underlying unconscious axiom—that in the case of Jews there is, indeed, some dynamic affinity, a mystical union that explains the extension of loathing from the one to the many, and itself derives from the notion that Jews as such are maleficent. In short, the explanations of mystical anti-Semitism as having a rational or quasi-rational, i.e., empirical basis are found plausible just because of the acceptance of the idea of a mystical, supra-individual Jewish collectivity.

To sum up, the philosophical, rationalistic, and juridical elements of the Enlightenment collided with powerful unconscious self-contradictions in the psyches of its architects. They also, of course, encountered stubborn resistance from society as a whole. It became clear that the forces of social inertia were much more powerful than had been foreseen by the naive optimism of the humanists and rationalists; perhaps it would be more accurate to say that the champions of the new ideas, unaware of their own self-contradictions, remained bogged down in traditions they considered outmoded.

This was reinforced by the realities of the Jewish condition. It was during the Enlightenment, which was grounded in the notion that rationalism had to overcome the ancient superstitions of religion and social parochialism, that the Jews, through their attachment to their religion, their ancient customs, festivals, and so on, through their fanatical absorption, as it seemed to the Humanists, in their Scriptures—themselves of an immemorial antiquity, including the Talmud, already more than a thousand years old, as well as the Kabbala, more recent but with a patina of age—came to seem more stubborn and more strange than ever.

Precisely to the degree that Christianity was released from its ritualistic and dogmatic fetters to become more nearly a "pure" religion, it could always be counterposed to the hidebound dryness, ritualism, and dogmatism of a negatively projected Judaism. Since the liberal critics of Christianity did not cease to become, in their own eyes and according to their own reinterpretation, believing Christians, the hostility to Judaism on this plane could become more and more vigorous.

Thus, at the very moment the newly aroused imagination of the Enlightenment elite was stimulated by the exoticism of ancient but unknown peoples—the Chinese, the Indians, the Persians, even the local gypsies—the Jews themselves, because of their origins and history, became the victims of this infatuation with the exotic. The Jewish quarters of cities all over Europe, the ghettoes that hitherto had been of no interest to outsiders, became objects of study. Many Christians now took pains to observe living Jews, herded into unhygienic buildings and narrow lanes and following strange customs that were nevertheless not remote, like those of the Indians and Chinese, but close at hand.

The benevolent response of a Rembrandt, astonished at finding, as he thought, the prototypes of his biblical figures in the alleys of Amsterdam, was atypical.

Some reformers were simply repelled outright; others drew a natural conclusion—reform! But in neither case did the mood change in favor of the Jews. The mere fact that they were no longer contemplated through the prism of theology was of little help to them. Some thinkers, to be sure, developed an interest in the Jewish history of the Diaspora itself, an interest that was quite alien to the Jews themselves, who generally had no interest in secular history at all, least of all in the Diaspora, for them a mere way station to some messianic transformation in the unknowable future. For them it was the destruction of the Temple in 70, understood, like everything else, as ordained by God, that remained a titanic caesura in Jewish history. For many religious Jews down to the present, indeed, secular history in general is meaningless. Throughout the later Middle Ages and the Enlightenment, champions of the Jews contented themselves with casual apologetics in defense of Judaism, as it were in the abstract.

In short, both friends and enemies of the Jews concurred in the view that what they needed above all was to be *changed*: both felt that in some profound way they were defective. The difference between the two camps was simple: friends of the Jews said that they could be reformed; enemies, that they could not. Both agreed that the Jews, as they were, did not fit into the hoped-for new society.

The theory of emancipation underlying the French Revolution pointed up these views of Jewish dislocation in society. The goal of "equality" was taken to mean dropping all previous divisions within society, such as the special rights of the upper classes: the emancipation of the Jews, therefore, was modeled on the notion that Jews as individuals were to be freed from special restrictions and accepted as citizens enjoying the rights of all citizens.

This was, essentially, nothing more than the philosophy of Natural Rights, identical with the theory embodied in the American Declaration of Independence (1776); thus, Jewish emancipation was only a natural consequence of the Declaration of Human Rights of the French and American Revolutions.

Since logic alone had brought about Jewish Emancipation, the Emancipation achieved in the French Revolution remained abstract. In real life the status of the Jews, now separated from theology, nevertheless became a major topic in European life. The friction between Jews and Christians was to become a constant theme in politics. In practically all peace congresses, for instance, after the Vienna Congress of 1814–15 that settled the aftermath of the Napoleonic Wars, the status of the Jews played an important role.

The general principles underlying the French Revolution had been affecting European life for some time: the Emperor of Austro-Hungary, for instance, Joseph II, had issued an Edict of Tolerance, legalizing Jews as residents of Vienna, Lower Austria, Hungary, and Moravia, long before the Revolution broke out. For that matter, Louis XVI had legalized the Jews of Alsace as his subjects in 1784. Thus the French Revolution merely crystallized ideas that were already in the air.

After the French Revolution, generally speaking, the continuing expansion of burgeoning free enterprise provided Jews with a social function that counteracted the blemishes thought for so long to inhere in Jewish economic activities as such, particularly usury. With the energetic expansion of the bourgeoisie and the upsurge of international trade and the money market, the Jews emerged from their segregation and easily found places in society.

This process was reinforced and enhanced by the fact that the French state emerging from the Revolution had inherited from the absolutist state it had shattered the same tendency toward centralization, and with a predilection for organizations that were as unitary as possible. (This tendency of course is now universal: all modern states resist "states within states.")

With emancipation, the Jews were entirely out in the open:

no longer a mere dogmatic concept, a legend, a theory, or the like, Jews, previously cooped up in ghettoes, so that they were actually seen close to by relatively small numbers of people, and then only through the prism of a narrow lens, could now be seen as simply another group, of outsiders still, to be sure, since despite the disappearance of the ghettoes it was a long time before personal relations with non-Jews became common.

Thus the Jews, after a long career as a hermetically sealed-off group, now became a minority directly relating to majorities. The tension naturally arising out of the demarcation of groups was heightened by the tension emanating from the relations between Jews and their neighbors as individuals. At the same time, of course, this mingling naturally broadened the area of friction between Jews and Christians, as the intertwining of social and economic activities brought countless Jews and Christians in closer contact with each other. In some ways the Jews became a "normal" phenomenon, without, at the same time, losing their singularity.

The emancipation of the Jews, which rapidly though fitfully filtered through Europe, was soon to demonstrate that the Manichean division of the world into Good and Evil, Light and Dark, articulated by Paul and seemingly congealed in the Church forever, had expressed such deep needs of the psyche of those brought up in it that even when the actual religion, the theology underlying the institutions, was radically eroded and eventually sloughed off almost entirely, the original polarization of values remained. The notion of an Evil Other persisted: many Christians who were no longer moved by or retained even a lukewarm allegiance to Christian theology nevertheless retained a powerful urge to identify that powerful Evil Other. For many, the Jews were to remain that Evil Other down to our own day.

The integration of the Jews in European society was complicated profoundly by a major consequence of the French Revolution—modern nationalism, together with the concept of the "people's sovereignty," paralleled by a similar concept in the American Revolution. The nationalist idea buttressed the resistance, often insurrectionary, of many European peoples to the advance of Napoleon, heir of the French Revolution.

The French Revolution had, in fact, a primordial influence

in strengthening or inspiring the concept of national identity, and, more important, in emotionalizing it, not only in Europe but throughout the world. In many respects the Jews, in some sense a nation after all, were to suffer from this, especially since the general critique of Christianity as a religion did not, of course, eliminate it, but merely modified its social setting.

At the same time, the concept of "people's sovereignty," ultimately derived, no doubt, from the axiom of human equality inherent in monotheism, steadily extended the participation of the general population in government, which had earlier been almost entirely the domain of the aristocracy and gentry. From the eighteenth century on, government kept spreading down from the top strata. From the nineteenth century on, the masses of the people came to be involved more and more pervasively in parliamentary systems until the emergence of totalitarianism after the Bolshevik putsch of 1917.

All the movements dominating the nineteenth century, indeed, came under the concept of "people's sovereignty" expressed in the liberal democratic theory of nationalism. The romantic tradition, especially, was inspired by the idea of the "folk" virtues inherent in national traditions. This led to a sentimental revival of the Middle Ages, expressed in a new love and sympathy for Christianity, now understood no longer as a theological system, but on the contrary, as itself an outpouring of national and folk traditions that were to justify, in the countless "interpretations" of the meaning of Jesus and so on generated by the Higher Criticism of the Bible, the application to contemporary society of the high ideals now found in the Gospels. This was accompanied by a revival of religion proper, whose influence on society expanded throughout Europe. Once again the state itself came to be conceived of as essentially Christian.

Romanticism also came to be linked to various ideas of "progress" and "evolution," an auxiliary of various forms of Darwinism or teleologically tinctured views: this general approach also provided an underpinning for the flourishing "science of history," that is, all phenomena were seen historically, not only in human life but also in nature. This was typical of the last half of the nineteenth century, and later, very naturally, came to include economics.

In this complex of social and historical views, biology and ideas of "race" intermingled with the basic concept of the "nation," and so on. All this menaced the Jews, especially since in the case of England, France, Germany, and Russia a potent element of "imperialism" was part of the mixture.

Thus the Jews found themselves pinpointed, for other reasons, as permanent outsiders by the upsurge of Christian tradition at the very moment that a cluster of nationalist movements, with their inevitable stress on emotionalism, came to involve masses of people. The net result was that the Jews, while emancipated and participating more and more vigorously in all aspects of public life as well as in the life of the mind, came to be seen as the chief target of this evolving fusion of religion and nationalism. The emancipation of the Jews was plainly a mere formality: it actually served to expand the area in which The Jew could be felt to be an alien.

Hence, even outside the strictly religious sphere the concept of the Jews as a group retained an integrity around which hostile sentiment could coagulate. The Jews came to focus emotions in European society; in a context that had changed only superficially from what had preceded, they served once again as ready-made scapegoats for practically everything that could go wrong in any sphere of social life whatever. Nor were they scapegoats in a mere technical sense: they retained the primordial magnetism Jews have always had for Christendom. They continued to represent an emotion-charged concept that pulsated with enough energy to fuel the hatred of masses of people.

Perhaps the most striking demonstration of the infusion of emotion into allegedly rational theories can be found in the mysticism that, like the mysticism of the *philosophes*, was born as it were already incorporated into the ideas of the most radical branch of world reform engendered by the French Revolution —the Socialists and Communists (for generations indistinguishable terms).

From the very beginning of the Socialist movement, in the wake of the French Revolution, it was usual to take over the ancient stereotype of the Jews, rooted in Church doctrine, and dress it up in a more contemporary form as a way of describing the enemy, in this case the "class enemy." Since it was adopted at the very beginning of the movement, and expanded endlessly by the most successful Socialist thinkers, Marx and Engels, it has acquired a pedigree of total respectability among modern Socialists as well, notably, as we shall see, in the Soviet Union.

It is essentially the ancient view of the Jew as a usurer and parasite, which has survived the disappearance of individual Jews as usurers, and the growing abundance of Christian usurers—the modern banking system—over the past few centuries of the expansion of the free-enterprise system.

Charles Fourier (1772–1837), for instance, in his "Tale of Judas Iscariot," analyzed the mechanism by which Jewish businessmen down the ages could rove about bankrupting honest, upright Christian merchants. Even in Fourier's hatred of all business, accordingly, he nevertheless distinguished fundamentally between Jewish and Christian businessmen. Significantly, he took the figure of Judas Iscariot as the prototype of the operation, in which, as he also pointed out, "The Jews, by virtue of their dedication to trade, are the spies of all nations, and, if need be, the informers and the hangmen."*

Though Fourier, in some respects like Rousseau, was passionately attached to theories of social reform, he found it natural to imagine a better world—conceived along rigidly "rational" lines—without foreigners in general, and in particular without Jews.

He regarded trade as the "source of all evil," and, since Jews were the "incarnation of trade," it was natural for him to charge "The Jews" with every conceivable malefaction: their economic activities were parasitic, rapacious, altogether pernicious: there had in fact never been a "nation more despicable than the Hebrews."**

Curiously enough, he became a sort of premature Zionist; just as later on, during the burgeoning of the Zionist movement, many outright anti-Semites and Jew-haters thought Zionism a splendid way of unloading the Jews elsewhere, so Fourier

---

* Charles Fourier, *La Théorie de l'Unité universelle*, in *Oeuvres*, 14 vols., vol. 5, Paris: Anthropos Editions, 1966, p. 424, footnote.
** Charles Fourier, *Theorie des quatre mouvements et des destinées générales*, 1808, Paris: A la Librairie sociétaire, 1846, pp. 61, 253.

thought it would be a good idea to rebuild the "Hebrew nation" in Palestine on the basis of his chief innovation in social reform: the "phalansteries"*—a form of social structure in which goods and services were held in common—which was, to be sure, to be financed by the Rothschilds. His Zionism, however, remained relatively unknown, while his virulent anti-Semitism inspired many Socialist followers; during the Dreyfus case at the end of the nineteenth century, for instance, a Fourierist newspaper, *Rénovation*, was ferociously anti-Semitic.

Pierre-Joseph Proudhon (1809–65), one of the most influential of the early Socialists, considered the Jews, quite simply, Satan himself—the element of evil in the universe. He seems to have been the first to invent the "race of Shem" to explain this.

> The Jew is by temperament unproductive, neither agriculturalist nor industrialist, not even a genuine trader. He is an intermediary, always fraudulent and parasitical, who operates in business as in philosophy, by forging, counterfeiting, sharp practices. He only knows the rise and fall of markets, transport risks, uncertainties of returns, hazards of supply and demand. His economic policy is always negative; he is the evil element, Satan, Ahriman, incarnated in the race of Shem.**

Though Proudhon seems to have had some old-fashioned theological fixation at the back of his mind in vilifying the Jews—that is, the old-fashioned horror of Jews for rejecting the Savior—he inserted a strange twist in his reasoning by depriving the Jews even of their monotheism: in fact he contrasted Jewish polytheism and Indo-Germanic monotheism:

> It is a hierarchized polytheism . . . Monotheism is so little a Jewish or Semitic idea that the race of Shem can be said to have been repudiated by it; rejected; this is what the declaration of the apostles to the Jews, unyielding in their particularism, is expressing: *"Since you spurn the word of God*, of the universal God, *we pass on to the gentiles.* Monotheism is a

---

* Charles Fourier, *La fausse Industrie*, 1836, in *Oeuvres*, vol. 8, p. 224, and vol. 9, pp. 659 f. and 791.
** Pierre-Joseph Proudhon, *Césarisme et Christianisme*, vol. 1, p. 139, cited in Leon Poliakov, *History of Anti-Semitism*, vol. 3, transl. Miriam Kochan, New York: Vanguard Press, translation copyright 1975, p. 374.

creation of the Indo-Germanic spirit; it could only have come from there . . ."*

The Jews—an unsociable, stubborn, infernal race, First authors of that maleficent superstition called Catholicism, in which the furious intolerant Jewish factor always prevails over the others, Greek, Latin, Barbarian, etc., and has long tortured the human race . . . The influence of the Jewish element in Christianity is thus explained by the character of that nation.**

No doubt the most celebrated demonstration of this particular form of mystical anti-Semitism, whose mysticism is all the more obvious since it claims to be rooted in "science," is Marx's attempt to settle the question once and for all.

Descended from a long line of rabbis on both sides of the family, Marx, baptized at the age of six by his father, was evidently determined not to be distracted from his true interests by any comments on his origins. At the age of twenty-six he printed an essay, "On the Jewish Question," in a journal he and a friend were publishing, which represented a systematic attempt to remove the whole "problem" of the Jews from its theological background and relocate it in the domain of the special ideas he was working out, that is, what was to become "historical materialism." Because of the unique expansion of Marx's influence long after his death, these views were to give his own special sanction to the particular form of mystical anti-Semitism that was characteristic of so many radical reformers shaped by the French Revolution.

At the very opening of his essay on the Jews Marx declares his aim: "Let us consider, not the Sabbath Jew, but the everyday Jew. Let us look for the secret of the Jew not in his religion, let us rather look for the secret of the religion in the everyday Jew." Then he presents his conclusion: "What is the worldly ground of Judaism? Practical need. What is the worldly cult of the Jews? Bargaining. What is his worldly God? Money. Well then! The emancipation from bargaining and from money, that is, from real, practical Jewry, would be the self-emancipation of our age."

---

* Pierre-Joseph Proudhon, *De la Justice dans la Révolution et dans l'Eglise*, in *Oeuvres*, vol. 1, p. 445, cited in Poliakov, *History of Anti-Semitism*, op. cit., p. 375.
** Pierre-Joseph Proudhon, *Carnets*, cited ibid.

Marx's reasoning makes it evident that he was not thinking of individual real-life Jews; he was, it is clear, merely thinking of them as embodiments of an abstract idea. Yet at the same time he is singling them out, among all the peoples involved with economics—the human race—and casting them in the specific role of money-obsessed "bargainers."

No doubt Marx felt no hatred for individual Jews; for him, everything exemplified an idea of itself. On the other hand, this method of identifying Jews as such with some loathsome principle enabled "real" anti-Semites, who also expressed themselves, after all, in the same way, to assimilate his formulations.

In any case, Marx's method of reasoning was to set its stamp on all the sociological and political forms in which mystical anti-Semitism was to clothe itself from then on.

Even at that age, long before he had worked out his basic schema, long before he was obliged, by quirks of circumstance, to devote himself to scholarship in order to seek, and seem to find, his documentation, Marx's aim was the complete overhaul of "bourgeois" society, well established in England and France and already laying its foundations in Germany. Thus, as part of his general campaign to eliminate the "servitude of capitalist economy" and to show a way out of burgeoning "capitalism," he had to demonstrate the necessity of "freeing" society as a whole from the "fetters" of "capitalism" while demonstrating that this emancipation would in its very nature entail the elimination of Jews as Jews. Society, emancipating itself, would solve the "Jewish Question" automatically.

What preoccupied Marx was not, to be sure, the empirical situation he seemed to be discussing, but his determination to create a framework of theory for the world—history, economics, and society. Without discussing this large-scale view, it is enough to recall that 90 percent of European Jewry at the time were living as artisans, petty tradesmen and the like.

It is obvious from Marx's analysis of social, even historical events, with its rigorous "logic," that he is not describing a real-life situation, with all its imponderables, unknowables, and contingent potentialities, but a logical schema. Thus, when he predicts that the Bourgeoisie, by evolving, will create the Proletariat, and that the Proletariat will then "inevitably" overcome the Bourgeoisie, he is plainly articulating a chain of logic. That is, the Bourgeoisie is not the actual bourgeoisie—a large and disparate group of people, no doubt with similar but at the same time varying interests—but the Idea of the Bourgeoisie. Thus, the so-called rigor of Marx's thought, which he himself was particularly proud of, was based precisely on its "logical," that is, antiempirical character.

From this point of view, of course, he was not being "unfair" in his description of Jews; he was simply applying his own form of essentially idealistic logic (taken over unwittingly from his master, Hegel) and thus bringing order into the chaos of history, that is, of life.

For Hegel too, the fundamental nature and destiny of the Jews made them parasites permanently: they were slaves by nature, whose "great tragedy" can "arouse neither terror nor pity . . . but only revulsion": by nature incapable of appreciating Jesus, they were "bound to run aground his attempt to give them the consciousness of something divine, since faith in something divine . . . cannot make its home in dung. The lion has no room in a nutshell, the infinite Spirit none in the prison of a Jewish soul."*

This was, of course, the same reasoning followed by the Church: the Church Fathers were well aware of the real life of the Jews they were familiar with, but that seemed to them, steeped in abstract ideas as they were, to be entirely irrelevant. What was true was what was *real*: what was real was—ideas. Jews *really* represented, by virtue of their very *essence*, the will of Satan—a potent force.

Thus, for Marx as for the theologians who preceded him, the fact that Jews, as businessmen, were simply businessmen like any others, seemed to him entirely pointless, indeed meaningless: Jews in their essence *were* business! The essence of Judaism was identical with the essence of business.

Marx seems to have been unaware of the philosophical idealism he had wholly assimilated from Hegel. His famous claim

---

* Georg Wilhelm Friedrich Hegel, *Der Geist des Christentums und sein Schicksal*, 1798–1800, in *Werke in zwanzig Bänden*, vol. 1., Frankfurt-am-Main: Suhrkamp Verlag, 1971, pp. 297 and 381 (author's translation).

that he had stood Hegel, that "colossal old boy," right side up was a profound misconception of his own method, which consisted, very precisely, in retaining the full thrust of Hegel's logic and applying it fruitfully, as he thought, to the flux of real life.

> The Jew has emancipated himself in the Jewish manner, not only by acquiring the power of money, but by *money* becoming the world power through him and without him, while the practical Jewish spirit has become the practical spirit of the Christian peoples . . . What was, in and of itself, the basis of the Jewish religion? Practical need, egoism. Hence the monotheism of the Jew is, in reality, the polytheism of multiple needs, a polytheism that even turns the privy into an object of divine law. *Practical need, egoism* is the principle of bourgeois society . . . Money is the jealous God of Israel, before whom no other god may exist. Money debases all the gods of mankind—it turns them into commodities . . . The bill of exchange is the real God of the Jew . . . Even the relationship between man and woman becomes an object of trade! Woman is bartered away . . . The *chimerical* nationality of the Jew is the nationality of the merchant, of the financier above all. The law of the Jew, without reason or basis, is only the religious caricature of morality and law in general, equally without reason or basis.*

These views, formulated at the age of twenty-six, were clung to by Marx all his life. He never modulated them in any way; they remained the foundation of attitudes that in connection with individual Jews were generally expressed with a ferocious spite that was surely somewhat pathological. His voluminous correspondence with Engels, a German Protestant by origin, is full of the most malicious judeophobic gibes at almost every Jew mentioned, regardless of relevance. About a lifelong admirer, Ferdinand Lassalle, for instance, phrases like "kinky-haired Yid," "Ikey," "Baron Ikey," "niggerlike hair inherited from the niggers who accompanied Moses out of Egypt" recur with striking regularity.

Marx also subscribed to the general theory being developed in the eighteenth and nineteenth century of the Jew as parasite: for instance, he mentions the trading peoples of antiquity as

---

* Karl Marx und Friedrich Engels, *Werke*, vol. 1, Institut für Marxismus-Leninismus beim ZK der SED, Berlin: Dietz Verlag, 1964, pp. 373–75 (author's translation).

living in the interstices of the ancient world "like Epicurus's gods or the Jews in the pores of Polish society."

This was to become the classic Socialist method of attacking Jews: by identifying them with the reprehensible principle of finance capital, it was possible both to retain the "scientific" validity of their analysis and at the same time exploit the gutter anti-Semitism of the masses they were wooing.

The anti-Semitism expressed in this categorical form by classical Socialist writers did not repel Jewish Socialists, who either simply disregarded the anti-Semitism propagated by Socialist doctrine or else accepted it as part of that doctrine, which could be swallowed without qualms since Jews were not, after all, denounced as Jews, but because they exemplified something else. Thus even a practicing Jew—to say nothing of nonpracticing or nonbelieving Jews—could wholeheartedly denounce Jewry as being part of some cosmic malaise that Socialism had undertaken to get rid of.

The erudition attributed to Marx by his hagiographers did not extend to the Jews; he seems not to have read much about them. Apart from serving to epitomize some of his abstractions, they also provided him with epithets: in the most irrelevant situations he would go out of his way to sneer at Jews more or less as such, especially, of course, at financiers such as the Rothschilds. What distinguished him in this respect was his harshness. His feelings about Jews were by no means unique; he shared them with the other founders of the Socialist movement.

Ironically, perhaps, Marx's attempt, if not to camouflage, at least to distance, his Jewish background was signally unsuccessful: from the very moment he became famous, his personality crystallized in the minds of many the very essence of the world's corruption that was in any case blamed on the Jews. By the time of the Bolshevik putsch in 1917, which destroyed an entire social class and put into power a small group of intellectuals proclaiming Marx as their inspiration, it was possible for all forms of right-wing agitators and downright anti-Semites to point with indignation at the role of Jewry as the crowning horror of the Bolshevik regime.

Marxism became a natural way of describing a worldwide

Jewish conspiracy against the human race, and more specifically against whatever country was being discussed. In the Soviet Union, contrariwise, Marx's Jewish origins have been routinely concealed from the public, particularly, as we shall see, since the anti-Semitic campaigns after the Second World War.

SCIENCE AND MOCK-SCIENCE

CHAPTER SIX

T hough the agitation over the Jews troubled European society, and naturally appeared in the New World too, it might have been tempting, during the nineteenth century, to foresee a situation in which the "Jewish question" would finally receive some sort of "answer" that would relegate the whole discussion to the settled past. As it turned out, however, the past could not be settled so easily.

Eminent Protestant scholars, especially in Germany, probed into the origins of the Bible, both the Old and the New Testaments, as part of the history-mindedness of the age and, from the point of view of the more pious scholars, as a way of guaranteeing the basic truth of the texts by the discovery of more straightforward historical data. Yet though this in some way moderated the concept of the Jews as alien, by giving them a more or less normal historical background and so making them more "understandable," the very study of the Bible had a hostile element at its core.

The "Higher Critics" accepted, as it seems unwittingly, the New Testament and in particular the Gospels as the historical framework of the very documents they were analyzing. Thus, while tearing the texts of the Bible to shreds by conscientious analysis, they did not transcend the framework itself. In the case of the Jews, in particular, they treated the Hebrew Prophets polemically, taking pains to stress just those passages in which the Prophets flayed the moral shortcomings of the ancient Hebrews. Here too, accordingly, the enfeeblement of Christian dogma was compensated for by finding another justification for irritation.

It took a few generations after the emancipation of the Jews for the cluster of attitudes about them, ranging from disdainful to malevolent, to find expression in the behavior of large groups of people. While the "Jewish Question" preoccupied the summits of opinion in the mid-nineteenth century, it was not until the last third that broad-gauge opposition to the Jews began to be organized. Just as there may be an analogy—inadequate, like most historical analogies—in the length of time between the formation of early Christian theology and its permeation of the populations gradually converted over the centuries, so the various stages in the modernizing of the traditional attitude to the Jews took some time to set.

The process was signaled by the coinage of a new word, "anti-Semitism," in the 1870s. The word, precisely by seeming to replace one concept by another, epitomized the retention of the same primordial revulsion in a new guise.

Before the middle of the nineteenth century the notion of "race" had not meant much: the word itself was essentially fuzzy in English and for that matter all European languages—Shakespeare's "island race" implied nothing about English physique. Initially it was merely used in various theories of social origins, such as that the plebeians of a given country were the original inhabitants, while the rulers were descended from their conquerors.

It also came to be used in the study of language, despite the obvious fact that outsiders can easily and indeed effortlessly acquire any language by social osmosis. The study of philology, which in our own day occupies a powerful position in contemporary thought through the proliferation of various schools of linguistics, began its ascent in the nineteenth century as part of the study of the Indo-European and Semitic groups of languages.

Max Müller (1823–1900) found it convenient to use a Sanscrit word, "Aryan," for the Indo-European group of languages: harmless in itself, that usage was soon twisted out of shape by his extending it to the notion of an Aryan "race" that spoke the "proto-Aryan" language.

Similarly, "Semitic languages," a phrase invented in 1787 (by J. C. Eichhorn) as a refinement of the vague phrase "oriental languages," was now used to refer to the "Semites" who spoke a "proto-Semitic" language. This was all the more seductive since it could be integrated with the Higher Criticism of the Bible.

Both notions—"Aryans" and "Semites"—were swiftly taken up by writers, scholars, and above all pseudo-scholars of all kinds, wrenched out of the linguistic context and given some vague meaning as a sort of primordial, folklike, genetic category. It was felt to be all the more persuasive because of the attractiveness of the idea that however language originated, it must have been spoken initially by a small group united by blood. Thus clusters of language as such, despite their vast range in historical times, were taken to represent some sort of biological identity.

Nevertheless, the word "Semite" almost immediately came to mean nothing more than "Jew"; this notion also underlay "anti-Semite." Indeed, practically speaking, the only purpose of the theories about "race" that began proliferating in the second half of the nineteenth century—whatever their conceivable value—was to place a high focus on the Jews: they really supplemented attempts to cope with the Jews politically.

By mid-century these ideas were streamlined. A four-volume work on the "inequality of human races", by a French aristocrat, Joseph de Gobineau*, came out in 1855. Though not given much attention in France, it was taken up after Gobineau's death by his German admirers, notably Richard Wagner. It was to become

---

* Count Joseph Arthur de Gobineau, *Essai sur l'Inégalité des Races humaines*, four vols., Paris, 1853–55.

the keystone of all modern racial theories (as distinct from the study of race, whatever that may prove to mean).

Gobineau's book made a sustained effort to elevate historiography above subjective caprice by fitting it into the framework created by the natural sciences, the basic assumption being a simple one that "race"—never quite explained, to be sure—was the "cause" of all history.

In a sense, this supplemented and attempted to amplify Montesquieu's *Esprit des Lois* of the preceding century, but Gobineau thought the *Esprit des Lois*, which allowed some importance to "race" or something like it as a premise of history, fell short of the true scientific ideal: to Gobineau, "race" was the prime cause of literally everything.

This factor was, accordingly, given the status of a First Cause in empirical situations and proved able to elicit the same blind devotion as any other First Cause. Gobineau's determinist-naturalistic theory thus had fateful consequences: since the study of anthropology at that time was at a primitive stage, there was nothing to hamper the florid development of this basically vague and virtually indefinable notion, mingled as it has been with endless unassessable considerations of society, historical development, and language.

Gobineau believed that "races" in the biological sense existed, and moreover *meant* something. They were unequal: the best of all races was the "white race," not only the most gifted but in fact the only creative race, and within the white race, the Aryan race in turn was the most gifted, and within the Aryan race, the segment or subrace closest to the original Aryans was the Teutons. Hence the Teutons were the noblest race in the world.

This "Teutonic race"—tall, blond, blue-eyed, also, since the end of the nineteenth century, called "Nordic"—was taken up by Gobineau and his countless successors with growing frenzy as being, of course, the precise opposite of the presumably small, swarthy, uncreative, parasitic "Semites," who were entirely dependent on the achievements of the Nordic race. Thus the concept of the Jew as parasite returned via, so to speak, biology, to be reinstated as a loathsome excrescence on society.

Ernest Renan (1823–1892), a student of Hebrew and other Semitic languages, had in a way laid the foundations for this preposterous contrast between "Teutons" and "Semites" in a famous work on the Semitic languages.* This work, throughout its vast windy generalizations, subjected the "Semitic race" to a severe drubbing, though in a foreword Renan defended contemporary Jews somewhat by saying that *despite* their biological descent from the former inhabitants of Palestine, they no longer had much "Semitic" character left.

The word "anti-Semite" itself seems to have been coined by a Jewish scholar (Moritz Steinschneider) in a polemic against Renan. It was then taken up in 1879 by Wilhelm Marr, a German pamphleteer, and used for a purely political concept, aimed quite unequivocally not at the speakers of other Semitic languages— such as the Arabs, the Ethiopians, and for that matter the Aramaic speakers still in existence—but specifically and exclusively the Jews. It was, in short, plainly a euphemism, required as a scientific camouflage for a feeling that was, after all, very old.

The timing of the appearance of the word is itself significant: it was meant to lump together various reasons for objecting, politically and socially, to the Jews and to their function or alleged function in society: it was a euphemism too in the sense of avoiding a flat statement of what would have seemed "old-fashioned" to all those affected by the enfeeblement of the traditional scheme of values connected with the ancien régime: the loosening of the grip of the churches, the rise of the sciences and pseudo-sciences, and so on.

As early as the eighteenth century, the very word "Jew" had caused malaise. It pointed up their disadvantaged position, and in its overtones recalled their medieval travail. Thus this word "anti-Semitism," while camouflaging a new style of hatred, was also a concession to Jews, made hypersensitive by the evil associations of "The Jew" over many generations.

After the first few decades of the Enlightenment the Jews were, in fact, longing to pay off the mortgage, so to speak, on

---

* Ernest Renan, *Histoire Générale et Système comparé des langues Sémitiques*, Paris: M. Levey Frères, 1847.

the word "Jew": they were casting about for alternatives, of which there were not, to be sure, very many. "Israelite" was one: this seemed to echo the Old Testament and was not burdened by the associations shadowing the word "Jew"; others were straightforward escape-hatches, such as the phrase common around this time in Germany, "adherent of the Mosaic faith," which was part of the attempt being made by Jews striving for assimilation to establish themselves as a merely religious association and not as a "people."

Thus, the word "anti-Semitism," polite and socially acceptable, was also in harmony with the scientific temper of the age. It sounded rather scientific, as though it were part of the vocabulary of the newest biological science, or of the race theories now beginning to proliferate. The suffix "-ism" played a role: it gave the vulgar aversion to Jews a lofty cachet among those whose faith had shriveled but in whose unconscious the deposit of hatred left by the debris of theology had calcified the infernal conception of Jewry.

Curiously enough, it was this euphemistic quality that made the word repellent to an outstanding judeophobe, Eugen Dühring, who rejected the word "anti-Semite" just because, as a euphemism, it veiled the true odiousness of the Jews: he wanted to attack them openly as such. Later, to be sure, he abandoned his opposition to the word and accepted it as achieving his own aims just as well as the more obvious, historical word.

The formulation of this notion of "Semitic race" by Renan, followed by countless other intellectuals, created what was in fact an indispensable substitute, in the incipient scientific and pseudo-scientific age, for the conceptual succession to the theological notion of the Jews as doomed by their satanic role in the world. That role was now expressed by their genes: inferior, uncreative, unimaginative, and persistently noxious socially.

The erosion of traditional Christianity itself, oddly enough, was given a "racial" basis, since it was claimed that even the monotheism hitherto regarded as the handiwork of the Jews was no more than a reflection of their sterile, arid character, shaped by the desert.

As long as the Catholic Church was unchallenged the Jewish role had been clear and logical: as a group that had denied and indeed killed God, the Jews were naturally under a curse: but each individual could redeem himself through his own free will, abandon his obduracy, and achieve salvation by conversion. This was still Luther's view: even though his castigation of the Jews as a group was remarkably virulent, it was still possible, according to his own logic, for individual Jews to be saved in the old-fashioned way.

But the mock-scientific stigma now made that impossible. Thus the effect of the "racial" generalizations about the Jews from the 1840s on was easily summed up: the curse of the Jews, made eternal through biology, was inescapable; now there was *no way out*.

The debates over Jews before and during the Enlightenment had taken it for granted that the question was one of improving the real-life Jews of the period: enemies thought it unlikely, friends thought it possible. Those repelled by scenes of daily life in the Jewish quarters, the ghettoes and so on, could, even as they were expressing repulsion, still say that since people in general could be improved, the Jews could too. Those skeptical about the possibilities of reforming the Jews before or even after their emancipation were eventually outweighed by those liberal humanists who simply clung to the obvious common-sense idea that people in general really could be improved. Even after the Emancipation, the question of the Jews could have a practical, reasonable form: had the Jews been bettered *enough?*

But of course the race view, held with growing force by many people in Europe and America in the nineteenth century, made the whole question of "reforming" the Jews downright senseless: if they were condemned to pernicious inferiority by their own biology, that is, their *nature*, what could be done about it? The race view eliminated all hope. From the middle of the nineteenth century on, the Jews were totally condemned: the curse of God had taken on a new form; the Jews were racially inferior; wholly unredeemable; it was just the way they *were*.

The unchangeability of their character, the assumption that they were in fact a race in a biological sense—for that matter, the notion that races are themselves inherently unchangeable—was of course reinforced by the success of Darwinism, another branch of science that suited the racists and more particularly the enemies of the Jews. After Darwin it became axiomatic that acquired characteristics were not inheritable; this reinforced the inalterability of the doom now assigned the Jews.

It was this atmosphere of "science"—longed for by all social theorists of the nineteenth century and since, especially, of course, by Marx—that stamped the new version of mystical anti-Semitism, and made it distinct, as it has seemed to some scholars, from the original, theological concept of "The Jews." Yet this would surely seem to be a provincial deformation of scholarship. After all, the target of animosity in mystical anti-Semitism of both the theological and the "racial" varieties has been the same group of people: that could hardly be an accident.

The transition from theological to "racial" anti-Semitism was imperceptible to many people; it was not disturbing emotionally. It was even fashionable. Nevertheless, it involved a substantive change of principle. The satanism of the Jews was originally an integral part of a ramified theory, a crystallization of Paul's ideas (minus the motor of history, which for Paul made it all hang together). Theology was a *system*: the satanic function of the Jews was mandatory, rational, coherent—part of a Divine Plan for which their existence remained necessary: when converted, ultimately, as they were bound to be, they would, like all mankind, be reborn in a regenerated universe.

Believing Christians could not, after all, be called unbalanced: theology gave a rational organization to perceptions of cosmic scope, providing a framework for psychic equilibrium, emotional and intellectual.

By the time theology had shaped the world picture of masses of people, it was able to rationalize profound emotions: hatred too could be expressed as a fusion between an emotional explosion and a conceptual rationalization. Within that framework the hatred of the Jews could be expressed in a unitary, balanced manner: it was legitimate to hate what was in its essence hateful, since the Jews were thought of as an enemy of the Sublime— God and His Son.

In the Middle Ages the mob violence in which Jews were plundered and massacred was sporadic and brief. The less violent plebeians would come to their senses; the upper Church strata and the nobility would prevail; calm would be restored.

In spite of everything, the theological stance of the authorities maintained a balance.

When the humanists of the nineteenth and twentieth centuries no longer took theology seriously, the edifice began to crumble: the emotions surfacing in mystical anti-Semitism were left without a foothold in a larger sustaining intellectual structure. Though initially the Jews had been symbolized by a theological concept, the symbol itself proved capable of dislocation to a nontheological sphere without loss of potency. Hatred thus became autonomous, its own justification, so to speak, and since it remained wholly phantasmagorical—Jews are not, after all, emanations of Satan—it proved a locus for true dementia.

The degradation of the Jews became as it were absolute. The Jews became, precisely for unbalanced, demythologized Christians, objects of total horror—a target that could focus, within limits, any form of paranoid pathology. This would be the difference from believing Christians, who would not necessarily be mystical anti-Semites, since the theology contained a cardinal element of hope—that when the cosmogony was consummated all would be harmonized. In principle Jews could be regarded with indulgence, as they have, after all, been regarded by many Christians.

But Christianity does not sum up Christendom: it is merely a conditioning factor. The permeation of Christendom by theology had deposited in the minds of untold multitudes a special psychic entity: a fusion of symbol-idea-person. In the event, that psychic deposit, so to speak, withstood the obsolescence of its rational, structured, theological ingredient. Jews remained a symbol of Evil even after Satan himself and the theology he was part of ceased to be taken seriously by the conscious mind. Thus all those within the Christian world view, even those hostile to Christianity as a religion—perhaps even *especially* those—have inherited the mystical obsession with the Jews independently of theology.

If it is true that there is a deep urge in the psyche that lends meaning to the contention between Good and Evil, then Christianity focused that urge so profoundly within its theology that even when this crumbled, the focus remained a structural element within Christendom—minus the theology. Even atheists, for whom the notion of "The Jew" is literally senseless, feel that Jews remain the emblem of Evil—as long as such atheists are ex-Christians.

When theology became obsolete through the cooling of faith and atheistic indifference, the Jews became *pure* Evil. There was then no rationale for their existence—no reason they should *not* be exterminated. They no longer had to be sustained as Witnesses to the Truth of the Cross. They no longer *meant* anything: in the imaginations of all those released from the sustaining, harmonizing force of theology, the Jews were simply monsters, and nothing else.

This creates, of course, a rationale for extermination: monsters should not be. And in the psyches of countless unbalanced people that was surely an adequate reason for active hostility. Thus the debris of theology had brought about the replacement of one rationale by another—a material rationale grounded in a sort of social prophylaxis that is necessarily boundless: monsters must be got rid of for the good of all.

And of course this limitless revulsion was well established even when society was governed by the coherent, balanced system of Christian doctrine. For what theological concept could have been in the mind of a medieval peasant during an access of horror at the sight of a Jew, say, in some social eruption? Even though the double vision of the Jew—a real-life view and a suprahuman, eerie view—had been grounded in theology, during a social eruption an actual human being could be looked at, in real life, as a mask of Evil. This was, after all, the justification for violence to begin with. Thus, even though the Evil had been grounded in a mystico-theological world view, it was now independently palpable.

The masses in the Middle Ages who plundered and killed Jews were living in a society full of magic, devils, demons, witches, and personified evil generally: the Jews personified one more such category—with a greater degree of intensity, to be sure, since the peasants also believed, perhaps profoundly, in the world view of their religion, which thus gave the Evil inhering in Jews unique power. The murky, unspeakable lusts lurking in the unconscious were given a sacral legitimation.

Practically speaking, after all, despite the theological difference between a satanic Jew who could be converted and the "biologically" different nonhuman Jew who should simply be killed, Jews as such remained freaks in the minds of ordinary people. During the Middle Ages plebeian mobs obviously thought it natural to savage Jews despite the restraint enjoined by the Church. The "science" and "race" theories that sprang up in the nineteenth century mainly affected the educated classes: *they* could now bypass theology with a good conscience.

Perhaps the most devastating irony in this mocktransmutation of values is the obvious fact that the very notion of "race," however defined, as a category that can intelligibly be described as "evil," is incomprehensible except as an unconscious borrowing from theology. "Race" theories about Jews, at the very moment of seeming to abandon the purely Christian notion of the special status of Jews, are in fact retaining it—but in a preposterous context. For just as the *philosophes* had inherited a theologically based loathing of the Jews that survived their attempts to erode Christian theology, so the racists also retained the concept of the special maleficence of the Jews.

Thus racism, at the very moment of introducing a new, "scientific" definition of Jews as a biological community, in fact assigned them the same importance, in addition to their Evil nature, as they held in Christian doctrine. For after all, if Jews had merely been excluded from the possibility of becoming civilized by their defective genes, Christendom might not have been seriously threatened, since there were so few Jews. Hence the "racial" category created for them in the nineteenth century had to be founded on their importance—their ability to wield the same occult power that had been bestowed on them by theology.

Yet while religious believers can rationally regard people holding pernicious beliefs as themselves pernicious, how can it be comprehensible for a people scattered through time and space and no longer defined by beliefs to be biologically predisposed in any specific *moral* direction?

Though in a way a quantitative increase in the common habit of characterizing countless numbers of people by one adjective or another, the biological criterion intensifies this habit so extravagantly as to make it literally senseless. Fundamentally, it is understandable only as a plausible pretext for unavowable longings.

It may be an odd irony that the terrain for the preposterous racial theories of the nineteenth century might have been prepared unwittingly simply by the very name of the Jews: if "The Jews" could be called responsible for the rejection of Christ, and for that matter for his crucifixion, it was obviously a natural transition from "The Jews" as a community of religious believers in Judaism to a community linked by blood ties. Since Jews are after all descended from Jews in a sense that is felt to be quite different from the way in which, for example, Buddhists reproduce Buddhists, it was always easy to make the transition even when religious conversion was taken seriously.

Thus, for instance, under the Inquisition the category of "purity of blood"—though logically extraneous to the concept of conversion—was felt as somehow being valid as part of the background of conversion, in any case suspect because of the element of coercion, so that even after a number of generations of people descended from converts to Catholicism doubt could still be cast by a suggestion that the "blood" was still not quite "pure." For that matter, individual churchmen even in the modern era can be swayed by a passion of hatred similar to that of a mystical anti-Semite in the grip of pathological "racism."

As recently as 1965 Bishop Luigi Maria Carli, Bishop of Segni, in a weekly addressed to the Italian clergy, could write of the Jews' role in the death of Jesus in this way: "[Jews of today are still] accursed and rejected of God ... the whole Jewish people at the time of Jesus was responsible for the crime of Christ's murder, even if only the leaders, followed by a part of their supporters, actually carried out the crime ... in this very precise sense even the Jewry of the times after Our Lord objectively share the responsibility for the murder of Christ insofar as this Jewry represents a voluntary continuation of the Jewry of that time."* One can imagine John Chrysostom chuckling with delight.

---

* In *La Palestra del Clero*, March 1965, cited in Friedrich Heer, *God's First Love: Christians and Jews over Two Thousand Years*, transl. Geoffrey Skelton, New York: Weybright and Talley, 1967, p. 391.

The "racial" form of mystical anti-Semitism evidently did not replace the theological form: they ran parallel or convergently, or intertwined. The age-old stigma of the Jews was easily shifted from beliefs to genes, a shift that permitted passions to be expressed without the brake of theology.

The withering of theology had, in fact, left behind a pulsating sack of bile in people predisposed to the formation of bile. In times of tension that sack could burst. As life in the modern era grew more complex, the masses could vent on the Jews all their fury at the countless afflictions of the early and intermediate stages of industrialization. The role of scapegoat assigned the Jews, congealed in the status of outsiders, was inevitable: all the subliminal and actual content of all aspects of Christendom, alongside the religion proper, had fixed the figure of the Jew as the natural repository of the odd, the alien, the loathsome, the evil. And without the superstructure of a theological concept that made Jewry meaningful as well as degraded, there was nothing, in times of crisis and tension, to withstand destructive hostility.

Thus the abandonment of the Christian religion left a void in which all forms of outright pathology might find a foothold: Hitler may well be the outstanding example of a nontheological, mystical hatred of Jews, with all the intensity that, as we shall see, characterized his career.

An epigram may be in order: with the "racist" theory, mystical anti-Semitism became a disease of Christians, as well as an affliction of the Jews.

There were also, of course, mundane factors that intensified the emotion required to transfer the stigma on the Jews from theology to the earthier realm of biology.

The success of the Jews in permeating Western society made them extremely conspicuous. After having been abstracted, so to speak, from European society for so many centuries, and then spreading with such rapidity throughout the bourgeois world that was expanding in the wake of the Industrial Revolution, Jews were becoming more and more noticeable in Germany, Austro-Hungary, France, Great Britain, and America.

Classical Church theory, which insisted that Jews must survive, but in "abject circumstances," was now absurdly irrelevant. Though the great bulk of Jewry was far from affluent, the many

Jews who had scaled the heights of society obviously made the Church's theory quite obsolete, aside from the absence of any mechanism to enforce such "abject circumstances."

And the success of many Jews was achieved against a background of social upheaval: peasants were becoming workers, traditional activities obsolescent; countless individuals were shaken up, family life was transformed. All these complex processes necessarily distressed large numbers of people. The recourse to "race" was thus a satisfying outlet for many frustrations.

The way Jews were depicted in the growing campaign against them in the nineteenth century came to diverge more and more from the current situation of real-life Jews, and to acquire a sort of ideology, rooted in the notion of the inherent worthlessness, as well as perniciousness of Jews, and taken to justify what was proclaimed to be an "instinctive" revulsion.

By the end of the century the anti-Jewish movements in Europe had linked up all the arguments stemming from the debates of the preceding century with respect to the emancipation of the Jews and given them an infinite scope based on "science." The growth of this pseudo-scientific view of the Jews was rapid: Wagner's attack on the Jews in music was initially published anonymously in 1850: less than twenty years later he printed it under his own name.

From the last third of the nineteenth century on, anti-Semitism spread widely among the intelligentsia and the upper classes; that growth was paralleled by its practical consequences. Anti-Semitism became part of an actual movement, first in Germany, then spreading to many other countries—to the Austro-Hungarian Empire, torn by intractable ethnic conflicts, then to France, England, and the United States. Russia too began to be preoccupied by the "problem"; by the end of the nineteenth century it was being studied in the topmost strata of the Empire. Germany, to be sure, remained the focus of the agitation concerning the Jews, sharpened, perhaps, by the stream of Jewish immigrants from the East since the 1880s.

What was new about this political context was that anti-Semitism, in and for itself, now became the actual content of a political program, no longer serving merely as an auxiliary element in many religious, political, or social movements. From the end of the nineteenth century on, parties and movements appeared in Europe whose exclusive, all-encompassing actual program was a very simple one—against the Jews and against Judaism. This is all the more arresting if one recalls that the actual number of Jews in Europe in the mid-nineteenth century was some four million—slightly over 86 percent of world Jewry and only about 1½ percent of the population of Europe.

Thus, even though the Jews were a minute fraction of the population, the attention of numerous highly educated and influential Europeans could be concentrated on them to the point of making plausible a unique, all-inclusive political program organizing the aversion to the Jews on an impressive scale. It was a program, moreover, that leaped over national boundaries: Hungarian judeophobes, for instance, called for a sort of anti-Semitic league of nations as their major goal. Though before the First World War such movements remained relatively weak, they were considered an understandable form of political activity.

This curious combination of political extremism and ideological mysticism produced, toward the end of the nineteenth century, an extraordinary forgery that is still current today: the Protocols of the Elders of Zion. These purport to describe a secret meeting held by "rabbis" to organize the rule of the world under international Jewry, by the use of guile, the world banking system, and the world press, and, for good measure, the infiltration of the Freemasons. The Protocols crystallize the main theories of the late Middle Ages about the Jews: the notion of a conspiracy to wipe out or enslave all Christians as an explanation of the countless tales of well-poisoning, the spreading of plagues, and similar legends.

To a receptive audience they present a seductive picture of scheming Jews, their power, their incredibly close-knit organization, and their deep hostility to all mankind, especially to Christians. The very notion of a secret conference of "rabbis" —a theme also outlined in the late Middle Ages—was to have a catalytic effect.

The legends underlying the Protocols had taken on a political flavor from the Renaissance on; after Napoleon's convocation of a Great Sanhedrin in 1807, they acquired a certain vogue in France and Germany, though without becoming very popular; in France writers also linked Jews to Freemasons as part of the same alleged plot against Christians.

Strangely enough, however, the actual text of the Protocols was composed in Paris at the end of the nineteenth century not by reworking these ancient legends in a new form, but simply by taking an entirely different composition—an attack by a French writer (Maurice Joly) on Napoleon III for his dreams of world conquest—and changing the substance of it to make it point to "international Jewry" instead of Napoleon III.

The adapter of Joly's brochure is unknown: he seems to have been working for the Tsarist Secret Police (Okhrana), perhaps in order to influence the last Tsar, Nicholas II. In any case, the forger simply took Joly's brochure, *Dialogue aux Enfers entre Machiavel et Montesquieu* (1864), which has nothing whatever to do with Jews, and turned it into something entirely different: the alleged proceedings (Protocols) of leaders of world Jewry, claimed to be already in control of many European states, and so already close to achieving world rule.

Nicholas II, not abnormally quick-witted, saw through the brochure the moment he saw it; the first Russian public printing (1905) was scarcely noticed outside a few small groups. Yet after the terrible shock of the First World War it was to have a great future. In 1920 the Protocols soared aloft. The enemies of the Bolsheviks blamed the Jews for the whole catastrophe: the Russian text was published in Europe in numerous translations. The Russian edition itself no doubt played a role in the pogroms carried out in southern Russia during the Civil War (1918–20).

The Protocols gave a seductive explanation of the upheavals and carnage of the First World War and also, of course, of the Bolshevik putsch itself, which had decapitated a great state, exiled the upper class, and no doubt destabilized Europe. The Protocols seemed to explain the reality behind the mysterious otherness of the Jews, and to create a focus for understanding the apparent variety of actual Jewish behavior.

In the modern period Jews had begun fanning out through society as individuals, rapidly achieving distinction in countless activities. It would have been evident to any observer unbiased by ideology that so many individuals could not act in unison, especially since in any given activity they might ordinarily be competing with each other. It would normally have been assumed that similar origins would be expressed in family ties, friendly coteries, a general link of a common "background," and so on—that is, that there was no *national* interest. It was just this fragmentation and chaos of Jewish life that could not be harmonized with the ideas of both mystical anti-Semites and vulgar judeophobes. The Protocols, with their description of a hidden center *behind* the chaos, satisfied the need for an explanation of the seeming diversity.

Though their authenticity was exploded almost immediately—a correspondent of the *London Times* (Philip Graves) simply demonstrated their obvious dependence on Joly's innocuous dialogue between Machiavelli and Montesquieu—so that no furthur attention might have been expected to be paid to them, they had an enormous impact: the text was translated into the chief languages of the world. In the United States it was sponsored and heavily subsidized by Henry Ford until 1927.

The Protocols were widely accepted, in fact, by educated opinion all over Europe as well as North America. In Germany too, the Protocols were thought by many to convey a penetrating truth about history. They were, after all, a summary of what mystical anti-Semites had been saying for generations. Since they duplicated what anti-Semites already *knew*, they carried conviction as it were automatically. But their most enduring success, ironically enough, was to be achieved after the Second World War—and in Soviet Russia.

At the end of the nineteenth century the "Dreyfus Affair" highlighted and focused the tension surrounding the Jews.

A Captain Alfred Dreyfus, son of a rich textile manufacturer, had a position in the French War Ministry; in 1894 he was charged with treason (selling military secrets to the Germans); on 22 December he was convicted and sentenced to life imprisonment on Devil's Island, off French Guiana. The case might have been thought to be simple.

The tone of the press, however, was unusually vindictive; its theme was that Dreyfus symbolized the inherent disloyalty of French Jews to France. Anti-Semitic elements led the chorus of outrage not only in the press but in the expression of public opinion. This, coupled with severe doubts raised by extraordinary irregularities in the trial, created a violent counter-movement.

For twelve years all France—far beyond the circles of the intelligentsia—was polarized. "L'Affaire," a major element in national life, split France for a whole generation and more. Dreyfus's innocence—demonstrated a few years later—was merely one element in a bitter struggle between nationalists and left-wing anti-militarists.

The crisis in French life survived, in fact, the events of the Affair itself; it foreshadowed a permanent division in the country on the basis of conflicting loyalties and various types of extremism. The somewhat pallid figure of Dreyfus himself had catalysed a complex phenomenon of the modern age, and in one of the most advanced countries.

Despite the shortcomings of the Emancipation, the Jews, especially in Western and Central Europe and America, flung themselves into the life of society as a whole at a breakneck pace.

The large-scale molecular adaptation of individual Jews requires no analysis. Countless Jews found their niches in civil society in Europe and America, with results that are everywhere manifest. The assimilation of Jews, either outright—through conversion or intermarriage—or functional—Jews remaining Jews in the various accessible pursuits, notably in business, in the professions, and later on in the arts—has been equally evident. By the end of the last century, Jews were already playing a variety of roles, prominent and obscure, in almost all walks of life in America and the principal countries of Europe.

A natural consequence of this was a transformation of Jewish self-consciousness: the germination and spread of nationalist movements throughout Europe, and the emergence of new nation-states had a direct effect on the Jews, who were bombarded by movements comprehensively splintering traditional structures.

Aside from the outright assimilation of individual Jews, orthodox tradition, the norm throughout Jewry for many centuries, became increasingly subject to erosion. Religious values were sapped by rationalist critiques, or else replaced by various currents of world reform. These included blanket panaceas, such as liberal, socialist, or Marxist politics, or some version of global Jewish reform, such as the overhaul of Jewish life through settlement in areas in Russia where Jews could have autonomy ("territorialism"), or Zionism, a movement aimed at the restoration of Jewish sovereignty in Palestine (though "political" Zionism, too, showed some initially "territorial" wavering, that is, a short-lived speculation about the possibility of Jewish colonization in Uganda, in Africa).

In Western Europe, by and large, especially in Germany, there was large-scale assimilation after the Enlightenment, both from the direct loss of individual Jews in numerous conversions and from the weakening of Orthodoxy among religious Jews. It was the "Reform" movement, focusing on the ethical content of Judaism, as distinct from ritual, liturgy, and national allegiance, and intent on establishing Jews as citizens of the countries they were living in, that generated the concept of "German citizens of the Mosaic Faith" as a way of describing the Jewish community.

Various movements for world reform were launched by the French Revolution, of which the most successful was Marxism. By the end of the nineteenth century Marxism, in different varieties (militant, moderate, activist, quietist, and so on) had acquired a substantial following, including many Jews. In Eastern Europe especially, before Marxism touched masses of Russians and Poles, even the small Jewish minority could play a disproportionate role.

It seems plain, both in retrospect and today, that many Jews have been attracted to one variety of "universalism" or another through the malaise affecting individuals shaken out of a millennial, self-contained orthodoxy into a burgeoning, open, and dynamic industrial society. Ordinary Jews, to be sure, pursuing careers and establishing themselves in society, became organically integrated with it whether they remained devout or not. But many, especially in the intelligentsia, who were not quite settled in some stable occupation and not yet wholly or willingly integrated, were buffeted by general ideas. Marx, of course, was the outstanding example of such a Jew, but a great many others have felt the same attraction.

What "universalism" meant for Jews was summed up with magisterial precision by the most celebrated German-Jewish poet, Heinrich Heine, in 1824: "What is (the) great task of our own age? It is emancipation. Not only the emancipation of Irishmen, Greeks, Frankfurt Jews, West Indian Blacks, and other such oppressed peoples, but the emancipation of the whole world."*

This would surely seem to imply that the "emancipation of the whole world" takes precedence over partial emancipations. And of all the aspects of everyday group distinctiveness, this "universalist" predilection of Jews was to entail the most intimate interaction with the cosmic dimension of mystical anti-Semitism. Political universalism, in its abstract, disembodied intransigence, in its practical boundlessness, was to go a long way toward providing mystical anti-Semites with a real-life prop: Jewry as such could now be identified with sweeping abstract principles, alien through their very abstractness, their remoteness from ordinary people, and thus justifying strong reactions. For how could the inhabitants of a given country be expected to react to the insistence of universalist Jews that all mankind had to be emancipated before conditions anywhere could be ameliorated? That all improvements had to be global?

Yet just this attitude of aggressive self-effacement has been a characteristic response of many more or less secularized Jews who nevertheless retain strong Jewish feelings. It has made it natural for them to believe with fervor that the Jewish community too, and in particular the State of Israel, can be seriously helped

---

* S. S. Prawer, *Heine's Jewish Comedy*, Oxford: Oxford University Press, 1983, p. 130.

only by being integrated with a worldwide movement. It would seem to indicate a morbid absence of group morale that makes universalist programs seductive to Jews, perhaps even a way of subtracting themselves from Jewry at the very moment of maintaining that universalist ideals, properly understood, are actually the essence of Judaism. Other peoples, after all, can easily declare themselves to be universalists in the sense of looking forward to some utopia for mankind while at the same time balancing the ideal against the concerns of their own people: French, English, German, American universalists are common.

Leon Trotsky as a young man was once asked by another left-wing Jew just how he defined himself—"Russian? Jew?" he answered proudly, "Neither—I am a Social-Democrat!" It is obvious that Trotsky's retort, universalist in form and content, was for that very reason exclusively Jewish: only Jews are universal universalists. To outsiders, of course, it was just this boundless abstractness that constituted a source of ceaseless disturbance.

As Marxism expanded during the last third of the nineteenth century and became a mighty force both intellectually and institutionally in Central Europe, many Jews were attracted to this species of universalism, as well as to other varieties of world reform such as Tolstoyanism. Toward the end of the century, indeed, only Zionism was to begin a serious competition with Socialism among secular Jews and to some extent among pious Jews, some of whom became Zionists.

Zionism and "territorialism" may well represent a backlash against the persistent, molecular erosion of Jewry through the assimilation brought about by religious conversion, intermarriage, and cultural absorption.

The "territorialists" were active only in the Tsarist Empire, though their agitation was echoed in the foundation of Jewish agricultural colonies in North and South America. Their aim was simply autonomy somewhere in the vast reaches of Russia, where Yiddish would be the national language. In Russia too, the first shoots of Zionism appeared in the Eighties of the nineteenth century: from then on small bands of idealists began making their way to Palestine in order to settle there.

The theory of Zionism had been adumbrated a generation before by Moses Hess in his prescient *Rome and Jerusalem* (1862), but a precipitating factor was no doubt the reformulation of anti-Semitism toward the end of the century. Many Jews, enthusiastic about the prospect of its decline after the French Revolution, were bitterly disappointed by its recrudescence, and in an organized, violent form at that.

Some pogroms in Russia in 1881, though negligible compared with what was to happen a couple of generations later, left the most sombre impression: Leo Pinsker thought the "Jewish Question" inherently insoluble, indeed a "psychic aberration" of the Christian world, "a disease transmitted for two thousand years."*

Mystical anti-Semitism, whose origins, at least, had a theoretical framework, had become so attenuated in public expression that the transformation of its rationale to a secular basis was baffling to most students of the phenomenon, and perhaps particularly to the Jews. It seemed incomprehensible that after the crumbling of the theological framework, its ostensible rationale, an obsessive, motiveless hatred should remain. The feeling that Jewry still seemed to Christians a "ghost nation," whose eerie, landless survival had once again become a source of fear as well as loathing, oppressed early Zionist thinkers (Pinsker, Ahad Ha-Am, Nahum Sokolow).

Zionism was given a political formulation in *Der Judenstaat* (*The Jewish State*: 1897) by Theodor Herzl, himself an "assimilated" Jew—a well-known Viennese littérateur and playwright—whose initiative was a more concrete response to the growth of anti-Semitism. The fact that the emancipation of the Jews, called by Herzl the "crowning achievement of our century," had not brought about the blanket acceptance of the Jews on all levels of society, which might have been thought to be an inevitable consequence of their legal emancipation, indicated to Herzl that the only way out was political. That the

---

* Leo Pinsker, *Auto-emancipation*, transl. D. S. Blondheim, Philadelphia: Maccabean Publishing Co., 1906, p. 3.

Dreyfus Affair took place in a country like France helped crystallize Herzl's views.

Herzl took an unusual leap: he simply projected the restoration of Jews to their own land, that is, to political sovereignty in a certain territory, thus counteracting what he, like Pinsker, took to be the incurable malady of mystical anti-Semitism. However, though Herzl regarded the crisis facing the Jews at the end of the nineteenth century as urgent, his analysis was somewhat skewed by the inability he shared with most people to assess the true force of mystical anti-Semitism. He remarked (at the end of his *Judenstaat*) that in his day the whole "Jewish Question" was nothing but a dislocated chunk of the Middle Ages. This is surely a misperception of the theological factor, and especially of its psychological potency for those who have lost their religion; it is a failure to appreciate the main problem for the modern era—the transformation of a theological view (Paul, Augustine, Luther) into the unbridled bestiality of a secular view (Hitler).

This conundrum was no doubt rooted in a rationalistic prejudice, a would-be empirical misperception—a failure to grasp the point of mystical anti-Semitism. It was part of a general tendency among Jews to give rationalistic or sociological explanations of anti-Semitism, generally in self-centered terms. Though Pinsker's word "disease" seemed to point at least to a nonrational source, he and others, including Herzl, nevertheless linked anti-Semitism to actual Jews.

The explanation is evidently a form of exaggerated self-esteem: it makes anti-Semitism "understandable" because of Jewish superiority (God, Torah, Jewish family life, Jewish gifts, and so on). Inversely, in a minority of Jews, no doubt predictably, negative aspects of Jews (conceit, arrogance, pushiness) would be highlighted. Thus mystical anti-Semitism would unwittingly be "objectified" by locating its roots in the Jews themselves, which is, of course, what anti-Semites themselves have always maintained. This brought about, ironically enough, a convergence of the allegations of anti-Semites, including Christians who do not take Christian theology seriously, and the apologias of Jews who naturally do not take it seriously either.

In the same work Herzl gives a further judeocentric

explanation—"pressure naturally creates within us an hostility to our oppressors, and our hostility, in turn, strengthens the pressure"*—that seems heedless of the irrational factors. He not only assigns to the Jews the credit, so to speak, for mystical anti-Semitism, but entirely disregards the irrationality at the core of the problem he is concerned with.

Herzl's remark is, indeed, strangely wrong-headed. No doubt many Jews resent being discriminated against, but since resentment at a large majority is weakened by the very size of the majority, the "normal" wish of many Jews is to be assimilated by precisely that majority—at as high a level, of course, as possible. Even when the assimilation is not explicit, or total, Jews express a desire for it in a variety of ways, all subsumed under the notion of aping the majority (in dress, manners, and ideas). The gradations in this sort of imitation or quasi-assimilation are doubtless infinite.

Nevertheless, the Zionist movement, which had begun in the somewhat inchoate agitation among Russian Jews, influenced to some extent themselves by theories of social reform (Tolstoyanism and Marxism), and conceptually rounded off by Herzl's specifically political formulation, acquired momentum. In the space of a half-generation Herzl's personal lobbying became a political actuality. Herzl, in fact, was one of the most successful prophets in history: the State of Israel was founded only a few months after the fifty years Herzl had predicted it would take.

Herzl, unusually striking physically—with an impressive beard, burning eyes, and an air of compelling magnetism—constituted himself an apostle to the Gentiles: his self-composure, together with his gifts, presence, and conversational powers, led to introductions to the German Kaiser, to the Sultan, and to many eminent personalities in Europe, who seemingly accepted without demur his claim to represent "The Jews."

The Zionist movement was fought with great vigor by all other currents of Jewish opinion: Orthodox Jews, assimilationists

---

* Theodor Herzl, *Judenstaat*, 11th edition, Berlin: Jüdischer Verlag, 1936, p. 29.

of all kinds, liberal Jews, Socialists, Marxists—all opposed Zionism, each group from its own angle.

Perhaps Jewish Orthodoxy rejected Zionism with the greatest violence: though many Orthodox Jews were to reconcile themselves to Zionism, and later to the State of Israel, the rejection of Zionism has survived in some Orthodox groups, who to this day violently oppose the State of Israel root and branch. This opposition derives from the very heart of Jewish history for almost two millennia. The secular defeat of Jewry, incorporated in the oldest Jewish tradition since the Babylonian Exile, was given its "modern" form by the Zealot debacle in the Roman war of 66–70 and the Bar Kochba fiasco of 132–35. This led to a rejection of *all* political action, and that rejection, enshrined in the Talmud, proved to be a major obstacle to the spread of Zionism, whose aim after all was to move the Jews once again into the ranks of the "warring nations," and thus out of "God's hand." Many pious Jews considered this an outrageous impiety.

Zionists, of course, took the view that it was time for Jews to recover control of their collective destiny, and that the "normalization" of the Jews—by the restoration of territorial sovereignty—would automatically extinguish anti-Semitism, which Zionists generally considered a consequence of the "abnormal" situation of the Jews in the Diaspora.

Yet many Jews who were indifferent to "God's hand" still felt that the very fact of a Zionist movement might well stimulate further anti-Semitism. It is certainly true that many anti-Semites regarded Zionism, like any manifestation of Jewish initiative, as inherently baleful, though it seemed to others that it might well provide a modus vivendi with Jewish communities in various European countries (like Poland) whose difficulties with the "Jewish Question" might be solved by removing the Jews altogether: if Palestine was their destination, so be it.

By the time of the First World War, the Zionist movement was strong enough in Europe and in America to become a factor in the Versailles Peace Congress; in 1917 the British Government issued the Balfour Declaration, which provided for a "Jewish National Home" in Palestine, including the present-day State of Israel and Jordan, and was integrated with the British Mandate for Palestine. The mandate provided for the mass colonization of Jews. For some time the problematics of the Middle East situation were not foreseen—or, perhaps, foreseeable.

Taking a long view, if one surveys the arc of anti-Semitism since the emancipation of the Jews, it is difficult to avoid the impression that until the appearance of National Socialism in Germany the mystical obsession with the Jews had been, by and large, on the decline. Despite the numerous manifestations of anti-Semitism from the nineteenth century on, despite its potency as a factor in European politics, despite the persistence of age-old anti-Semitism in a new garb in Marxism and all the movements derived from it, despite the survival of mystical Jew-hatred rooted in Christian theology among people indifferent to the theology, it had been steadily declining since the Middle Ages. Therefore it might well have seemed possible to agree with all those optimists, Jews and non-Jews alike, who foresaw in the obsolescence of theology, the spread of humanism, and the expansion of secular democracy a termination of mystical anti-Semitism as well.

The daily interaction between Jews and Christians was pervasively tinctured, to be sure, by a deep, unavowed, unconscious element of mystical anti-Semitism, so that personal and social rivalries and competition, conflicts of ideas, political divergences overlaying the whole of the social spectrum would also be colored, somehow, by varying degrees of dislike on the part of Christians that would have to be regarded as excessive. This situation is still current; no doubt it characterizes the general attitude of society toward the emancipated Jewries of the West.

Nevertheless, the relative balance between mystical anti-Semitism and ordinary, "normal" group frictions seemed to be tilting toward the normal. One might have expected, accordingly, a gradual attenuation of mystical anti-Semitism. What had begun, when the theological odium was in full vigor, as a sort of horror of Jews, seen bifocally, as it were, both as they were in real life and as symbols of the horror itself, was slowly diluted to an aversion to Jews as a group because of their symbolic identification with something else (ideas, political movements, social trends). This was then weakened still further into a miasma of dislike of the sort called "instinctive" precisely because it has no foothold in reality, symbolic or otherwise.

The last stages would have been amorphous social sneers, malicious but without excessive emotion, in which Jews in the abstract might be blamed for something or other, while at the same time the Jew one was talking to would feel assured he or she was not personally a target. The penultimate stage would be when Jews as a collectivity would be meaningful, perhaps, as a subject of conversation, but would have no overtones of "profound" significance. The final stage would have been negative —that is, Jews would be thought of just as people like any others. This may well be the case in the modern world already: in some milieus Jewish identity may actually be of no particular interest. It would be hard to generalize this further, to be sure: human nature attributes social importance ipso facto to whatever many people are talking about.

The hyperbole in Heine's remark a century and a half ago may retain an element of insight: Jews can be freed from their own self-consciousness as well as from the world's awareness of them as special only when the whole of Christendom is freed from mystical anti-Semitism. It seems to foreshadow, in a loose, sentimental way, Friedrich Nietzsche's later, much starker formulation, to the effect that only with the extinction of Christianity itself will the Jews be regarded without bias.

Nevertheless, at the turn of the century it might have seemed reasonable to think that mystical anti-Semitism was truly dying down. Even special cases, such as the critical situation of the Jews in Poland between the two World Wars, with the constriction of economic life owing to the sharpness of the competition between educated Jews and the formation of a parvenu Polish middle class, could have been seen as transitory. Similarly, the numerous survivals of traditional anti-Semitism in the East of Catholic Europe, as well as among Protestants in Germany, England, and America, could have been seen as isolated vestiges of basic mystical impulses in Christendom that in the main had already exhausted themselves.

Hence, the advent of National Socialism in Germany, spearheaded by the unique personality of Hitler, must be viewed not as a culmination of vast forces gradually swelling to the dimensions of the Holocaust, not as a resurgence of mystical hatred in the masses of the population, but as the convergence of disparate factors: A biological anti-Semite whose career was based on national politics became the head of a great state whose people, familiar with conventional anti-Semitism, both mystical and vulgar, were blind to the pathological extremism of his obsession. When the war began to founder, the violence in Adolf Hitler's psyche broke out in a matchless mass murder.

HITLER

CHAPTER SEVEN

Hitler's interest in religion was marginal, indeed minimal. His occasional remarks to Church leaders that in fighting the Jews he was "doing God's work" were merely opportunistic.

For him the dialectical tension of theology meant nothing: the "Aryan race" did not confront the Jews for them both to be ultimately "reconciled": Jews were simply outside humanity—unclean, the diabolical opposite of Aryan "purity."

At the same time, Hitler's fixation on the Jews could hardly have developed without his Catholic upbringing; his obsession manifestly stems from an otherwise forgotten Catholicism. He was an extreme case of a renegade who has retained the negative elements of what he has abandoned; in his case, the adverse view of Jews was intensified by hatred, independent of anything in his personal life, and shaped to accommodate the fashionable "racism" of his era. His "fanatical" anti-Semitism is taken for granted, to the point of obviating comment. Yet since, aside from the Jews, it was, as we shall see, an integral element in the crippling of Germany, it deserves more than a glance.

Hitler's countless references to Jews all make it plain that "The Jew" was in no way a real-life figure—in this one respect it was a kind of theological concept, freed, to be sure, from its theological context and hovering, so to speak, over Hitler's unconscious. In Hitler's mind, The Jew was bent on universal destruction: since he was essentially nothing but a parasite, he used his universal power in order to destroy all mankind, and so bring about his own annihilation.

The omission, accordingly, of self-interest in an organism allegedly scheming to rule mankind indicates that the nature of The Jew was merely a diabolical projection: what can be the point of an ambition that destroys its originator?

All this was colored by a sexual fantasy also quite indifferent to a true sexual interest; it merely reproduced a sort of cartoon: "The black-haired young Jew lies in wait for hours, satanic glee on his face, for the unsuspecting girl whom he then defiles with his blood and thus steals from her people."

Hitler's well-known hatred of the aristocracy, whatever its origin, was linked to his obsession with the Jews: he blamed the aristocracy for having condoned the Jews' diabolical bloodsucking and protected these leeches against the wrath of the people instead of freeing the German nation from them. This complicity was their fundamental crime: "the aristocrats made an alliance with the Devil." Whereas the people perceived "instinctively the alien organism in their own body," the princes even allowed the court Jews to insinuate themselves into the hereditary nobility to continue their work of universal destruction.

This concept of Absolute Evil, mindless and boundless, aiming at the destruction of mankind at the price of its own destruction, enabled Hitler, like other mystical anti-Semites, to soar above what might realistically be considered the antithesis between, say, "capitalists" and "Communists." For mystical anti-Semites of the "racist" variety, both these seemingly different groups could be reconciled as representing two different techniques for playing out the same satanic role: the annihilation of the human race whose blood they are sucking.

For Hitler, the Jew "is and remains the eternal parasite . . . that like a horrible bacillus spreads more and more the moment it is invited in by a favorable medium. The effect of his existence, however, is just like that of parasites: wherever he appears the host-people dies out sooner or later."

This is far removed from any notion of Jewish inferiority: it was not at all like Hitler's feeling about the Slavic "subhumans":

> Two worlds confront each other! The God-man and the Satan-man! The Jew is the counter-human being, the anti-human being . . . the creation of another god . . . The Aryan and the Jew . . . are as far removed from each other as the beast is from the human being. Not that I am calling the Jew an animal. He is far further from the animal than we Aryans. He is a being alien to and remote from nature.*

Of course this boded no good to the Jews. In 1922, long before he was in a position to implement his deepest feelings, Hitler said to a journalist:

> When I am in power the annihilation of the Jews will be my first and most important task. . . . I shall have gallows erected in the Marienplatz in Munich, as many as can be fitted in without stopping traffic. Then the Jews will be hanged, one after another, and they will stay hanging until they stink and the last Jew in Munich has been destroyed."**

There is no trace of experiences in Hitler's youth that might have caused an "exaggerated" aversion to Jews; there is no suggestion of any events that could explain any strong feelings whatever. Even the legends, soon circulated, to the effect that Hitler was himself part Jewish, and hence "overcompensating," have no link to real life.

If one surveys the arc of Hitler's evolution, which after his early youth took a few years to turn, first, toward politics in general and then to his own brand of politics—the campaign for a Greater Germany, the annihilation of France, the defeat of England, the smashing of Russia, and the installation of a new order ruled by Germany in Europe and then in the rest of the world—we see that the first phase in the growth of *all* his ideas

---

* Hermann Rauschning, *Gespräche mit Hitler*, New York: Europa Verlag, 1940, p. 228.
** In an interview with Josef Hell, an editor of *Der gerade Weg*, a weekly magazine, cited in Charles Bracelen Flood, *Hitler: The Path to Power*, Boston: Houghton Mifflin Co., 1989, p. 244.

was, in fact, a very simple loathing of Jews. At the outset, in Vienna, he thought they were strange, odd-looking, repulsive; then this simple idea was swiftly transformed into a notion, rooted in the "race" theories of the middle and late nineteenth century, that the Jews were actually "bacteria," a mortal danger to mankind.

This metaphor is a remarkable achievement; it seems tailor-made to explain away the problem, for mystical anti-Semites, of obvious Jewish helplessness in the face of the awe they feel for whatever it is in their psyche that they identify with Jewish "power." The aura of invisibility, of insidiousness, of unfathomable mystery with which the metaphor surrounds the activities of actual human beings gives it a magical force. Rationally, of course, it cannot be defended; how can human beings, in fact, be bacteria? But in the psyches of unbalanced mystical anti-Semites, rationality can be replaced by magical metaphors.

It may well be, as I have suggested, that in Europe all "race" theories of the kind that were integrated with ideology stemmed from a preoccupation with the Jews; in Hitler's case this would seem particularly obvious. On the basis of mere physique, for instance, it would be hard to understand his contempt for the Poles, who are, after all, predominantly "Nordic," like many Russians for that matter, as well as Letts and Lithuanians. Many Germans are not, after all, especially "Nordic," nor are the Japanese extravagantly so. And even though Jews are generally part of the "Caucasian" race, that did not, in Hitler's eyes, help them.

It was natural for Hitler, enthralled by "absolute" anti-Semitism, to seize on the Protocols of the Elders of Zion as an expression of his own view. In their boundlessness, indeed, in their dreamlike paranoia the Protocols weld together, logically, the mystical anti-Semitism rooted both in Christian doctrine and in the "racial" anti-Semitism of the modern era.

The Protocols were to have a special effect in Germany: as a dividend, so to speak, of the picture of horror they present they also provide an explanation of the German defeat in the First World War (the "stab in the back").

How completely the whole existence of this people depends on one continuous lie is incomparably shown in the "Protocols of the Wise Men of Zion," so bitterly hated by the Jews. They rest on a forgery, the *Frankfurter Zeitung* keeps groaning to the world—the best proof that they are genuine. What many Jews do unconsciously is here consciously made clear. . . . It is a matter of indifference what Jewish head these revelations come from; the important thing is that they uncover the nature and activity of the Jewish people with absolutely horrible accuracy, and show their inner interconnections as well as their ultimate aim.*

The destruction of the Jews was, in fact, one of Hitler's two major ambitions—the other was world rule following the German mastery of Europe. On the face of it the two ambitions were not linked: they seemed independent ambitions on two different planes of reality, as well as performing different functions in Hitler's psyche. If Hitler had achieved world rule, or at least the mastery of Europe, he could of course have realized both ambitions, but the destruction of the Jews, politically and militarily pointless, played a real role only within Hitler's psyche.

In any case, anti-Semitism was not a mask, a rationalization, or a modality for Hitler's realization of other aims; it was, from the very beginning, a prime ambition. In Hitler's psychic economy it was potent enough, as we shall see, to be discharged, eventually, in an explosion of mass murder. It turned out to be a cardinal element of his character, though its dimensions were veiled until the war—more specifically, until the first real defeat of the German army.

It was not the mainspring of Hitler's success, to be sure: German politics did not revolve around anti-Semitism. On the contrary, while Hitler harped on the cosmic theory of the maleficent Jew, sucking the blood of mankind down the ages, this theory was superimposed on a wide range of mundane vexations. Not only were there reasons for gnawing discontent from large-scale factors—the awareness of the Bolshevik decapitation of the Russian people, the general churning up of the population in the social upheaval following the German defeat in the First World War, the financial crisis during the inflation of the 1920s—it was of course child's play to blame even those developments on the Jews. But beneath the cosmic cloud of psychotic

---

* Adolf Hitler, *Mein Kampf*, New York: Stackpole Sons Publishers, 1939, p. 299.

hatred, countless Germans could find a malign influence in Jews who were rivals in professions, competitors in business. Upstart Jews could be blamed not only for cosmic problems, but also for objectionable manners, loud clothes, pushiness, cleverness.

Hitler, well aware of the wide range of social distress, could embroider on this theme with his right hand while his left pounded away on the bass: the universal significance of it all. He held out many marvels to a remarkably broad spectrum of Germans during the terrible period after the First World War: a restoration of order and the economy, a regenerated Germany leading the world.

Jew-hatred was only one among many attractions. The impact of Hitler's mystical anti-Semitism was small: no doubt it galvanized into real action only the pathological fringes, that is, people like himself. It was of course natural for Hitler to secure the collaboration of anti-Semites in Germany and Austria, in all the other countries of eastern Europe, and also to some extent in France and England, though there he probably overestimated its appeal: by the time news of the atrocities was broadcast, even fervent anti-Semites in the West were put off.

Among the Germans the intensity of mystical anti-Semitism varied widely, from strong, in the lower and middle classes and intelligentsia, to slight in the working class and still less in the upper classes. In terms of ordinary, polite, "drawing-room" anti-Semitism, it would surely be an exaggeration to single out the Germans as against, say, the French, the English, the Russians, the Poles, the Rumanians, the Hungarians, and for that matter, the Americans.

Hitler had the double vision peculiar to mystical anti-Semites: he could maintain two contradictory ideas simultaneously without discomfort—both the helplessness and the power of Jews.

If he had believed the Jews were really so powerful, he might have taken pains, after becoming head of state, to exploit their power for the benefit of Germany, and not treated them harshly, at least for a time. He might have thought it prudent to conciliate them until his other, equally fundamental ambition had been achieved. Yet he immediately contrived to lose for Germany some of the ablest scientists in the world, spearheaded by Einstein. Many important non-Jewish scientists also left Nazi Germany; many who had come to Germany to study now stayed away. The center for atomic research shifted to America. In 1933, in short, Hitler turned the ability and zeal of the Jews, mostly sincere German patriots, from a credit to a debit.

At the same time, in terms of Hitler's dreams, these were no more than pinpricks. At first, in fact, he paid no more than lip service to his profound obsession with the Jews. His initial vilification, harassment, and menacing harangues, while blood-curdling if taken seriously, were in fact often shrugged aside, by Jews and Germans alike, as mere talk, soon to be submerged by his governmental concerns. Moreover, in the euphoria of his first overwhelming success—the winning of a predominant role, soon to become a monopoly, in the German state—with the prospect of grandiose further achievements, the Jews might have seemed to him a peripheral issue.

And in fact, the only public action against the Jews in the beginning was trivial. Aside from some minor disturbances on 1 April 1933, a few months after he became Chancellor, more than five years went by before, on 9 and 10 November 1938— celebrated as "Kristallnacht" (broken-glass night)—German Jewry was dramatically attacked: passers-by were beaten up, windows broken, shops smashed.

Yet the very fact that these brutal attacks were carried out by agencies of the Nazi Party, and not by the population at large, demonstrates the cardinal feature of the mass murder of the Jews that was to be launched later, during the war: *it was not a pogrom.* The German masses did not succumb to a frenzy of homicidal passion, fall on the Jews in their midst, and tear them limb from limb.

Still, against the background of the rapid escalation of Germany once again into the status of a first-class military power, this extravagance too might have seemed trivial: though the ill treatment of the Jews after the accession of the Nazis to power dismayed Jews everywhere and disturbed liberal circles in the West, Hitler's conviction that there was enough anti-Semitism in France and Great Britain, and no doubt in America, to make his actions in principle not entirely unwelcome may have had a kernel of truth.

It may well have been Hitler's failure on *Kristallnacht* to kindle popular enthusiasm against the Jews that prompted him, from 1942 on, after the conquest of Poland and the opening of the campaign against Russia, to establish the death-camp operation in the depths of Poland, which for years enabled the Nazi regime to keep the murderous program as secret as it could be, and, more important, to keep it from ordinary Germans or, at worst, to enable them to pretend to themselves, to each other, and later to outsiders that they knew nothing about it.

The smashing of France after a year of "phony war" achieved one of Hitler's major objectives; the attack on Russia, which was to prove a debacle, did not at first seem preposterous. It was not absurd to count on a swift victory. Indeed, the potential for the dissolution of the Soviet regime had already been demonstrated most dramatically by the early, relatively effortless victories of the German Army during the first few months of the offensive, when many hundreds of thousands of Russian soldiers surrendered the moment the Germans appeared. This should have made it obvious to Hitler, very astute on a mundane, non-mythological plane, that the Stalin regime might have been unpopular enough to make its dismantling perfectly feasible.

Hitler's political evaluation of the Bolshevik regime had always been the underpinning of his military plans: his statement (in *Mein Kampf*) that "the giant empire in the east is ready for collapse" might very well have been accurate.

The Soviet regime could legitimately have been considered to be on the verge of disruption: the top strata of the Red Army had been annihilated by Stalin's murderous "purges" of 1936–39 and tens of millions had been slaughtered, from the slaughter of the peasantry in 1929–32 to the extermination of millions under the umbrella of the Moscow Show Trials of 1936–38 and the "purges." What rallied the population to the Bolshevik regime was not patriotism alone, but perhaps even more, the unbearable brutality of the Nazis' "colonial policy."

From the outset of the war, Hitler's successive campaigns of murder were of course well known:

The very day the war broke out all invalids in Germany were killed out of hand. This order of Hitler's—in writing, to boot—was not, in fact, suspended until August 1941.

That was when the indiscriminate mass shooting of Jews in Russia and Poland began: large numbers of Jews were killed in this way, perhaps two million; this somewhat indiscriminate method lasted until the Final Solution was launched in January 1942.

Many gypsies had been rounded up and killed, beginning in September 1939 in Germany and spreading to the eastern territories after 1941. In 1945 only 5,000 gypsies were left alive in Germany, out of 25,000 before the war. On the other hand, the gypsies were not completely wiped out, which in view of their small numbers would have been easy: there was no blanket order for their extermination; much was left to the initiative of local authorities.

In October 1939, at the end of the German campaign in Poland, Hitler immediately set in train the extinction of the Polish elite, two and a half million officers, functionaries, and educated people of all kinds. Not only was the elite largely wiped out, the population as a whole was restricted to the most elementary schooling, with the avowed aim of incapacitating it for civilized life.

This senseless attack on the Poles highlights a major feature of Hitler's vindictiveness: During the formation of Hitler's ideas on politics he had allotted to Poland as well as to England the privilege of becoming a German auxiliary in the march against Bolshevism; when the Poles failed to live up to their mission, they were decimated, tortured, and barbarized. Thus, despite the manifest value of a great people he could control for a campaign against the East, Hitler still kept the German Army at war with Poland for five years after the lightning victory of 1939.

The same policy vis-à-vis the Slavic "subhumans" was applied in Russia after the start of the Russo-German war in 1941; all Communists who were found were immediately killed, the population as a whole enslaved.

It was the German defeat outside Moscow in December 1941 that transformed Hitler's perspective. It had, of course, objective factors: the unprecedentedly cold winter of 1941–42 was not a figment of Nazi propaganda, but a fact: calculating on a swift victory in normal winter weather, the Nazi planners had failed to provide the troops with even ordinary winter clothing.

But the German army was not destroyed; Hitler, with the French army annihilated, was still master of Europe.

It may be that he had had in mind a sort of aesthetic scenario for the war against Russia; he had visualized it as being won by one titanic "hammer blow" that would pulverize all resistance.

Hitler might, if he were successful in the initial phase of the Russian war, have hoped to persuade the British that with Germany now in control of the continent and well able to sustain its position in the East, an early peace would be attractive. Then Hitler's hope of bringing Great Britain round to recognizing his conquest of Europe could have been realized.

Hitler's dark side had been quiescent for a time, which was expedient; it would have been hopeless to expect a rapprochement with England, which he had always sentimentally longed for, if the vast crimes already committed by the Nazis—the mass shootings of Jews, Poles, and Russians, still camouflaged as part of the military operations "in the field"—had been broadcast. In any case, however, the decision he made on 6 December 1941, upon learning of the defeat outside Moscow, was to prove fateful, especially for the Jews.

The first thing he did, a few days later, was to declare war on America, without giving the slightest hint beforehand even to his closest entourage. Rationally speaking, this decision was absurd, if only because there was no conceivable way for the German armed forces to get at America: Hitler had merely enabled the Roosevelt administration to overcome the strong antiwar sentiments of many Americans and generate a flood of troops and supplies for Great Britain and Russia. The notion that he did this from a feeling of solidarity with Japan, which had declared war on America on 7 December 1941, would seem ludicrous.

The following month the suicidal decision to declare war on the United States was succeeded by one still more suicidal, as we shall see, and involving at once the German armed forces and their logistical underpinnings—the Final Solution, set in train by the Wannsee Conference in Berlin.

Not only was the Final Solution not a pogrom; it was a strictly controlled state operation carried out as clandestinely as such a massive enterprise could be. By the time the news, in credible form, reached outsiders, including Jewish leaders in Palestine, London, and New York, several million Jews had been slaughtered.

We know from Hitler's autobiography that he had brooded on wiping out the Jews from his adolescence, long before the germination of his vast strategic ambitions. His obsession with the Jews had merely been subordinated, for a time, to grander projects, but when those projects did not work out, as it were artistically, he abandoned them and succumbed to his lust for killing.

When the defeat outside Moscow in 1941 destroyed the hope of a rapprochement with England, together with the hope that America too could be discounted as a military factor once that had been accomplished, the last practical, "commonsense" inhibition of his bloodthirstiness was removed. His dreams of a world-shaking victory destroyed by the defeat in December 1941, which led to the collapse of his practical, down-to-earth planning for the English rapprochement and the avoidance of America's entry into the war, Hitler could now live for his secret vision.

From January 1942 on, accordingly, Hitler devoted the capabilities of the German army not to waging a war for victory in Russia, but to the camouflage of what had now become his paramount—though unavowed—objective, the extirpation of the Jews.

The mass murder of European Jewry required the use of vast quantities of rolling stock, desperately needed for the Russian front, and several highly trained divisions, all focused on corraling, transporting from all over Europe, and murdering in expensive factories unarmed individuals—women, children, untrained men of all ages—who were not, in fact, enemies of Germany at all, and in any case were scattered and unorganized—a military zero. And this at a time when millions of German soldiers were locked in a titanic death struggle with heavily armed Russians.

And what could have been the goal of such a slaughter, the very antithesis of a military operation? What collective purpose was served by the death of millions of soldiers, deprived of supplies and reinforcements that were deflected to the destruction of unarmed, scattered civilians?

Thus, while the mass murder of European Jewry was obviously an atrocity—and on a scale, moreover, that beggars all historical precedents—it was also, from the point of view of Germany, and for that matter of the Nazi Party itself, a suicidal atrocity. It destroyed the Nazi Party, shattered the German state, brought about the death of millions of soldiers, and left Germany divided, after the loss of a third of its territory, into two rival states, one of them de facto integrated with the Soviet Union for forty-five years.

It would seem obvious, whatever the institutional complexity or chaos of the Nazi state, that the only person in Germany who could have imposed such a "Final Solution," which while failing in fact to wipe out all Jews, did accomplish the destruction of Germany and its relegation for a generation to second-class status, was Hitler—in wartime, uniquely powerful.

It may be difficult to quantify the effect of the mass murder of Jews during the Russian campaign; that is, to *prove* that Germany, if not for the Final Solution, might well have won the war. But there can be no doubt that in the mind of Hitler the aims of the war were subordinated to this bizarre, antiwar enterprise, and that its immediate effects—the loss of countless German soldiers and the devastation on the eastern front—were palpable.

It may be illuminating to distinguish between rational and irrational atrocities. It was surely an atrocity to murder the hopelessly sick people, the Polish elite, the Russian prisoners of war. But that did not endanger the German state; to Hitler, and indeed, perhaps, to Nazis in general, the Polish elite and Russians of military age and training might have seemed to be inherently enemies of German national expansion.

The Russian campaign, grounded in the notion of "living space," proclaimed with vehemence by Hitler during the 1920s, might have been considered an authentic geopolitical enterprise.

However atrocious the treatment of the population, ideological Nazis and even militant German nationalists who believed in the primitive idea of "living space"—in the twentieth century!—might have considered it a necessary measure for clearing the indigenous people from the territories to be conquered. In this respect the slaughter could be conceived, if not as an act of war, properly speaking, at least as an act of brutal national expansion, with its "justification" lying in the remote future.

Some atrocities have a commonsense purpose: they are meant to benefit the perpetrator. It is certainly deplorable that people do terrible things to advance their putative interests, but it is stultifying to lump together all morally detestable behavior: to do so obfuscates the understanding of politics. War itself, after all, is atrocious, all the more so the countless atrocities perpetrated in wartime. In this century the establishment of the Bolshevik dictatorship, for instance, brought about many atrocities as the Bolsheviks attempted to control the huge country in which they found themselves isolated.

I have referred to the slaughter of many millions of peasants during the "collectivization" program of 1929–32; the mounting repressions and massacres of the 1930s; the unpublicized elimination of millions before, during, and after the well-publicized Moscow "Show Trials" of 1936–38, which saw the summits of the Bolshevik Party itself destroyed.

It was quite natural—that is, nonpathological—for the Bolsheviks at the outset to stress social classification, not personal guilt, as the basis for massacres: in 1918 Martyn Latsis, one of the first heads of the Cheka (the initials in Russian of the Bolsheviks' terror organization, the "Extraordinary Commission"), said: "We are engaged in exterminating the bourgeoisie as a class . . . that is the quintessence of the Red Terror."

This was Bolshevik policy—initiated by Lenin, who founded the Cheka—not because the Bolsheviks were demented but because they had taken power as a tiny group in a huge country, that is, they represented a minority and *could not admit it*. Thus it was natural for them to kill their opponents as "enemies of the people," to conceal the fact that it was they themselves who were the "enemies of the people." But since the Bolshevik theory was that they had taken power not in a putsch, but through an "upsurge of the masses," the pretense was inevitable.

The characteristic behavior with which Marxist-Leninist regimes throughout the world—China, Cambodia, Ethiopia—isolated in the midst of vast populations who are not, after all, Marxist-Leninists, feel it vital to establish themselves, by surgically amputating whole classes of the population, highlights the essence of a rational atrocity: such leaders are simply establishing the conditions necessary for the realization of their ambitions.

Thus it was rational, while atrocious, for the Nazi regime, too, to kill off the Polish elite, vast numbers of Russian prisoners of war, Socialist and Communist leaders, and so on. Given Hitler's stated goal, living space, these atrocities were, so to speak, inherent in the aims themselves.

Even the massacre in the First World War of large numbers of Armenians, carried out in a pogrom-like manner, though not systematically—that is, the army was turned loose on ordinary people—was a rational atrocity: some high-level Turks had designs on the Turkic-speaking areas of southwest and central Siberia; Armenia lay athwart an intended advance into the Russian interior. Feelings were, in addition, inflamed by the anti-Turkish agitation of Armenian intellectuals, supported by Russia and France. The atrocity, accordingly, had some sort of self-seeking purpose, and in any case by no means threatened the Ottoman state.

These practical, rational atrocities tell us nothing new about human nature—they simply highlight the statecraft of the twentieth century, in which modern technology enables ambitious rulers to manhandle their subjects with impunity.

Students of society have occasionally attempted to link Hitler's obsession to some actual situation, for example, his outrage at the news of the Bolshevik atrocities that came flooding into Germany shortly after its defeat in the First World War. In the spring of 1919, for instance, Munich was flooded by horrible stories of deportations and killings in Russia. In Munich itself, the short-lived Bavarian Soviet Republic had many Jewish leaders. All this might be considered a real-life element in the genesis of Hitler's fantasies about Jews.

But if the early atrocities of the Bolshevik regime had in fact been a predominant element in Hitler's conduct after he came to power in 1933, he would have eliminated Marxists—not just a few leaders, but millions of Communists and Social-Democrats, and not unarmed women, children, and old men, most of whom were not, after all, Marxists at all. Such a "real-life" explanation, aside from its radical inadequacy as an analysis of Hitler's psyche, does not reach the paramount issue—the diverting of desperately needed military personnel and supplies for the purpose of killing unarmed Jewish civilians.

There have been some attempts to shift the responsibility for the decision to wipe out Jewry from Hitler to Himmler. Aside from the inherent absurdity that under Hitler's dictatorial monopoly such an enterprise as the diversion of rolling stock and veteran divisions could have been carried out without Hitler's approval, Hitler himself, in the course of 1942, explicitly boasted of it publicly five different times—1 and 30 January, 24 February, 30 September, and 8 November.* The last occasion indicates the transition from the threat he had made before the war to what we now know was the actual implementation of the threat:

> In case Jewry imagines that it can trigger off an international world war for the extermination of the European races, then the outcome will be not the extermination of the European races but the extermination of Jewry in Europe.

(This speech, which repeats the substance of a speech he had made at a session of the Reichstag before the war, differs only in the substitution of "European races" for "Aryan peoples.")

Hitler's unique role is also all the more striking since one of the strange facts about the mass murder of the Jews in wartime is that the wording of the fundamental directive to implement the "Final Solution" was so vague, so essentially impracticable that no decisions involving its execution were provided for in the budget, for instance: it was left to local authorities—army and Nazi Party commanders—to make ad hoc improvisations.

It is unimaginable that such sweeping decisions involving the fate of the army and the state could have been made by anyone but Hitler himself. An explanation of the mass murder of the Jews that excluded Hitler would entail the assumption that collective dementia had broken out in the summits of the state and

---

* Sebastian Haffner, *The Meaning of Hitler*, transl. Ewald Osers, Cambridge: Harvard University Press, 1982, p. 138.

army. That is quite fanciful: there is not the smallest evidence for it.

The fact that many thousands of individuals were involved in the horrible details of the mass murder is, after all, irrelevant: Bestial human beings are easily come by—in wartime, no doubt, more readily.

The moralizing that seems inevitable in discussing mass murder can find no target in the behavior of large numbers of people: the carrying out of the slaughter by Germans, Ukrainians, Letts, Rumanians, and so forth tells one nothing. Individuals cannot be distinguished; they cannot be brought to book; they are part of the impenetrable flux of mankind.

It may be appropriate to recall that the rational atrocities of the Communist Party under Stalin, programs of extermination that were vaster and extended over a much longer period of time, were carried out on native soil in peacetime, with no resistance of any kind. (Estimates vary around a figure of sixty million; since the end of the 1980s Soviet sources, laughably low at first, have been inching up toward this figure.)

Hitler's murderous hatred is a unique illustration of the transition from "classical anti-Semitism" to the "racist" anti-Semitism of the modern era. The intensity of his obsession with the Jews is sometimes considered mysterious because of the absence of any actual experiences with individual Jews that, as in the case of some mystical anti-Semites, might be thought to explain it.

Still, his family background may justify some inferences. Two things stand out: the well-established fact that as a small child he was beaten, savagely and regularly, by his father, and that his father, himself beaten as a child by *his* father, was both illegitimate and perhaps half-Jewish. The uncertainty about the latter was all the more disturbing, both to the father and doubtless to Hitler, just because it could not be resolved: it was grounded in the fact that Hitler's maternal grandmother had become pregnant while working for a Jewish family, and was also treated with special kindness after she left them to marry Hitler's father.

Thus we have a source for a rage in Hitler that because of his father's unchallengeable authority in the family could not

be expressed by the child even to himself. The hatred was necessarily repressed, shunted into substitute mechanisms and
stoked with all the greater intensity. Also, it may have made the
growing boy ambivalent toward his mother for not shielding him
against his father.*

It might also, of course, have stimulated a determination in
the grown man to exercise absolute authority while unconsciously seeking a suitable target for his accumulated hatred.
That target was, naturally, the Jews; we may take as evidence
Hitler's own explanation:

> Since I had begun . . . to take cognizance of the Jews, Vienna appeared
> to me in a different light. . . . Wherever I went, I began to see Jews, and
> the more I saw the more sharply they became distinguished in my eyes
> from the rest of humanity. Particularly the Inner City . . . swarmed with
> a people that even outwardly had lost all resemblance to Germans. . . .
> All this . . . became positively repulsive when, in addition to their physical
> uncleanliness, you discovered the moral stains on the Chosen People.
> . . . Was there any form of filth or profligacy, particularly in cultural life,
> without at least one Jew involved in it? . . . Gradually I began to hate
> them.**

The last sentence highlights Hitler's gradual, though no
doubt rapid, discovery of a suitable outlet for his repressed rage.

The complex phenomenon of repression may also shed light
on his oratory. For some time it has been universally acknowledged that countless small children are savagely beaten and must
repress their suffering because of the father's unchallengeable
authority, endorsed by the full weight of society. This may explain how Hitler, whose speeches were ground out with profound
internal travail at the very moment of eruption, could commune
with an audience that unconsciously empathized with his feelings while consciously approving of his ideas. This may have
been what enabled Hitler to sway multitudes: for them his or-

---

* Alice Miller, *For Your Own Good: Hidden Cruelty in Child-Rearing and the
Roots of Violence*, transl. Hildegarde and Hunter Hannum, New York: Farrar,
Straus & Giroux, 1983, pp. 142–97.
** Adolf Hitler, *Mein Kampf*, pp. 56 ff., quoted from Joachim Fest, *Hitler*
(English), New York: Random House, 1973, p. 39.

atory was not mere speechifying, but the product of suffering shared by them. Thus his intensity may have been due to the dynamic force created by the repressed, redirected accumulation of rage, given a special effectiveness through his singular fusion of talents.

That repressed rage may also explain, somehow, his lack of sexual activity. The documentation for this is, to be sure, negative: in the decade between 1923 and 1933, that is, between the ages of thirty-four and forty-four, when he had become a celebrity (after the abortive Munich putsch) but was not yet protected by the government, scores of eager journalists followed the trail of his itinerary looking for a "story." After interviewing great numbers of innkeepers and private individuals, they failed to come up with the smallest indication of any sexual activity whatever.

Still, what is of importance for the study of mystical anti-Semitism is that whatever the source of the wounds to Hitler's psyche, whatever the shattering experiences repressed in infancy and childhood, his passionate revulsion against the Jews reflected the traditional function of mystical anti-Semitism.

Hitler was a real-life example of how a phobia, originally encapsulated and balanced by the harmonizing structure of theology, could express itself without restraint in psychopaths who had found an outlet for their idiosyncratic paranoias in the concept of a mystical Evil Jew, created by the abstractions not of theology but of a mystically conceived "racism."

Hitler, just because of his gifts, demonstrated the deadly power of this warping of the mind. Of the many psychopaths who cherish lethal fancies about faceless collectivities, he was the one who, because of his unique situation as wartime dictator, could play out those fantasies in real life.

At the same time, to be sure, the quantum jump Hitler had made from "classical anti-Semitism" to the boundless extremism of biological anti-Semitism was acceptable to his own entourage, as well as to the German public, because of the cultural legacy of theological as well as biological anti-Semitism. Thus, although practically speaking Hitler was the necessary and sufficient cause of the mass murder of the Jews, he could carry it out only because the propaganda leading up to it was not unusual, while the realities were filtered through the horrors of war.

It is strange, after all, that Hitler's obsession with the Jews was not seen as the self-defeating extravagance it was. Its boundlessness, its absoluteness, its suicidalness, its psychotic view of the Jews did not appear to many people as simply demented—at any rate, in wartime—but as no more than "fanatical," a mere exaggeration of something almost banal.

Toward the end of the war Hitler's sobriquet of *Oberfanatiker*—"top fanatic," a pun on his being both the head of state and an extremist fanatic—in its own way commended his firmness of purpose, when in fact that firmness had long since been transformed into a death wish for Germany. If Hitler's blood lust, for instance, had been fixed on any other group—say, redheads—it would have been instantly obvious as real dementia, and would never have got off the ground.

It was, no doubt, just the ingrained feeling about Jews in a very broad public, nurtured for centuries, as I have indicated, by all forms of culture, that restricted the interpretation of Hitler's extravagance to an extreme form of mere "fanaticism." "Top Fanatic" sounded merely satirical; it did not entail outright dismissal as sheer madness.

In short, mystical anti-Semitism had permeated culture in general so comprehensively that it was easy to disregard the pathological extremism of Hitler's true feelings and to shrug aside his radical anti-Semitism as no more than a variant of "normal" dislike of Jews.

Nevertheless, Hitler's determination to sacrifice the German army and state in order to destroy millions of irrelevant civilians was dementia in a pure form. Its not being noticed as such by his colleagues, by other Nazis, and by the upper stratum of society at large, the failure of the public to be horrified by his departure from the "normal," historical, relatively innocuous anti-Semitism of traditional Christendom, merely demonstrates the hypnotism of convention, made compelling during the war by fear and by buzz-word psychology—philistinism—since then.

Curiously enough, the fate of the gypsies is, from the point of view of finding a meaning in catastrophes, in some ways the most poignant of all. Poles and Russians were victims of the war with Germany; Jews were familiar with a millennial tradition of persecution. But the killing of large numbers of gypsies, though not comprehensive, was utterly pointless as either a rational or an irrational atrocity. "Aryan" of course through their Indian origins, and for that matter "white," their suffering had no ideological point of any kind. On the margins of society, they were no doubt felt to be simply superfluous—also inferior, parasitic, and so on—and in a period of comprehensive murderousness were simply swept along sporadically as obviously appropriate victims.

Toward the end of the war (on 2 April 1945), after the German catastrophe—the shattering of the army and state, the death of many millions of soldiers and civilians—Hitler summed up his own view: people "will be eternally grateful to National Socialism for my having wiped out the Jews from Germany and Central Europe." This simple remark casts in high relief the essential paradox of mystical anti-Semitism in its extremist form: the double vision I have referred to above.

Hitler, having demonstrated in his own immediate experience the ease with which Jews could be exterminated, clung to the view that they were nevertheless such an overwhelmingly powerful enemy of mankind that the destruction of Germany and the death of millions of Germans were well worth it.

The German sacrifices, after all, had not been caused by Jewish strength. Compared with the power of the German army and state, the scattered, unarmed masses of Jews, consisting largely of old men, women, and children, were helpless and harmless. The task of corraling and exterminating them was merely technical, administrative.

Yet even after this wanton slaughter on such a scale, Hitler could still feel it to have been a meritorious struggle for the sake of mankind. Hitler's judeophobia, which seemed to conform with "ordinary" anti-Semitism, was in reality nothing but psychotic hatred, to the exclusion of all rational restraints. It was just this bizarrerie, extremism, and absoluteness, and finally the stupendous horror of the massacres, that made Hitler the devastator of half of Europe as well as the destroyer of a third of the Jewish people.

After the defeat before Moscow in December 1941, the war still looked as though it were being carried on, after a setback. Though for Hitler the war as a whole had shifted its axis, no one, even in his immediate entourage, as it seems, suspected this. Hitler did not necessarily discuss his decisions with his generals even on a technical level; his supreme authority in the totalitarian state he had created was unchallengeable, the skill and devotion of the German armies were formidable; there were individual, spasmodic, small victories. How could anyone guess that from that December date on, he was driven by only one aim—a macabre personal-pathological aim?

In November 1941 Hitler had already mooted the possibility of a German defeat in a conversation with the Danish and the Croat foreign ministers, to whom he said icily that if Germany proved incapable of living up to its glorious mission it could just as well go under: he "would shed no tears for it."

From December on, accordingly, when Hitler gave up his dream of world conquest, he could, unfettered by practical calculations—by politics in its broad sense—devote himself to what was now his only remaining goal, indeed, his deepest longing—the extermination of the Jews.

There have been many accounts of the end of the war in 1945 describing the "Twilight of the Gods" mood that prevailed, in which Hitler is generally portrayed as a sick and helpless wreck, his mind going, willpower wavering, all sense of reality skewed by illusions. Nothing is further from the truth: from the end of August 1944 to the final collapse in April 1945, Hitler's energies were remarkable; his powers of decision, his physical and mental activity, despite failing health, were formidable. And all his energy was now directed at the goal he had implied in his remark to the Danish and Croat foreign ministers about "shedding no tears for Germany."

All accounts of Hitler's behavior from January 1942 on emphasize his high spirits: he was content, self-satisfied, indeed merry. Having reconciled himself to the unattainability of world rule, his primary ambition, he was now gaily consummating his other, true, final, uninhibited, and fully deployed obsession.

He had entirely disappeared from the public scene: he made scarcely any speeches; there were no visits to the front, no scrutinizing the cities being bombarded, not the smallest contact with the masses. Hitler was up to his ears in military planning at army headquarters, where he was of course still the total dictator—total power in his hands now, during wartime, more than ever. He now made all military decisions quite alone. All questions of strategy had gone by the board: the very concept of strategy was in effect neutralized, since there was, after all, nothing to fight for once Hitler had privately made up his mind that basically all was lost and the question was only one of time—to see how many Jews he could wipe out before the Allied armies, now swelled by the vast power of the United States, overtook his lethal yearnings.

Concentrating now on his now paramount objective, the extirpation of the Jews, he was happy to hear that the trains were rolling into the death camps day after day with human freight from all over German-occupied Europe.

From the end of 1941 on, accordingly, politics, which had, after all, been the medium of his remarkable career, was dead for Hitler. In the spring of 1945 he apparently told von Ribbentrop: "Politics? I don't do politics any more. It disgusts me so." Hitler gave up politics for military activity—with no aim in his mind now but the destruction of the Jews and finally, as we shall see, the destruction of Germany as well.

Hitler's disappointment in the German people, which was linked in some profound way with their failure to exterminate the Jewish "bacteria," had the most fateful consequences for Germany and the world. When the German army and its Nazi auxiliaries failed to carry out the grandiose mission hailed by Hitler as the immediate goal of the Thousand-Year Reich—the destruction of Russia and, at least, the extermination of the Jews—Hitler "turned on" Germany as he had on Poland. In the last months of the war he did his best to ensure that Germany would not survive.

He was now bent on two tasks—the extermination of the Jews and the destruction of Germany. These lay within his scope just because the area of any conceivable international influence had shrunk for him. There was no longer any hope of a compromise with the Allies on the military or diplomatic front; his decision to destroy the Jews in vast numbers made that impossible.

The war itself was now "fanatical," and the inevitable result was the Allied slogan of "unconditional surrender," a slogan that entailed, to be sure, many sacrifices on the part of the Allies as well as of the Germans, but that was felt by the Allied leaders to be unavoidable. By 1942–45 it was obvious to all observers that what was talked about propagandistically as "war crimes" were in fact nothing but titanic crimes, pure and simple.

Hitler proceeded against Germany both politically and militarily.*

On 22 August 1944 he arrested five thousand notables of the Weimar Republic and insulated them against contact with the Allies: no one was now left for the Allies to deal with but himself.

He also launched two suicidal offensives: At the end of August he called up the "Volkssturm" (national assault), a mob of untrained boys of sixteen and men over sixty, to the fanfare of a fantasy about some magic weapon. The mob was supposed to build up both the eastern and the western fronts—both of which, by the end of August 1944, were practically nonexistent.

In November 1944 he decided on the final operation, an advance into the Ardennes, in the West. For this "Battle of the Bulge," scheduled for 16 December, the German army, with far fewer troops than the Allies—an offensive by its nature requires a decisive numerical edge—also faced overwhelming Allied superiority in the air.

Hitler had to strip down the already skeletal forces in the East just at the moment when, as he knew, a great Russian force was being assembled. It was obvious that the defeat in the West, unmistakably foreseeable, would inevitably be duplicated in the

---

* Military summary in Haffner, *The Meaning of Hitler*, op. cit., pp. 151–56.

East. The disaster on both fronts was simultaneous and total: Hitler, by no means a military novice, had deliberately leaped into a yawning abyss.

The sole purpose of both these militarily pointless offensives lay in Hitler's psyche. By destroying the German army he frustrated the universal longing for an end to the war—more particularly, an end that would ensure the continued presence of the Allies, already in Germany, and the exclusion of the Russian troops. The Battle of the Bulge doomed that longing irremediably. Nor could this battle, from the German side, in any way be called a "last-ditch" heroic stand; it was quite simply a deliberate sacrifice of the last vestiges of the German army, all of which it utterly wiped out.

The goal of these operations was consummated by Hitler's final directives on 18–19 March 1945; these were plainly intended to eliminate Germany as a state.

The Germans, facing an imminent conjunction of the Russians and the Americans, from East and West, were naturally fleeing the Russian advance pell-mell; in the West they were hanging out welcoming ribbons for the longed-for Americans, British, and French. At this point (18 March) Hitler ordered the instant evacuation of all Germans in the West, and the total destruction of anything that might help the enemy in any conceivable future—in short, of everything.

These two decrees of 18–19 March had even less to do with a last-ditch stand than the Battle of the Bulge. Their rationale had nothing to do with heroism—it was the rationale, so to speak, of Hitler's private mania.

His words are revealing: "If the war is lost, then the nation will be lost also. There is no need to show any consideration for the foundations needed by the German nation for its most primitive survival. On the contrary . . . the future belongs exclusively to the stronger nation from the East. In any event, what remains after this struggle are only the inferior, for the good have died in battle."* (The last sentence, the "good have died in battle,"

---

* Haffner, *The Meaning of Hitler*, op. cit., p. 159 f.

echoes a basic theme of Hitler's: during the First World War, he said it was outrageous for "vermin"—that is, the Jews—to prosper when the "best ones have died at the front.")

If Hitler's aim had been realized, no Germans would have been left at all. But at this point his immediate subordinates balked; his two final orders were only partially carried out.

And meanwhile, until the final hour, trains from all over Europe were bringing their freight to the death factories in Poland.

By 1945 Hitler's judeophobia had turned Germany into a shambles—countless corpses, ruins, debris, homeless millions roving about scavenging for food. The state was annihilated, the administration shattered. Seven million soldiers had been killed (a figure exceeded only by the losses of the Russians, and far more than any other country, including Great Britain and France). Germany was truncated; the Soviet Union became a superpower.

Hitler's extremism, always evident, could have been considered the expression of a tempestuously unbridled psyche that expressed itself in violence only rhetorically. But when his political schemes—which, apart from their ingenuity, their brilliant penetration of his opponents' weaknesses, their strategic flair, their skillful exploitation of German abilities and emotions, always had a dreamlike element—collided with an intractable reality, his murderous fantasies, held in abeyance during the years of success, broke through to the surface.

Suicide, which had always been at the back of his mind as ultimately the only appropriate way out for him, had a natural inevitability. His extinction of a third of the Jewish people, to which he had sacrificed the German people, the German state, and his own person, in the event proved to be his only achievement: he is the greatest mass murderer in history.

It is a macabre irony that if Hitler *had* been rational about the defeat outside Moscow in December 1941, if he had not declared war on America, if he had tried to dismantle the Bolshevik despotism by political as well as by military means, if he had, in short, defeated Russia, then all the Jews in Europe and the Middle East would have been wiped out.

For run-of-the-mill anti-Semites, too, Hitler became indigestible. Even those Nazis who were pathological anti-Semites like Hitler himself, and who might have approved of his exterminating the Jews, could hardly have considered the slaughter of large numbers of Jewish civilians worth the destruction of Germany. Hence, just as the most ardent Nazis at the outset and during the halcyon years of his success considered Hitler the savior of Germany, so they would have been repelled at the replacement of patriotism by dementia.

If fanatical superpatriots are considered to have been the core of the Nazi Party, how could they have sponsored the destruction of Germany attempted by the Führer?

The minification of Hitler's role has, in fact, radically skewed the comprehension of the mass murder of the Jews. Aside from the unfashionableness—mainly because of Marxism—of considering individuals important, the determination to "explain" the mass murder, even if only partially, as an aspect of the German "spirit" represents the same type of "essentializing" so familiar from mystical anti-Semitism.

Yet the difference is profound: The identification of the Jews with some evil principle has been an integral part of theology, a vast conceptual system: the alleged empirical basis of "The Jews" as a concept is in fact mythical.

But there is no conceptual category for the Germans: generalizations about them, as about other "peoples," must be substantiated by alleged empiricism. Such generalizations, originating in any domain of the humanities—history, social analysis, mass psychology—will turn out to be fantasies, persuading only those predisposed to persuasion.

The very notion of inculpating a large and inchoate collectivity such as a "people," the universal habit of lumping together vast groups, does no more than create a framework, altogether imaginary, for the focusing of emotion. It is an excrescence of the "racism" that became endemic during the latter part of the nineteenth century.

The only goal ardent Nazis had in common was a form of

superpatriotism: they were otherwise diverse. Indeed, one of Hitler's achievements was the contrivance of a net in which to entangle multitudes. It is the destruction of the six million Jews that has created an emotional need to blame something *tangible*, in this case—with Hitler dead and the Nazis undone—a great collectivity whose very size makes blame meaningless.

One need only recall Churchill's aphorism: "The Hun is either at your feet or at your throat." Such absurdities, which the British manipulated with great success during the First World War, did neither them nor others any good in the Second. Aside from the grotesquerie of calling, in the First World War, the Prussians "Huns" and then transferring this silly notion of aristocratic Prussians to the guttersnipes, thugs, bohemians, pseudo-intellectuals, and outright nut-cases of the Nazi milieu in the Second World War, such generalizations are no more than a form of demagogy that hamstrings understanding.

The flimsiness of this racist view of the Germans stands out when one recalls its novelty: it is only a century or so since the Germans have been discussed this way, that is, since the emergence of Prussia as unifier of Germany. The generations of German societies previously—when, for equally flimsy reasons, they were normally described as a nation of "dreamers, musicians, and poets," and so on—are simply forgotten. In any case, all this represents a sacrifice of politics—the interaction of institutions, personalities, ideas, and contingencies—to the mysticism of "national" and "racial" essentialization.

After the Second World War a wide-ranging debate sprang up in Europe and America over whether or not the mass murder of the Jews was, in fact, unique. The discussion has been curiously lopsided. Two tendencies have converged in a joint claim that it was nothing more than one genocide among countless others: the classic figure of "six million" has been amplified to as much as eleven million (to include Poles, Russians, and gypsies, more or less), with parallels of smaller genocides retrieved from many places and epochs.

One tendency resulting in the "normalization" of the genocide of the Jews stems from Soviet propaganda. From the very beginning, the Soviet Executive set out to downgrade the genocide of the Jews altogether and to maintain that the Nazis killed no Jews whatever—"Fascists" had merely killed people in general. Thus, despite Hitler's utter frankness even as early as *Mein Kampf*, the Kremlin and its numerous spokesmen omitted any mention of Jews as such in all accounts of Nazi bestiality.

Outright anti-Semites, to be sure, have also supported this: the "revisionist" view of recent history—such as that of the Nazi sympathizers in America and Europe—goes even further along these lines by maintaining that the whole story of the mass-murder of the Jews was nothing but a hoax plain and simple.

There is another tendency, specifically Jewish, that also universalizes the Jewish genocide. This goes far beyond the attitude of those Jews who as sympathizers or partisans support the Soviet line automatically. It takes in Jews who are disturbed in the depths of their being by the thought that somewhere in the world there are people who, without knowing them personally, regard them, somehow, as an emblem of something mysteriously odious, and are, in fact, prepared to kill them.

This plain fact—with a background of many centuries, embodied in all aspects of Christian culture, hovering over even banal manifestations of polite, "parlor" anti-Semitism—has proved indigestible for many Jews. It is almost impossible for such Jews, aware of themselves as people with ordinary faults and virtues, to realize that they are regarded, compulsively, by huge numbers of other people, in whose midst they feel nevertheless at home, as no more than the exemplars of a principle.

For devout Jews, to be sure, this is hardly a psychological problem. The traditional attitude of the past two and a half millennia, ever since the Babylonian Exile, has enabled them to go on accepting Jewish suffering as natural in this world—until the Messiah comes. For them, the mass-murder of European Jewry, regardless of its dimensions, is merely one among the many afflictions inherent in the Jewish condition.

But for Jews who have been brought up with a shallow or peripheral attachment to their ancestral religion, the mass murder of Jews in our era is uniquely painful. Lacking the built-in defence of faith, which for secular Jews has been replaced by various fashions (good works, high-mindedness, ideas, culture), they are forced to confront the fact that because of some stranger's pathology they are considered freaks, monsters, or madmen.

They balk at yielding to the evidence that sophisticated culture has attenuated only superficially the ancient obsession with the Jews as being not quite human.

Thus there is a broad functional spectrum in the modern world, any of whose angles will produce a plausible reason for misperceiving the attempted genocide of the Jews.

NEO-BOLSHEVIK RUSSIA

CHAPTER EIGHT

All Socialist parties had always condemned anti-Semitism in principle: it was summed up as merely one more pernicious attribute of a putrescent "capitalist" system. In the immediate wake of the October putsch of 1917 the Bolshevik regime proscribed anti-Semitism absolutely, as a "counter-revolutionary" crime.

Practically speaking, on the other hand, the facility of Socialists in continuing the theological, aesthetic, and philosophical castigation of Jews by finding some other locus for Jewish perniciousness made it natural for them—especially the Marxists—to identify the Jews with an evil concept: Marx's "spirit of money," the profit motive and the like, or, with somewhat less zeal, with a category of wrong-headed politics, that is, nationalism.

The Bolsheviks shared this general view. Thus, while formally banning anti-Semitism, they could plausibly regard the Jews as exemplars of some odious principle. Very early on they revived Charles Fourier's characterization of Jewish business-

men as incarnations of Judas,* and treated both Jewish orthodoxy and Zionism as virulent enemies. Membership in any
Zionist organization became a capital crime; Zionists were
hunted down throughout the country; the use and the teaching
of modern Hebrew were forbidden.

The Jewish community—entrepreneurs, traders, merchants,
artisans, professionals—was ferociously uprooted and economically extinguished from the time of the Bolshevik putsch on. To
some extent this was a natural consequence of Bolshevik statecraft; it was carried out, in the main, by the tiny handful of Jews
who were themselves Bolsheviks or their allies.

But harsh treatment of Jews on the basis of Marxism alone
was a mere residue of attitudes predating the acquisition of
power: the breakneck pace of Bolshevik evolution soon imposed
on the Jews—a collectivity independent of beliefs, activities, or
professions—their classic role as Enemy.

By the middle of the 1920s, the Bolshevik terror, founded by
Lenin and the core of the Party at the very outset as an indispensable adjunct of the dictatorship—a tiny minority aiming at
a radical overhaul of a great society—realized its potential under
Stalin, until his death in 1953 surely the most powerful man in
history. By the end of the 1930s Stalin had consolidated the
Bolshevik regime by realizing the potential of Lenin's
innovations—a Party monopoly based on institutionalized terror.

Marx had taken pains to avoid predicting what would happen
after the advent of Socialism, and since Marxist debate is inherently endless (because of its fundamental element, the di-
alectic), a method had to be found of making decisions that were
justified by some Marxist sanction. Stalin solved the problem:
he would listen to consultants, make decisions, have them endorsed by a mock-executive, and implement them as the "Party
line."

The concept of a "line" in the confusion of survival was
essential just because it was evident that while projecting the

---

* In an article by Friedrich Engels, with an introduction by David Ryazanov,
an authoritative Bolshevik (Jewish) historian, published in *Pod Znamyenem
Marksizma* (Russian), Moscow: Materialist Publishing Co., April 1922, pp. 23–
57.

mirage of "building Socialism," the "line" was really a series of zigzags, and since this fact could not be admitted, all criticism had to be banned. The ban itself, of course, had to be located in Marxism. It was natural for Stalin, a former student in a Russian Orthodox seminary, to set up an actual canon of Marxism (the "Short Course of the History of the Communist Party") that contained all the selections from the texts of the Founding Fathers (Marx, Engels, Lenin) that were permissible.

Thus, for the very reason that critics could surely have found somewhere in Marxist writing a good reason for criticizing the "Party line," they were restricted to quotations from the Short Course: any other source made them instantly suspect, and in fact liable to imprisonment or execution. In practice, of course, the total conformism imposed by the very nature of the dictatorship made the Short Course merely a symbol of the ecclesiastical structure of Marxist authority.

The chief victims of this formula, which began to be applied in the 1920s, were at first the "Trotskyites," the followers of Leon Trotsky, who were still clinging to the Marxist dogma, adhered to by all Bolsheviks too, before, during, and after the putsch of 1917, that The Revolution was bound to erupt in an advanced industrial country, not in a backward agricultural country like Russia. From the classical Marxist point of view, accordingly, the Revolution had still not been properly launched, and hence had still to be promoted worldwide.

Since this Marxist cliché had proved a dead end, Stalin, in 1924, simply banned it: to implement his decision marxistically, he had tame intellectuals, agitators, pamphleteers, and speakers assert it by quotations, arguments, and so on that baffled the Trotskyites, whose faction could not be organized. All oppositionists were met with a torrent of verbiage, inhumanly boring both in itself and through repetition, that swamped all Stalin's critics and made their counter-arguments even more stupefying to the rank and file of the Party.

For some decades Stalin's Short Course played the role of the canon in Christianity. Toward the end of the 1920s, it came to be the textual foundation for the formalization of a category of "counter-revolutionaries." The Short Course encompassed all criticism: by the middle of the 1930s, it covered a wide variety

of crimes, ideologies, ideas, and activities. In this way it articulated and reinforced the monopoly of the Bolshevik Party.

The celebrated "Moscow Show Trials" of 1936–38 charged
all the "Old Bolsheviks" except Stalin—that is, Lenin's
entourage—with membership in a conspiracy directed by Trotsky, at the time a helpless exile, to destroy the Bolshevik government and restore capitalism, with the help of Hitler, the
Mikado of Japan, the British Secret Service, and Wall Street.
Their methods were said to be universal sabotage and
assassination.

The outstanding feature of the court proceedings was that
the defendants not merely confessed—their confessions were in
fact the only evidence—but went even further in inculpating
themselves than did the prosecution, whose style was itself a
model of hysterical ferocity.

The Great Charades of 1936–38—the Moscow Show
Trials—were given all the fanfare available to a major power.
Many foreign visitors were invited; all reported on the judicial
rigor of the procedures and the convincingness of the confessions. The court transcripts were translated verbatim into many
languages and distributed worldwide.

At the same time, under the umbrella of the Great Charades
but with no publicity whatever, a vast comb-out of the population
took place, in which eight to ten million people were eliminated
as "Trotskyites." All the "apparatuses" of the Soviet regime were
combed out, and the whole of the population as well: the categories selected for inquisition, torture, and confession were all
dissident or potentially dissident left-wing groups and all nationalist groups. Right-wing people and monarchists were not
touched.

Though the Great Charades included a preponderance of
well-known Jews, and it was common knowledge that the Jewish
element in their background was important, explicit anti-
Semitism was not publicized. After the Second World War, however, a campaign of open anti-Semitism was launched by the
Soviet Executive. In the late 1940s a concentrated movement of
agitation against "passportless wanderers" and "cosmopolitan
intellectuals" was initiated by the official organ, *Literaturnaya
Gazeta*. In the vast literature devoted to this theme, countless

Party people came under attack, their original Jewish names regularly revealed in parentheses accompanying their conventional Party pseudonyms. At the same time, the attack on them specifically as Jews was still muted.

This campaign was soon supplemented by Charades in three Soviet satellites, beginning in 1949, that extended the concept underlying the Moscow Great Charades of 1936–38.

These Charades—of Rajk and others (Budapest 1949), of Kostov and others (Sofia 1949), and of Slansky and others (Prague 1951–52)—were conceptually identical with the Moscow Great Charades of 1936–38, except that the demonological motif underlying the whole enterprise was enormously heightened by the explicit, reinforced theme of classical, indeed medieval, anti-Semitism.

In the Slansky Charade the previous taboo inhibiting the attacks on Jews was dropped. For instance, eleven of the fourteen defendants were Jews; the name of each Jewish prisoner, called "Zionist," was followed by the phrase "of Jewish origin." Since the defendants were not religious Jews, and in civic terms were either Czechs or Slovaks, this evidently meant a "racial" differentiation.

As adults, all the Jewish defendants had always been violent opponents of all forms of Jewish nationalism, including Zionism: calling them "Zionists," accordingly, evidently stigmatized them as members of the worldwide Jewish conspiracy that was one of the durable elements of classical anti-Semitism, and that had of course been a major obsession of the Nazis.

The worldwide conspiracy was articulated at the Slansky Charade to mean the State of Israel, all American Jewish leaders, all Jewish relief organizations, and a whole network of Jewish agents of "imperialism" allegedly working in sabotage and espionage services for years before the Second World War.

Thus the Slansky Charade, modeled structurally on the Great Charades of 1936–38, also took in the content of the Protocols of the Elders of Zion. Essentially the same procedures were made use of in the Sofia and Budapest Charades of 1949.

The fundamental mythical theme of the Great Charades of 1936–38—the Bolshevik *turned* traitor, the idea of Judas, of course—was extended by the notion of the Bolshevik Jew *born* traitor. Stalin had created a remarkably flexible, potent device: the expansion of the primordial Judas image through the satanization of whole groups of enemies, or alleged or potential enemies, was bound to be useful to a regime propped up on a vast apparatus of police control required to monitor and control its helpless subjects.

In the Great Charades of 1936–38, the "Prosecutor" had gone to great lengths to make somehow plausible the motive that lifelong Bolsheviks might have for betraying Marxism in order to restore capitalism. The reasoning, laughable in essence, had been seductive to many dupes of the regime, not only in the Soviet Union but throughout the world.

In the satellite Charades, however, this was entirely dispensed with: Stalin's establishment of Bolshevik "orthodoxy" had borne fruit. Within the Soviet system it was now possible to achieve conviction, at least for public purposes, merely by laying the charge. The mythological elaboration of the concept of Judas-(Jew)-Bolshevik was advanced enough to make the category itself, as it were, objective: an established fact that merely had to be referred to for it to be evident. Once the idea of a Bolshevik having been a spy from birth was taken for granted, there was no need to explain why he had become one: just as spying was in his nature, so the role of Party leader was his natural mask.

This mythologizing process, inherently indifferent to factual data, had shown itself in 1936–38 in the idea of "espionage services." Since these exist, after all, it might have been thought sensible to deploy some genuine evidence. But this never happened: on the contrary, the word "espionage" was treated as a slogan, evocative and persuasive. By the time of the satellite Charades in 1949 and 1951–52, the slogan was part of an artificial nightmare: no evidence was even alluded to. All naturalism had been obliterated in the construction of the myth, in which for decades the Jews were to play a more and more conspicuous role.

From the time of the Slansky Charade in 1952 on, accordingly, the public was prepared for the exploitation of mystical anti-Semitism, which had begun with the attack on Zionism as "bourgeois nationalism"—part of the general proscription of nationalism in which pejorative words like "Jew" were avoided—and gone on to the satanization of Jews as such. In the Slansky Charade, it was already possible to make hundreds of pejorative references to Zionism and Israel and to the defendants as Jews, coupling all references to the charges so as to make them explanations for the depravity of the defendants. Throughout the Charade, all political and other naturalistic data were subordinated to a concept of "racial" solidarity highlighted by the change of names.

In the Soviet Union itself a trial was fabricated by Stalin just before his death in March 1953. Known as the "Doctors' Plot," it involved several dozen doctors who were arrested in January 1953: nine doctors were named in the communiqué; six were Jews. They comprised all the leading doctors of the Kremlin hospital, including the physicians to Stalin himself and most of the Soviet leaders. They were all accused of murdering some of their patients on the orders of the British and American "intelligence services."

The element of complicity with foreign powers indicated another political charade in the offing, accompanied by a tidal wave of overt anti-Semitism in the Soviet press: Zionists, the (Jewish) Joint Distribution Committee, and Jews as such were vilified: all Jews were labeled both Zionists and agents of "American imperialism."

The Doctors' Plot launched a flood of denunciations, arrests, and demotions of Jews throughout the Soviet Union: trials of prominent Jews were prepared; huge numbers of ordinary Jews were sent to concentration camps. In East Germany a "Zionist plot" was uncovered; "alien and unproductive" elements were deported from the cities of Hungary and Rumania, thousands of Jews starving to death en route.

Throughout this large-scale operation a flood of propaganda denounced Jews as being by nature traitors, spies, embezzlers, imperialist agents and out-and-out murderers.

Later there were rumors that Stalin had in fact been preparing a true pogrom against all Jewry in the Soviet Union; the mob was to be incited against Jews, who were to be "rescued" by the Political Police and killed while in custody.

But Stalin's sudden death stopped it at once. The Charade of the "Doctors' Plot" was denounced as a fabrication.

Here we can see a commonsense exploitation of mystical anti-Semitism: it was no doubt prudent on the part of the Soviet apparatus to drain off the the masses' hatred of the government and focus it on the Jews in the Soviet apparatus as well as on the Jews as such. There were a disproportionate number of Jews generally in the intermediate strata of the bureaucracy, where they had the most immediate contact with the people. It was natural for the anti-Semitism prevalent among both the masses and the Party bureaucracy—and affecting, for that matter, Stalin himself—to be discharged with maximum benefit by making the target of popular hatred not the state but its Jewish agents, as well as Jews generally.

Stalin's remark to Lion Feuchtwanger, the German-Jewish novelist, in 1936, at a time when Stalin was personally fabricating the Moscow Charades of 1936–38, that "you Jews have always been able to produce a Judas"—to say nothing of the meek acquiescence of Feuchtwanger, desperate for a refuge from Hitler—illustrates the point with precision.*

There can be no doubt that Stalin had a strong component of mystical anti-Semitism in his nature. This had practical consequences for Jews insofar as it enabled him to utilize, with composure, the anti-Semitism of others. And the formation of a plan for the extirpation of vast numbers of Jews toward the end of his life was surely fueled by some profound source of energy.

He resembled Hitler in having inherited from a Russian Orthodox background this one element of doctrine, the adverse feeling about Jews, and intensifying it into hatred. Still, it is hard to quantify its extent. While utilizing banal anti-Semitism against various targets, both personal and political, it might have helped more generally to mitigate his own foreign origins (as a Georgian with a heavy accent in Russian): "At least he's not a Jew!"

---

* Lion Feuchtwanger, *Moskau 1937*, Amsterdam: Querido Verlag, 1937, p. 113.

On the other hand, there was no risk to him, nor was the state endangered. Even the vast, murderous police operation he intended to implement before his death would hardly have affected the security of the state or even of the Bolshevik Party.

In any case, the ancient stereotype of Jews as agents of Satan, the basic formula of medieval anti-Semitism, was absorbed into Soviet mythology. The concept of the Jew as Satan, in his contemporary incarnation of "anti-Soviet counter-revolutionary," could also absorb with ease not merely "Trotskyite," but "Zionist," "tool of Israel," "tool of Wall Street," "tool of American Imperialism," and so on. The theological structure established by the Bolsheviks soon after their putsch, and streamlined by Stalin as his entourage engulfed the Party apparatus, evolved a supple and pivotal instrument for the use of any Communist administration. No doubt the satanization of opponents on a quasi-theological basis, reminiscent of the Middle Ages, was Stalin's major contribution to the statecraft of self-proclaimed Marxist parties.

During the Six-Day War of Israel against Egypt and some other Arab states in 1967, anti-Semitism became official, public Soviet policy. Since then books, pamphlets, newspaper articles have been published by the Party organs—all public institutions in the Soviet Union were Party organs—in many millions of copies focusing on the same theme: Jews, Zionism, and the State of Israel.

While political hostility to Israel need have nothing to do with mystical anti-Semitism, it is evident, nevertheless, that since 1949 the Soviet Executive made use of the whole panoply of classical anti-Semitism in waging its war against Israel. The Six-Day War of 1967 merely streamlined the identification of anti-Zionism and anti-Semitism.

From then on, the attack on the Jews and on Zionism was integrated with the chief mythological element in Marxism—its pretension to science. In 1967 the Department of Public Science of the Presidium of the Soviet Academy of Science established a Permanent Commission for the "disclosure and analysis of the history, ideology, and practices of Zionism." The government published a stream of "scientific" books put out by "science" publishing houses, all with "scientific"-sounding titles (e.g., *Ide-*

ology and Practices of International Zionism), whereas the broad public was deluged with brochures and pamphlets with much catchier names, such as *The Zionist Octopus of Espionage*.

In the Soviet Union writers never wrote for an uncertain market; the most cursory examination of the literature on anti-Semitism indicates that the same handful of writers wrote both the "scientific" book for the elite and the popularizations for the masses.

The most striking thing about the "scientific" publications "disclosing and analyzing" Zionism was that they were all grounded, in fact, on the Protocols of the Elders of Zion, rejected by Tsar Nicholas II, taken up by the Nazis and other right-wing ideologues and developed under full throttle by the Soviet Executive. Thus the resources of a huge apparatus were thrown into the revival as science of a notorious fraud, itself a work of fantasy.

The Protocols were supplemented in Soviet usage by various anti-Semitic remarks made by Marx himself, together with some of Lenin's sallies against one Jewish organization (the Bund), with which he had been at odds long before the Bolshevik putsch. Thus Lenin, even though he had no personal feelings against Jews, confirmed the "scientific" themes harped on in the Protocols and in contemporary Soviet politics.

The changes in the content of the Protocols were altogether trivial, purely cosmetic, and meant to bring them up to date with respect to the existence of the State of Israel. What used to be called, for instance, the "worldwide Zionist conspiracy" in gutter literature was given the scientific baptism of the "Jewish branch of imperialism." Lenin's theory of imperialism as the "last stage of capitalism" (itself borrowed from J. Hobson's *Imperialism*), was modified so as to make Zionism the "final stage of capitalism."

Accordingly, what purported to be (in Hobson's and Lenin's books) an analysis of various socio-economic processes within the "capitalist mode of production" was dropped altogether and replaced by a simple demonological concept, part of the transition from medieval theological anti-Semitism to the secularization of the same theme.

The focus of this worldwide conspiracy of the "Jewish branch of imperialism" was the State of Israel, whose goal was world rule. This ramified Soviet campaign integrated ancient visual stereotypes: numerous illustrated Soviet publications reprinted a celebrated caricature from the Nazi periodical *Der Stürmer*, showing a Jew with a horrible face stretching elongated clawlike hands to clutch the world, each palm displaying the Shield of David.

The Soviet press constantly exhorted the "healthy powers" of the world, spearheaded by the Arab states, to gird themselves for the decisive battle menacing the human race: this menace was all the more formidable since the Zionists controlled 80 percent of the Western mass media, in addition to vast funds: it was nothing for them to spend $400 million in an attempt "to liquidate Socialism in Czechoslovakia" in 1968.*

The invective used against the Israeli army, unmatched for ferocity in Soviet history, even outdid the language used for the Nazi invaders in the Second World War: Israeli soldiers were routinely and exclusively called "thieves, animals, pirates, murderers."

Soviet propaganda also linked Israel, fountainhead of intrigues aimed at world rule, to a basic theme of the Protocols— that the medium for world conquest by Jewry was the world banking system. All the big Jewish investment firms and brokerage houses (Wall Street firms such as Lazard Frères and Bache & Co.) were lumped together as members of the conspiracy: this "bourgeoisie of Jewish origin" was a subdepartment of the "Bourgeoisie."

This was built up by another motif of the Protocols: all these investment firms representing the "Jewish bourgeoisie" were supposed to be linked by blood ties among the individuals in charge: "the international amalgamation of finance capital," for instance, was symbolized by "firm ties."** *International Zionism,*

---

* M. B. Mitin, *Ideologiya i Praktika Mezhdunarodnogo Sionizma* (Ideology and Practice of International Zionism), Moscow: Izdatel'stvo Politicheskoy Literatury (Political Literature Publishers), 1978.
** In an article by V. I. Kiselev, published in *Mezhdunarodny Sionizm: Istoriya i Politika* (*International Zionism: History and Politics*, Russian), Moscow: Institut Vostokovedeniya, 1977.

published in the summer of 1977 and given special fanfare by the news agency Tass on 22 July, laid the groundwork for the last phase of the Soviet world campaign of anti-Zionism and anti-Semitism.

In resurrecting the Protocols from having been totally discredited, as one might have supposed, by the Nazis' use of them, the Soviet Executive put them in fact to far more effective use than anything Hitler had dreamed of. It may be that Hitler himself, a mystical and, for that matter, "physiological" anti-Semite, did not need the prop of the Protocols to the same degree—his private lusts sufficed. For the scientific needs of Soviet statecraft, however, the Protocols proved to be a fruitful device.

The ramified, virulent Soviet campaign against Zionism as a macabre iniquity was evidently modeled on the concept of The Jew, rooted in the earliest phase of Christian theology and developed, as we have seen, in the Middle Ages and in its secular form since the French Revolution. Zionism, the quintessential expression of an Evil People, is both universally potent and satanically evil, powered by a demented urge for world rule. Thus it could in its nature encompass all the evil forces in the Soviet universe, from "Wall Street" to the "secret services" of the "capitalist states." The only bulwark against this satanic array was the Soviet Union, like the Church in classical Christian theology.

This Soviet "Marxist-Leninist" echo of Christian theology was a precise rendering of St. Paul's original conception of the God Forces, the Forces of Light, arrayed against the Devil Forces, the Forces of Darkness: at the end of the cosmic contest the Soviet fatherland, champion of the Forces of Light, would emerge victorious, with Zionism and Jewry underfoot.

Any distinction made in Soviet propaganda between anti-Zionism and old-fashioned anti-Semitism was manifestly no more than lip service to the unfashionableness, in "scientific" circles, of classical anti-Semitism, now replaced by a basically identical anti-Zionism, but up-to-date and politically more fruitful.

Within the Soviet Union too, Jewry became the target of a defamatory campaign. A characteristic instance of the scapegoating of Jews was the explanation of the Stalin terror of the late 1930s (the Moscow Show Trials and the purges discussed above) that targeted Trotsky as a criminal, a Nazi agent, and an arch-fiend.

In 1978 a novel,* given an initial printing of 1,600,000 copies and containing (like much fiction of its kind) the "findings" of Soviet specialists on Jewry, explained that the architect of the Great Terror was—Trotsky himself, who, though in exile, had been commissioned to carry out his work of universal sabotage by the Gestapo. Though Trotsky had been living outside the Soviet Union for eleven years (before he was assassinated by one of Stalin's men), it had proved possible for the "Jew Trotskyites," after infiltrating the political police, to instigate the atrocities of the 1930s, and thus bewilder the millions of sincere, upright Communists obeying Stalin.

This device was emulated, indeed outdone, by a claim that had been broadcast by the Soviet government for decades—that it was the Jews themselves, through the machinations and self-interest of the Zionists, who had collaborated with the Nazis and brought about the destruction of millions of human beings, including Jews. Thus the Nazi atrocities, which included millions of non-Jewish victims, were blamed directly on the Jews.

More broadly, Stalin's other major contribution to Marxist statecraft—the blanket fabrication of history, as distinct from its mere slanting—was also focused on the Jews. All Russian history, considered pernicious before the advent of "Marxism-Leninism," was explained as having been stage-managed by Jews, whose actual involvement in the Socialist movement before the Bolshevik putsch was summed up as a mere "counterrevolutionary role" when they were not merely hired agents of the police.** All mention of Jews was removed from all ancient and medieval history.

The only exception was the extravagant publicity given the U.N. Resolution passed in November 1975, equating Zionism and racism. With remarkable speed (by 1976), this resolution, in whose genesis the Soviet representatives at the United Nations

---

* A. S. Ivanov, *Vyechny Zov* (The Eternal Summons), Moscow: Sovietskii Pisatel', 1978.
** M. B. Mitin, *Ideology and Practice of International Zionism*, ibid.

played an executive role, was printed in Soviet textbooks and given the usual high-profile treatment.

From the very inception of the dictatorship in 1917, the arbitrariness of the tiny Bolshevik core, its lack of any mandate from the population, and the active or passive enmity of the people obliged the rulers to explain the massive miscalculations of the Bolshevik planners by projecting a vast range of enemies: from the real White Guards of the Civil War in the early 1920s to the fantasied White Guards in the 1930s, to corrupt engineers, maniacal saboteurs, Mensheviks, Social-Revolutionaries, Trotskyites, Bukharinites, nationalists of all nuances, and especially Zionists—all plotting day and night.

Stalin's contrivance of a single quasi-theological grab bag of Evil for all dissidents and opponents was tailored to the satanic stereotype of The Jew; no doubt it was suggested to Stalin by the same tradition. And just as during the proliferation of heresies in Christian history the words "Jew" and "judaizing" became commonplace epithets in a theological sense, so in the Soviet Union the word "Jew" could be used alone as an epithet; actual Jewish origins were irrelevant.

The concept of The Jew as Devil proved ideal for the Soviet system. The very essence of mystical anti-Semitism, the notion of The Jew as ubiquitously and mindlessly evil to a degree that soared far beyond self-interest—that is, Absolute Evil for its own sake—provided an ideal seedbed for scapegoating. The Evil Jew could be used in an endless variety of circumstances: just because the concept, once absorbed by the dupes of propaganda, obviated commonsense questions of self-interest, the Evil Jew could be blamed for literally anything. No plausibility need be striven for: Evil Being generates Evil Deeds.

Thus the theory of Judas (Jew)-Bolshevik-*born*-traitor— worked out during the Great Charades of 1936–38, focused more precisely during the Show Trials in the satellite countries in the late 1940s and early 1950s, and soon reaching full spate, without embellishment—riveted the attention of the Soviet public on the Eternal Jew as the Adversary par excellence and, in the secular realm, as the manipulator of American power.

In the mid-1980s the whole of Soviet life seemed about to be churned up. The utilization of mystical anti-Semitism was suspended, perhaps terminated, as part of a movement of reform that flaunted large-scale proposals for sweeping away the whole Soviet system—the Party monopoly and the state management of the economy. As part of the reform movement, far more comprehensive than the reform movements that had periodically cropped up in the Soviet Union, official hostility to the Jews was abated; a concession made in the past to allow Soviet Jews, in varying numbers, to leave for Israel was reinforced. The number of Jewish emigrants shot up.

The resentment of the Arabs at this balancing by the Soviet reform administration of Israel's demographic disadvantage was evidently ignored in favor of the psychological benefits gained from this further instance of the Soviet Executive's softening vis-à-vis Jews and Israel and its concomitant abandonment of terrorism in the Middle East.

In the Soviet Union itself, to be sure, the immediate effect on local Jews of the highly publicized reform campaign was an abrupt rise in the violent display of vulgar anti-Semitism, a natural side effect of instability and uncertainty. The relative freedom of expression permitted in the atmosphere of reform made it possible for the hatred of the Soviet system to be put in traditional terms: the Jews could be blamed once again, and with greater insistence, for the whole mess: having started the Russian revolution to begin with, they were now, to boot, sneaking out of the country. Hostility to Jews rose sharply throughout the Soviet Union.

It seems likely that in dropping its use of mystical anti-Semitism, the Soviet Executive was pursuing mundane, rational, power-political goals. Mystical anti-Semitism having been exploited in order to kindle useful passions, it might have exhausted its potential for the statecraft of the Soviet Executive.

The agitation instigated in the mid-1980s steadily expanded. The media were stuffed with accounts of economic chaos—acute shortages of all kinds, the inability of the top-heavy bureaucracy to distribute even what was on hand, the pervasive incapacity of agriculture as well as industry. The conclusion seemed obvious: the comprehensive planification of the economy for more than a half-century had been a dead end and there was now only one way out—democracy plus free enterprise.

On the other hand, despite the harping on themes of "reform," "democracy," "free markets," and "privatization," no free elections were held, while the fundamental elements of a free market were still assumed to require implementation by the swollen bureaucracy. The absence of elections meant that all governmental functions were in fact being performed by Party veterans.

The problem confronting the Party nucleus was essentially simple: how to convince the West of a radical change of heart while preserving an enormous arsenal. The wholehearted cooperation of the major media made it possible to soar above these facts of life—the arsenal and the absence of elections—while carrying on endless discussions of attractive prospects: an economy regenerated by the free market, a comprehensive democracy (eventually) and, above all, world peace, now accessible because of the neo-Bolshevik leaders' new intentions.

The practical benefits for the reformers were evident: offers of financial credits and technological assistance on the broadest scale, vital if a stagnating economy, crippled by decades of self-destructive planification, were to realize the longed-for perspective of "catching up with and passing" the West in a world economy based on the industrial societies of Japan, the United States, and the European Community.

In addition to broadcasting the general themes of democracy and reform, the new regime introduced many as it were psychological innovations. It stopped its sponsorship of terrorism in the Middle East, suspended military aid to Syria, supported the annulment of the 1976 U.N. resolution equating Zionism and Racism, and softened its behavior toward Jews and the State of Israel, which led to a resumption of diplomatic ties. More particularly, it turned a high beam on Soviet history—basically an attack on Stalin—while distancing itself from Marxism, changing "Leningrad" to "St. Petersburg" and allowing the toppling of some statues of Lenin.

All this enabled the foreign media to ignore both the arsenal and the lack of elections. The very size of the arsenal was bypassed, no doubt because it was impossible to reconcile an economy coming apart at the seams with its ability to sustain a huge arsenal and its infrastructure. It was also difficult to conceive of a state, perhaps especially the neo-Bolshevik state, that would exaggerate its weaknesses for some purpose not readily conceivable. Attention was focused, accordingly, on abstractions such as the collapse of "Communism" instead of on the interests of real people engaged in grappling with real-life problems. This was all the easier since the upper stratum of the Russian elite had not taken Marxism seriously for many years.

It was repeated over and over that real reforms would be a long time in coming, and that the attempts of the reformers to reshape the administration of the country were bound to inflame the "hardliners," that is, the Party hacks, the military, and the KGB.

Six years after the emergence of the reform movement, this leitmotif seemed to be confirmed by an abortive putsch (18–21 August 1991) led by military and KGB leaders with vast military forces at their disposal. It was entirely ineffective. The reformist leader, Mikhail Gorbachov, President of the USSR, who had been supposedly detained on vacation, returned a few days later. The "putsch" had lasted three days.

The abortive putsch, whatever its substance, was to set the neo-Bolshevik state on a new course that very soon culminated in a dramatic transformation.

Boris Yeltsin, one of six Party members put up by the Communist Party for President of Russia in June 1991, had been elected in a vote whose results, even in this huge country, were somehow known overnight. It was the only "free election" bestowed on any Party veteran.

A few months after the August putsch Yeltsin set about a comprehensive restructuring, or at least rebaptism of the neo-Bolshevik state: the Communist Party was declared extinct; the Union of Socialist Soviet Republics was renamed the Commonwealth of Independent States. In a couple of weeks the Commonwealth, consisting at its inception of three "Slavic states"—Russia, Byelorus, Ukraine—absorbed all the members of the former USSR except the three Baltic states and for a time Georgia.

The West, satisfied that the arsenal was still in the hands of a central authority, was indifferent to the absence of elections. The Russian Republic (with a population half that of the USSR) inherited the USSR seat on the United Nations Security Council.

Throughout the vociferous agitation about reform, democracy and the free market, even during the spate of catchwords about the disintegration of the Soviet Union, at no time was any doubt cast on its status as a Superpower, despite the flaunting of its lack of viability even as a normal government. With its huge arsenal and superabundant resources, the country as a whole, despite all the surface froth, obviously remained a superpower and was in fact treated as such—as a power, moreover, with a natural right to a role in all matters of world concern, especially the Middle East. This was made arrestingly evident during the war against Iraq led by the American coalition in 1990–91, when Gorbachov, President of the USSR, intervened to save its ally, Saddam Hussein, from annihilation by the coalition. He also co-chaired a Middle-East conference in Madrid between Israelis, the Palestinian Arabs and a few Arab states.

It was only natural for the Commonwealth of Independent States to inherit the ancient Russian as well as the neo-Bolshevik interest in the fate of the Persian Gulf and the Middle East.

Meanwhile multitudes of Russian Jews, distraught over their possible dislocation in the wake of tentative, still-inchoate projects for reform, focused their hopes on emigration to Israel. Even though such a way out was clouded over by the sharpening conflict with the Arabs, the vulnerability of Russian Jews to social upheaval in a country with mystical anti-Semitism woven into its present as well as its past made them more restive than ever.

EPILOGUE

Marxism might have been dented institutionally in the neo-Bolshevik upset of the 1980s and 1990s, but the multitudes in whom it had been indoctrinated since the Bolshevik putsch of 1917 were a major factor in the world, especially, perhaps, in Asia, South America, and Africa. And the confluence between Marxism and Christian doctrine—two systems of thought long considered incompatible—was to have an effect on Jews at large, including the State of Israel. The Kingdom of God idea, which in its various interpretations had a permanent effect on the fate of the Jews, had been revived by the foundation of the Soviet regime in 1917.

This could reasonably have been regarded as an attempt, by a fragment of the international Socialist movement, to create a new world based on justice and compassion. It shook up the great Christian churches, polarizing opinion in both the mainline Protestant confederations and, particularly since the Second World War, in the Roman Catholic Church, as well as to some extent in the Greek and Russian Orthodox Church. Many believing Christians were moved by the proclaimed ideals of the

Bolsheviks to revise their traditional views in order to accommodate what many felt to have been a great gap in the Christian view of the civil order.

Thus the Kingdom of God, an idea that as we have seen agitated Europe for centuries during the Middle Ages, returned in force. The idea of the Kingdom of God became a sort of decompression chamber, in which Marxists on the one hand could agree that the Kingdom of God, insofar as it involved the alleviation of suffering in this world, was entirely acceptable to the humanistic ideals of Marxism, while on the other hand Churchmen could agree that since the Kingdom of God was still tarrying and no doubt still lay in the remote future, it would be charitable, indeed very Christian, to give some thought to the reform of society in this vale of tears.

Thus Marxism as a system was stripped of its ideological scaffolding, its structure, its point, and refocused on an alleged preoccupation with the "Poor." Once this was established, the atheism inherent in Marxism was disregarded, while as a movement involving the Poor it mesmerized the most influential branches of the Christian Church. (It is ironic to recall that Marx, proud of his ruthless, "scientific" hardheadedness, despised those sentimentalists who were concerned about mere human suffering while blind to what was needed: an analysis that would show how the Proletariat, *not* the Poor, could overthrow the Bourgeoisie and inaugurate the new world.)

For decades younger churchmen had been chafing under the traditional detachment of Christian doctrine from the problems of social welfare. This changed radically after the Second World War: a tidal wave of social involvement engulfed the Church, both Protestant and Roman Catholic, not only in Europe and America but, most dramatically, in Latin America, Africa, and Southeast Asia.

The churches themselves were penetrated by social activism, largely Marxist in nature, either implicitly, or, more and more often after the 1960s, quite explicitly. They yielded to a transposition of both rationalism and social panaceas to the milieu hitherto reserved for abstract religiosity. In other words, a weakening of faith in the adequacy of the Church as a whole fostered a concomitant growth of enthusiasm for social reforms. This was the foundation of the many colloquies held since the end of the Second World War between Roman Catholic spokesmen and Marxists.

Great numbers of younger priests, nuns, and ministers, chafing at the pallidness of the Christian presence in the contemporary world, have become, in fact, apostles of upheaval conceived along lines that until only a short while ago would have seemed confined to Marxist agitators. Such churchmen have actively promoted a revolutionary social ferment—directed in the most general terms against poverty, corruption, and exploitation by the "feudal structures"—in Latin America, Africa, and Southeast Asia. There are many priests, nuns, and ministers who are actual Marxists of one shade or another, or, if not, are sympathetic to the professed aims of Marxist activists, who in these undeveloped parts of the world were, of course, guided by various dependencies of the KGB, both local Communist parties and other agencies. Because of the broad scope of the professed aims of the Communist parties in such countries, and because of their idealistic language—few people defend poverty or corruption—it was quite possible for idealistic young people to accept the benefit of KGB organizations while pursuing their own idealistic aims.

This large-scale development among the mainstream churches has had a direct effect on the State of Israel, which is uniformly regarded by all those under Marxist influence as a bastion of "imperialist" reaction: since Israel was the chief enemy of Soviet activities in the Middle East, and since Soviet invective took a form that was palatable to churchly social reformers, it was natural for the mainstream churches to lend their support to all campaigns against Israel on behalf of the oppressed Arab and Muslim "masses."

The mainstream church campaign against Israel, accordingly, would seem to represent a dramatic convergence of two powerful tendencies: the obvious, open attack on behalf of idealist objectives that Israel is alleged to oppose, and, without a doubt, a deeper, unavowed prejudice drawing its strength from the primordial wellspring of mystical anti-Semitism. Thus the manifest idealistic reasons for opposing the State of Israel camouflaged, in effect, the ancient, primordial strand of anti-

Semitism I have been distinguishing. The ancient legacy of The Jew provided additional dynamism for the achievement of cosmic panaceas, or for that matter, the run-of-the-mill social objectives of the Church idealists.

It is certainly a fact that anti-Semitism, cloaked very thinly by anti-Zionism, once again became an aspect of ordinary life throughout Europe, West and East, as well as in North and South America. The activities of the State of Israel, its ripostes to attacks, its military successes, its harsh measures against enemies, have had the effect of generating flurries of attacks on Jews in western Europe, from Scandinavia to Italy to France, while the media have played an indulgent role by comparing, for instance, conditions in Beirut during the Israeli incursion into Lebanon in 1982 with the Nazi reduction of the Warsaw Ghetto, and in general linking Nazi idioms to Israel's policies vis-à-vis the Arabs in its midst (referring to Israel's "Final Solution" for the "Palestinian problem," calling the Israelis outright Nazis who are persecuting the Palestinian Arabs, themselves turned into "Jews" as a counterweight to the Israeli "Nazis," and so on).

The appearance of a younger generation for whom Marxism had again become fashionable and the genocide of the Jews forgotten, and the dramatic military victories of the Israelis since 1967, taken together, have made it easy to disregard the mass murder of the Jews altogether and revert to stereotypes of unabashed animosity. This mood makes it easy for propaganda to convince people, already predisposed, that the Arabs, despite their vast numbers and still vaster oil reserves, are somehow the "underdog" vis-à-vis Israel.

One of the great ironies of the survival of anti-Semitism in movements of the Left is the presence of large numbers of left-wing Jews, especially in America, France, and Israel itself. Such left-wing—or "left-liberal"—Jews have their own complex, sometimes tortuous, reasons for opposing, with vehemence, the State of Israel. In effect, they legitimize, as it were, all those opponents of Israel who do indeed have an element of mystical anti-Semitism beneath their seemingly practical, mundane hostility.

But while the reasons for the ardor of anti-Israel feeling

among left-wing Jews are very various, they may all be derived ultimately from the attitude given lapidary formulation by Heine a century and a half ago—about Jewish emancipation being possible only after the emancipation of the whole world. The discussion of this "self-hatred," if that is what it is, or of what may be considered more generously a longing for the benign disappearance of the Jews, may prudently be postponed indefinitely.

If it is true that mystical anti-Semitism, even when secularized, remains anchored in the division of the universe into the Light and the Dark, the difficulties of assessing its current status may be insurmountable. It is hard to say whether what seemed to be the gradual decline of anti-Semitism around the turn of the century represented a genuine long-range tendency, or a very slow shift, on a somewhat mysterious axis, in which the eruption of Nazism and the Communist resumption of traditional anti-Semitism were sinister portents of the future.

The difficulty inherent in the assessment of anti-Semitism today is heightened by the varied reactions to the establishment of the State of Israel in 1948, some of which, as I have indicated, camouflage a potent strand of traditional mystical anti-Semitism.

The magnitude of the forces arrayed against Israel is undeniable: the spectrum is vast—from the mystical anti-Semites still active in many countries (ideological Nazis, Catholics, and Protestants), through countless elements of the Third World and the left wing influenced by neo-Bolshevism and Marxism, the Muslim intelligentsia as a whole and, more particularly, the twenty-one Arab states, many elements in the Roman Catholic Church, and some of the most important Protestant confederations.

It would no doubt be preposterous to say that all opposition to Israel is motivated by anti-Semitism. Just as a dislike of or aversion to Jews, within "normal" bounds, is like other forms of xenophobia—Freud's "narcissism of petty differences"—so hostility to Israel may well have a mundane, "natural" source: the rivalry between the great powers and the patriotic hostility of the surrounding Arab states require no mystical explanation; neither does the Realpolitik in neo-Bolshevik conduct, nor the overall attitude of Marxism to nationalism.

Arab hostility to Israel, for instance, is a prime example of collective enmity independent of mystical anti-Semitism, at least in the case of Muslim Arabs. Despite the second-class status in traditional Islam of Jews, Islam has no theory of anti-Semitism. The role assigned the Jews is not sinister. The odium is not theological. At the very outset Muhammad proclaims the message of Moses—the One God. He dropped, of course, the other half of Judaism, the covenant between the One God and His Chosen People, the Jews: Muhammad replaced the Jews with the community of the Believers, just like Christianity, which replaced the historic Israel with the True Israel embodied in the Mystic Church of the Savior of Mankind and Lord of the Universe.

Yet that did not change the nature of Allah, who, all-powerful, all-knowing, Creator and King of the Universe, like Yahweh, stands outside his creation. The sacral is not on earth. There is no mediator between Allah and his people, nor is an intermediary conceivable. The concept of the Incarnation, of Redemption through a Divine Son sacrificed as a vicarious atonement for others—these fundamental concepts are as alien to Islam as to Judaism. Hence there is no place in Islam for The Jew as the personification of primordial Evil: without the Incarnation, without the Universe of God counterposed to the Universe of Satan, there is no cosmology to serve as framework for the satanic role of the Jews.

The hostility of Muslim Arabs today to Israel today, accordingly, however ferocious, is not a form of mystical anti-Semitism. Its theological root is merely the conviction that Jews *should* be subject to Islam—like everyone else: the Jews are not *special*.

In the Qur'an the Jews play a dual role: on the one hand, the whole of the Qur'an is based on the "message of Moses" and on the Final Judgment—also, after all, a Jewish idea. Then, for real-life Jews during the lifetime of Muhammad, there is resentment, expressed in venomous comments that evidently stem from personal or political conflicts. These comments have no conceptual, philosophical basis; they cannot be explained by some general principle.

The restoration of Jewish sovereignty over a small territory that has been part of the realm of Islam for generations is of course irritating, because of the recrudescence of Islamic self-consciousness in the past hundred years, accentuated, among Muslim Arabs in the past two generations, by the specific formation of the Arab national movement.

In principle, of course, Christians too are second-class, like all non-Muslims. In this case, however, Islamic theorizing has been obliged to accept the facts of life, at least as far as practical politics is concerned: there could be no question of a religious war against Great Britain and France; nor can various institutions of higher learning, much frequented by aspiring Muslim engineers, scientists, and businessmen, simply be disregarded by old-fashioned cultures caught up in a crisis of modernization. Even in its early faith-imbued phase, after all, Islam made a tremendous concession in India, where the Hindus—for Muslims, arch-pagans—should in theory have been either converted or slaughtered on the spot.

That is, of course, ancient history: even the most fanatic Muslims could not undertake a campaign today against the non-Muslim world—five-sixths of mankind—despite outbursts of rhetoric as in Iran, where a fundamentalist Islamic revival, backed by the Soviet Executive, to some extent rearranged Muslim politics.

Still, while the restoration of Jewish sovereignty in Israel has galled Muslim dreamers, and in particular, maddened the neighbors of Israel, for Muslims the existence of Jewry has nothing mysterious or awesome about it.

When Muslims meet Jews, they do not see anything eerie, supernatural, behind their appearance; they do not regard them as freakish or strange. For Muslims, Jews are not leading a secret life—running the world on behalf of Satan. The mysterious odium that has had fateful effects on the Jews in Christendom throughout the centuries is entirely absent from the Muslim world.

Because of this, the Jews have never felt "strange" under

Islam: while they have been disadvantaged, often inconvenienced, and on occasion afflicted, they have never been obliged to internalize a mystical factor. Within themselves, Jews could feel perfectly normal: they were inferiors, but for social and political reasons, not for metaphysical ones. All was in the open: on occasion there could be ordinary personal relations, even friendships.

Both Christian and Muslim Arabs, to be sure, are quite willing to believe Jews are *influential*: that is, indeed, their principal explanation of the State of Israel's victories in five wars. They may well believe that Jews represent a far-flung conspiracy of powerful activists, with occult channels to the governments of the Christian West; that Jews play disproportionate roles in the economy of the world, especially in the world banking system; that they are, in short, a hidden power.

But the power is not hidden because it comes from Satan, or from the identification of Jews with some maleficent principle. Arab opposition to Israel is on the level of ordinary politics and warfare: its mystical penumbra is no more than the everyday mysticism of ethnic grievances heightened by a primitive utilitarian theory—the sort of commonplace prickliness attached to speculations about the Freemasons, the Mafia, the "military-industrial complex," and so on.

Since the establishment of Israel in 1948, many Muslims have succumbed, for instance, to the lure of the Protocols: the late Egyptian leader, Gamal Abdel Nasser, fervently proclaimed their authenticity; the Saudi Arabian kings have had millions of copies handsomely printed in many languages, and have made a point of handing each visitor a copy in his own language.

Nevertheless, Muslims do not share the psychic predisposition of Christians, for many of whom the Protocols echo the primordial horror anchored in the classical Jewish role of Satan's surrogate. Muslims may simply accept the Protocols on the superficial level of real-life conspiracy, reinforced by a somewhat one-sided view of the West. Among Muslims, accordingly, the use of the Protocols is a ploy, a simple-minded maneuver. The Muslim leaders who became Nazis before and during the Second World War considered Hitler an effective leader who would get rid of the British, the Jews, and the Russian Communists. The

Final Solution was, for them, a solution to a specific problem: the restoration of Jewish sovereignty in Palestine. They welcomed the destruction of six million Jews, the reservoir of Jewish colonization in Palestine, as a practical benefit. Their enmity lacked precisely the outsize, mystical dimension ultimately rooted in theology.

For Muslims the resurgence of Jewish sovereignty is, in short, a major annoyance that has merely been added to the other annoyances, by now myriad, that mar the stark simplicity of the idea of world rule underlying Islam. The number of Muslims who still cherish this ideal, to be sure, must be small, although since Islam is, after all, a sixth of mankind, now rapidly becoming a quarter, this ideal is not necessarily irrational.

Pious Christian Arabs may retain the mystical anti-Semitism embedded in Christian theology: this may account for much profound anti-Israel sentiment. In addition, many Arabic-speaking Christians who have in fact abandoned their religion have hurtled into Marxism, both theoretical and practical, that is, into a working alliance with the Soviet Executive (like the bulk of the PLO).

This is, to be sure, just the situation of many Muslims: despite the self-confident assertions of many Arabists and Islamologists that Islam is "inherently" alien to Marxism, the Soviet Executive has had no difficulty in solving the problem both of Muslim alliances and, more broadly, of Muslim "fronts." Not only have many Muslims, zealously catching up with the West, become Marxists, Leninists, Trotskyites, and so on, but many Muslims sincere in their faith have been seduced into fronts on the model of the many made familiar in the West since the Bolshevik putsch of 1917.

With respect to Christendom, on the other hand, it cannot be denied that the existence of the State of Israel, together with the general erosion of theology, has also had a side effect of defusing, as it were, mystical anti-Semitism. In this one respect, perhaps, the hopes pinned by some of the early Zionists on the "normalization" of the Jews may have been partially realized. Many Christians who in a previous era might have been susceptible to anti-Semitism, nowadays look at Israel from the point of view of *Realpolitik*. If, in their case, the erosion of theology has not left a "deposit" of a morbid complex to nourish some pathology, they can look at Israel objectively, cold-bloodedly, as one factor among many in a complex situation. Many Arabic-speaking Christians, for instance, look upon Israel as an ally, actual or potential, against the encroaching sea of Islam. Many military theorists in the western powers also take a practical view of Israel as an effective ally, though its efficacy is naturally lessened as long as the broad-based Arab opposition, and more particularly the restiveness of the Arabs directly under Israeli rule, remains unresolved.

It may be a curious fact that the mass murder of the Jews by the Nazi regime, though sometimes invoked rhetorically, has been swallowed up by history; its institutionalization as a scholarly pursuit, and the consequent production of an extensive literature, have failed to give it any resonance in practical affairs.

It is difficult to see how this could have been otherwise. In the turmoil of the twentieth century, the natural indifference of the great public, even among the Jews, despite the deep feelings underlying its ceremonial remembrance, must surely have prevailed.

In addition, the mass-murder has produced a reaction of some scope, because of the double vision I have mentioned. The very fact that the helpless have survived, to become a force once again, is to many an enigma that only mystical anti-Semites can explain to themselves satisfactorily. For them, and no doubt for many of those more or less under their influence, the survival of the Jews, and the existence of the State of Israel, are taken in and of themselves to reveal their occult power. The corpses can be shrugged aside, or for that matter denied outright: what remains is a striking fact: the major military power in Europe failed to exterminate them, and there they still stand, with a state of their own, to boot. And doubtless in control of the United States government.

Even Muslims, free of the distortions of mystical anti-Semitism, may find it natural to look upon this with awe.

It may be an unconscious element fortifying the remarkable weight of the State of Israel in world politics, one of the reasons it has been so easy to rivet the attention of the West on the Arab opposition to the State of Israel. It has even been easy to detach the Arab-Israel conflict from its statistics, so to speak, and present it as a problem of cosmic significance.

If one looks at its quantitative aspect, this seems bizarre: with Arab states, whose population is approaching 200 million, covering an area of five million square miles, it would seem hard to understand how so much energy can be generated by a few million Jews perched on 10,000 square miles. It can be understood, indeed, only from the point of view of Christendom, where Jews somehow remain important, and where, more particularly, the notion of Jewish territorial sovereignty may arouse a profound and perhaps unconscious malaise.

The media generally have concentrated public attention on Israel and its immediate vicinity. It proved possible, in the aftermath of the Six-Day War of 1967 between Israel and its neighbors, by defining the "Palestinians" as a unique people that remained, somehow, an integral part of the "Arab Nation," to create a precise counterweight to the claims of Zionist Jews to what remained of the land originally proposed to them in the Balfour Declaration of 1917, and thus to make the conflict seem insoluble.

It is surely an irony that this quirk of the western world view, a political windfall for Arab activists combating Israel, should be something of a conundrum for Muslims. It is no doubt a further irony that until the modern era it was common for Jews to be called "Palestinians." It was quite normal for Kant to use the word in one of his diatribes, as a polite reference to their ancient origins. While the British Mandate was in force (1919–48), all citizens were called "Palestinians" with a qualifying addition: "Jew," "Christian," "Muslim," "Druze," and so on.

The interaction of the currents of feeling outlined above defies quantitative assessment. It is impossible to say whether the decline in mystical anti-Semitism that seemed evident around the turn of the century was fundamental or episodic.

The factors weakening theology—notably science and humanism—must be balanced against the stupendous fact that a third of mankind is Christian, with all religious instruction still stemming from the sacred books. Even if the Christian elite has become too sophisticated for its religion, there are hundreds of millions of real believers. And if Christendom loses a few recruits to other religions—Hinduism, Buddhism, Zen—in addition to the losses due to scientific and humanistic erosion, the process may well be piecemeal, spasmodic, staccato—in a word, explosive, which in and for itself may bode ill for Jews.

Hence, regardless of the erosion of theology, both Jewry and Israel may continue to serve as scapegoats, partly because of the usefulness of scapegoats in general, and partly because even ex-Christians may begrudge the loss of their very rationalization of mystical anti-Semitism, and blame the Jews for that too.

Nevertheless, the traditional sources of mystical anti-Semitism are slowly drying up. Even if the Christian Scriptures remain the groundwork of mass instruction, that instruction will necessarily be gradually subjected to a more history-minded orientation. Texts themselves may become museum pieces, while the Christian faith, as distinct from theology, will recover its Kingdom of God, now lost in an endless future, and integrate it with the Here and Now.

OTHER FROMM HISTORY TITLES:

THE SECRETS OF MARIE ANTOINETTE
A Collection of Letters
by Olivier Bernier

TALLEYRAND
A Biography
by Duff Cooper

OUTCAST
A Jewish Girl in Wartime Berlin
Inge Deutschkron

THE END OF THE WORLD
A History
by Otto Friedrich

THE GRAVE OF ALICE B. TOKLAS
And Other Reports from the Past
by Otto Friedrich

J. ROBERT OPPENHEIMER
Shatterer of Worlds
by Peter Goodchild

THE AILING EMPIRE
Germany from Bismarck to Hitler
by Sebastian Haffner

ARCHITECTS OF FORTUNE
Mies van der Rohe and the Third Reich
by Elaine S. Hochman

A CRACK IN THE WALL
Growing Up Under Hitler
by Horst Krüger

THE CONQUEST OF MOROCCO
by Douglas Porch

THE CONQUEST OF THE SAHARA
by Douglas Porch

HENRY VIII
The Politics of Tyranny
by Jasper Ridley

ELIZABETH I
The Shrewdness of Virtue
by Jasper Ridley

THE HERMIT OF PEKING
The Hidden Life of Sir Edmund Backhouse
by Hugh Trevor-Roper

ALEXANDER OF RUSSIA
Napoleon's Conqueror
by Henri Troyat